Children Using Computers

Children Using Computers

Second Edition

Anita Straker
and
Heather Govier

Nash Pollock
Publishing

First published 1989
Second edition published 1996 by
Nash Pollock Publishing
32 Warwick Street
Oxford OX4 1SX

9 8 7 6 5 4 3 2 1

A catalogue record of this book is available from the British Library.

ISBN 1 898255 12 1

Typeset in 10.5/13 pt New Century Schoolbook, by Can Do Design, Buckingham.

Printed in Great Britain by Redwood Books, Trowbridge

Contents

Acknowledgements   vi

Primary Matters: Editors' preface   ix

Introduction   1

1   Children using information   17

2   Some information-handling software   30

    Databases and graph-drawing packages   30

    CD-ROMs   42

    Word processors   46

3   Problem solving and investigation with a computer   60

4   Programming: a creative activity   74

5   Using the computer for control   108

6   The computer in particular areas of the curriculum   127

    Language   128

    Mathematics   134

    Science and technology   145

    Social and environmental studies   156

    Creative arts   163

7   Cross-curricular topics   177

8   Planning and organisation   211

9   Children, parents and teachers   228

10 Evaluation and assessment   243

11 Into the future   257

Appendix: the National Curriculum   264

References   269

Index   270

Acknowledgements

I am conscious that many enthusiastic and talented people have been involved in developing exciting uses of computers in primary classrooms. I am particularly indebted to those whose work I have drawn on for the purposes of this book: Jean Ashcroft, Janet Banner, Judith Baskerville, Janine Blinko, Ivor Broad, David Brown, Pat d'Arcy, Nicola Davies, Richard Harrison, Keith Hemsley, Margaret Hutton, Joe Johnson, Mary Lomas, Zena McNiven, Alan Parr, Terry Pullen, Christine Robson, Chris Rowlatt, Linda Samson, John Thorne, Jo Waddingham, Andre Wagstaff, Peter West, Ian Whittington, Julia Williams, and Carol Wisely.

I am also indebted to the children in the following schools, and filled with admiration for their work.

All Saints C.E. Infants' School, Reading
Augustus Smith Middle School, Berkhamstead
Broad Town C.E. Primary School, Swindon
Bryn Deri Primary School, Cardiff
Chater Infants' School, Watford
Coryton Primary School, Whitchurch, South Glamorgan
Crockerton Primary School, Warminster
Emmbrook Junior School, Wokingham
Gabalfa Primary School, Cardiff
Grafton Primary School, London
Great Gidding C.E. Primary School, Huntingdon
Guthrie Infants' School, Calne
Southfield Junior School, Highworth
Lansdowne Primary School, Norfolk St Canton
Lethbridge Infants' School, Swindon
Longleaze Primary School, Wootton Bassett
Manor Way Primary School, Sussex
Peckham Rye Primary School, London
Penlan Comprehensive School, Swansea
Sir Thomas Abney Primary School, London
Springcroft Primary School, Blythe Bridge
Stadhampton Primary School, Oxfordshire

The Lea JMI School, Harpenden
Westbury Laverton Infants' School, Wiltshire
and primary schools in Avon and Somerset.

I am grateful to Doubleday and Company, Inc., for permission to quote from 'Earth is Room Enough' by Isaac Asimov, copyright © 1967.

Last, my thanks are due to my four sons, Nick, Tim, Andy and Simon, who gave up their arcade games in order that I could use the word processor, and to my mother, who provided endless cups of coffee.

Anita Straker

Primary Matters

Series editors Leone Burton and Henry Pluckrose

Children Using Computers Second Edition   Anita Straker and Heather Govier

Children and Technology   Katrina Blythe with Richard Bennett and Andrew Hamill

Children Learning Science   Lyn Sylvester Bradley

Children Making Music   Tricia Binns

Children Learning Mathematics   Leone Burton

Children Learning History   Henry Pluckrose

Performing Arts in the Primary School   Pauline Tambling

Environmental Education in the Primary School   Philip Neal and Joy Palmer

Primary Matters: Editors' Preface

It is hard to find an acknowledgement of how recent are primary schools whose curriculum and management reflect the particular emotional, social, intellectual and physical needs of young children, nor of how far they have developed in a very brief time span. Indeed, there are teachers in today's primary schools who remember that in 1949, five years after the famous Butler Education Act, 36% of children of secondary age were still attending schools which also housed children under 11. Those same teachers have seen the development of primary schools through the Plowden era in the 1960s, the building of open-plan schools which aroused such intense international interest in the 1960s and 70s, and in the 1980s and the 1988 Education Reform Act.

This Act made far-reaching changes. The introduction of a national curriculum was a radical development and brought in its wake consequences unforseen by its designers. Teachers were quick to discover that the syllabi which had been constructed in such detail were impossible to build into an effective curriculum; tests for 7 and 11 year olds which had been devised to give the curriculum credibility became a focus for parental and professional discontent. Persistent re-writes led finally to a 'reform' of the new curriculum by the Dearing Committee in the early 1990s. This was an attempt to make manageable what was unmanageable, hastily introduced and overburdened with bureaucracy.

These recent changes and upheavals must be set against the slow emergence of a realisation that the needs and aspirations of young people are not necessarily the same at 7 as they are at 13, and that the way in which knowledge is acquired and becomes useful must relate to particular phases in personal development and rhythms of growth.

In the years following the first world war, successive Government committees examined the educational needs of adolescents, of boys and girls in the middle years of childhood (7-11) and of children of infant and nursery age. These committees reported between 1926 and 1933 and their recommendations, though implemented in a piecemeal fashion, did lead to a considerable restructuring of schooling in England and Wales. The most profound effect of these changes was the acknowledgement that the primary years were a coherent and essential stage in the education process, and a stage which had distinctive needs and requirements. Before this children had been educated in all-age schools. Unless a child was fortunate to be selected at the age of 11 (usually as a successful outcome of academic competition), the school s/he joined at 5 years of age would be the school s/he left at 13. 90% of the school population attended such schools and it became increasingly obvious that they were failing to meet the different needs of the 5 year old, the child in middle years, and of the 13 year old school leaver. In the late `1930s primary schools began to develop, with secondary (elementary) schools providing for those children who failed the selective examination. The distinctive categories of secondary education were enshrined in the 1944 Education Act which established a comprehensive tri-partite system of secondary education, but even five years later this was still not fully realised.

It took, therefore, some twenty years from the mid-1930s until the 1950s and 60s for primary schools to become generally established and, with the population explosion of the 50s and 60s, primary school practice underwent many developments as the early years of schooling came to be regarded as an essential phase in the educational process. Experiments were undertaken in teaching and learning methodology, in the curriculum, in the organisation of classes (remember vertical or family grouping?), and, as already mentioned, in the architectural style of new schools. The curriculum became richer and more challenging to young children. Enthusiastic support for these changes was found in the report published by the Plowden Committee in 1967.

In contrast to this period, more recently primary education has been subject to critical appraisal and retrenchment. Academics (like Peters and Dearden), and politicians (like Boyson and Cox), as well as inspectors from local education authorities and Her Majesty's Inspectorate, and more recently the Office for Standards in Education (OFSTED) have focused attention upon the issues and assumptions underlying the work offered by teachers to young children. Are there things which *all* children should learn during their primary years? What constitutes essential knowledge for the primary-age child? What should be the balance between the teaching of facts, the development of skills, the understanding of the concepts which underlie knowledge, and the processes through which this knowledge is acquired and developed? How effective are different classroom approaches in developing thinking skills, social awareness and responsibility? How can the primary curriculum best address the fundamental technological changes brought about by the microchip? In what ways are social issues such as racism, sexism or disadvantage best addressed? How should the particular insights and experiences of the disabled child be incorporated? How can institutional barriers to the involvement of all interested parties, especially parents, in the education of each child be dismantled? How should religious education be handled within a society which is more and more secular but also no longer made up of only one major faith group?

Questions such as these are not asked in a vacuum. They reflect the anxieties (real and imagined) of parents, academics, politicians, employers, and, most of all, of the teachers themselves. That such questions are now being asked is, in part, a recognition of how far primary schools have come over the fifty or so years since they were first conceived. In a climate of concern and criticism, it is also easy to forget that British developments in primary education have been the focus of attention, respect and emulation in many other countries. Indeed, many have argued that it was a freedom from bureaucracy which gave English primary schools their unique character and made possible the kinds of thoughtful experiment which attracted an international reputation. At the same time, others have suggested that piecemeal development has led to idiosyncrasy. Hence the current demand for every school to follow a programme reflecting clearly defined national criteria. However, the need for the individual teacher to make choices, ask questions, and influence every child's development continues to be respected and, however centralised the curriculum may become, however much the school programme is evaluated, however regularly children are tested against performance norms, the thoughtful teacher will continue to ask questions about *what* John or Akbar, Mary or Mai-Lin will learn, how they will learn it, what particular needs they have and how their individual interests, attitudes and aptitudes can be accommodated into and contribute to the daily work of the classroom.

As we have already noted the national curriculum has undergone considerable changes since its implementation. Nevertheless it remains a reference point around which head teachers and subject co-ordinators construct the school experience offered to their pupils, a situation which is unlikely to change whatever party is in government. But the teacher is not powerless. The curriculum of a school has rightly been defied as 'everything that happens in a school day but leaves undefined the meanings which are constructed and attributed by the pupils'. Such definitions tend to embrace the content (the 'what'), the approaches to unspoken attitudes (the 'how'), and the learning strongly influenced by beliefs which underpin the relationship between school, home and community (the 'why'). The content (what should schools teach?) is the least difficult of these diverse elements to measure, although we have already noted the difficulties encountered by the national curriculum exercise. But what young people will learn by engaging with the content is not only problematic but a source of persistent questioning by effective teachers. The titles in this series acknowledge the centrality of subjects in any national curriculum but at the same time seek to show the many ways in which a prescribed curriculum can be vivified and enriched.

All the books in this series address aspects of the kinds of questions which teachers are asking as part of their concern to establish effective strategies for learning. Part of that concern focuses upon the links between the excitement of learning evidenced by young children, and the need to evaluate and maintain coherence in their experiences. Effective learning is the product of engagement as each member of the group struggles to make the learning process his or her own. At the same time, personal learning can still be limited unless it is placed in a broader context so that, for example, subject strands unite into a comprehensible and rational whole. Each author in this series seeks to indicate cross-curricular links, even though the titles indicate particular subject specialisms as starting points, so that the approach unifies rather than divides the child's experience of the curriculum.

As editors of this series, we wish to offer practising primary teachers a range of titles which recognises the complexity of the primary teacher's role. Each book gives shape and purpose to a specific curriculum area, dealing with issues which are particular to that specialism, presenting ideas for interesting and innovative practice in that area but, at the same time, emphasising the unity of the primary experience. Thus, each title is set against a broad canvas, that of the primary school as a living and vibrant place in which young children grow and learn.

Leone Burton

Henry Pluckrose

Introduction

Primary schools, like primary children, come in all sorts of shapes and sizes. The largest primary school will have more children than a five-form entry comprehensive school. The smallest will have only one class, containing children of all ages from 4 to 11 years. The oldest school building will date from the beginning of the last century. In an inner city area it may be built on three or four floors, each having individual classrooms with the very high ceilings we associate with Victorian schoolrooms. The newest school will have been planned by an architect working with teachers. There may not be any classrooms in the traditional sense. Instead, there will be open areas, mostly carpeted and linked one to another.

Inside all these classrooms a variety of things will be going on. There are very few primary schools nowadays which operate a formal timetable for the whole school. The class teacher takes responsibility for the timing of arrangements for teaching the class across the whole curriculum. One of the many advantages of this system is that activities which might take children any length of time from three minutes to three hours can all be fitted in. Although there are times in any primary classroom when all the children will be working at the same task, more frequently some children will be involved in some mathematics, others will be engaged in writing, a group will be working together on a large scale model, ...and four children will be having a heated discussion sitting round a computer.

It is hard to believe that the Department of Trade and Industry (DTI) hardware scheme for primary schools was only announced in 1982, and that before that date relatively few primary teachers had used a computer. There are approximately 22,000 primary schools in England, Wales and Northern Ireland, and a further 2,000 in Scotland. By the time the DTI scheme ended in 1984, virtually all these schools had acquired a computer. Since then the use of information technology in primary education has become so well established that the majority of schools have at least one machine in every classroom.

Throughout the same period over 50,000 practising primary teachers, in an unprecedented demand for in-service education, have attended introductory courses on computer use, although most of the primary teaching force have still not yet had the opportunity. Some may still feel uncertain whether or not they want it anyway! In some schools the only teacher who has been trained has moved elsewhere; in many there are classrooms where computers sit idle, gathering chalky dust because teachers are unaware of their educational potential. Head-teachers will be well aware of these kinds of problems. They will be aware too that an initial two-day course can do little more than concentrate on how to make the hardware function and how to operate a few small pieces of software. The real issues about possible new directions for the primary curriculum are only now beginning to be discussed.

The importance of information technology

Information technology, or IT, is the name which is given to machines which process information. It includes video recorders, telephones, calculators, cash tills and, of course, computers. Because information technology can be found in so many everyday devices it is affecting everyone's life. Whether we like it or not, it is here to stay.

Computers are probably the most versatile form of information technology. They are used very widely in industry and commerce, by the police, by hospitals, by newspaper publishers, and by designers of anything from a bridge to a wine glass. In the everyday world, they are used on weighing scales and cash tills in high street stores, to dispense money at banks, to store information at libraries or the telephone exchange, to control traffic lights or automatic doors, and to present graphical or tabulated information to the public at railway stations and airports.

A growing number of computers can be found in homes, where they tend to be used for writing purposes, or to support the running of a small business. Computers at home are also widely used for leisure activities. Some people - children as well as adults - enjoy programming as a hobby, perhaps drawing pictures and animating them to create a game, whereas others prefer playing the game itself. Surveys have shown that more than half of all primary aged children have a microcomputer at home, although girls are less likely than boys to have access to one outside school.

Anyone who has watched children working with a computer is impressed by the increase in their motivation and concentration. 'Computers,' said one 10-year-old recently, 'are meant for work and for having a good time on.'

Computers are fun to use because they are so versatile. They are cheap and very powerful tools; they will get cheaper and more powerful. They have pervaded offices and factories, homes and schools. The invention of the cheap computer will probably be as significant as the invention of the printing press in its effect on the lives of the children in our primary schools. Just as books can be used to enhance and extend children's education, so should computers be used. Just as children need to appreciate the versatility of books, and learn how to use them to fulfil their own needs, so they need to appreciate the versatility of computers, and learn how to control them to suit their own purposes.

FIGURE 0.1

A confidence and competence in using books is an acknowledged necessity for the present century. But we are now preparing children for life in the twenty-first century – a life in which everyone will come into contact not only with books but also with information technology in many different forms. The computers in our schools need to be exploited to the full in order to give children an equivalent confidence and competence in using these as they have in using books.

The place of computers in the curriculum

There is no specific book about information technology in the HMI Curriculum Matters series. Instead, there is the clear statement in *The curriculum from 5 to 16* (page 13) that: 'Information technology, which is having a profound effect on pupils whose adult lives will be in the 21st century, should find a place in all subjects which are able to take advantage of the facility to store and process information and to generate further information.'

In the same publication, nine areas of learning and experience are listed by HMI as the necessary components of a rounded education. Although computers are less likely to play a part in the **physical** or the **spiritual** areas, they can be expected to have an impact in the other seven:

in the **aesthetic and creative** area, as part of the processes of imagining, designing, composing, and inventing;

in the **human and social area**, in the collection and study of evidence and opinion from the local environment, and in the role play which takes place when children are involved in a simulation activity;

in the **linguistic and literary** area, in aiding the development of fluency and understanding in talking and reading, and in the composition and refinement of writing;

in the **mathematical area**, through the use of puzzles or strategic games, in the exploration of spatial relationships and patterns, in the solution of numerical problems, and in the management and representation of statistical data;

in the **moral** area, in questions about sharing time, taking turns, or the fair treatment of girls, in discussions about the use of computers to file information about people, or the use of robots to replace people at work;

in the **scientific** area, in the management and representation of information collected from observation, investigation or experiment, and in the simulation of processes which would otherwise be too dangerous, too time consuming or too expensive;

in the **technological** area, as a resource which can be used to bring about change or to exercise control over the environment.

To see how the use of a computer can integrate with these different areas of experience, consider what was done by one class of third-year juniors who used a piece of software which asked them questions about giants. Some of the questions required the children to enter measurements like the giant's height or weight; other questions required imaginative descriptions of the giant's personality or likes and dislikes. The children's responses were displayed, sometimes in the form of a graph to be interpreted, sometimes in the form of text to be read, and further questions about the giant were posed. Would it, for example, be able to lie down in the school hall, and what size shoes would it be likely to take? The use of the program inspired a great deal of excellent work on the theme of giants.

In the linguistic and literary area, the children read a variety of stories like *The BFG* (Big Friendly Giant) by Roald Dahl and *Giant Kippernose* by John Cunliffe. The watched a film of *Gulliver's Travels*, and started to think of giants as being relative to the size of the things around them. They read poems like Michael Rosen's *Giant Jojo*, then using a word processor they wrote and revised stories in which they imagined themselves either as a giant, or in the presence of one. As part of their work in the aesthetic area, they illustrated their stories using a variety of materials, including a computer program which allowed them to create giant-sized faces on the screen and then to print them.

In the scientific area, the children researched mini-beasts, and created a data file which would help them to identify a new mini-beast when it was discovered. Rory, who found a giant spider and looked after it for a week, started to consider moral issues. He wrote:

> **In the Autumn when I was only eight I found a giant spider. He was huge with black and white speckles and hairs on his legs. I found him in the corner of our yard. I made him a house from a biscuit tin with a piece of wood for him to hide under and some grass for his bed. My brother laughed and said Stupid nit, you cant keep a spider. But I did try. I fed him on ants and crums and I felt gentle towards him. For a whole week he lived and then one day I came home from school and looked in his tin and he was dead. He looked like a dried up bit of black cotton and I felt very sad. You would have liked my spider. His name was Fred.**

In the mathematical and technological areas of their study of giants, the children posed themselves a problem. In the corner of the school grounds there was a very tall tree. If a giant were as tall as the tree, what size would its slippers be? This problem involved the children in a range of skills. They estimated the height of the tree, and looked up different ways in which they could measure it. They used wood, string, glue and a small weight to make their own clinometer for finding the height of the tree. They collected information about themselves and their parents, and used the computer to produce and print out a graph relating their heights to their shoe sizes. By extending their graph they were able to come to a conclusion about the size of the giant's slippers. Their final task was to construct a slipper for the giant: first making plans and small prototypes, and then the full-scale production. The slipper, covered in blue and white checked wallpaper, was eventually placed at the foot of the tree.

Activities with computers will therefore permeate and stimulate many different aspects of teaching and learning in school, rather than the computer becoming an object of study in itself. The purpose of integrating computer use into the curriculum in this way is threefold.

• It allows teachers to extend and enhance the education of the children in their care.
• It allows children to acquire skills in the use of a computer as a tool for their own purposes.
• It gives children a better understanding of the range of ways in which their own lives will be affected increasingly by information technology.

Nevertheless, versatile and important though the computer might be, it is only one resource amongst many. There are some things which the computer does very well, but there are often occasions when children will learn more by other means. The use of software needs to be properly integrated with the whole range of other classroom resources: books, radio and television broadcasts, films posters, games and puzzles, apparatus and equipment for mathematics and science, materials for art and for technology, and so on. Most important of all, the use of the computer needs to spring from and relate to children's own direct experiences. There are times in any primary classroom when 'hands on' experience at the computer keyboard is valuable; but the time spent in related 'hands off' activities is just as important.

Making decisions: practice or problem solving

The curriculum from 5 to 16 (page 37) states its criteria for the selection of what children learn as: 'That which is taught should be worth knowing, comprehensible, capable of sustaining pupils' interest and useful to them at their particular stage of development and in the future.'

The questions which might help to determine what children should do with a computer in the classroom are therefore:

- Will the children do and learn things that are worth doing and learning?
- Is using the computer the most effective way of doing and learning these things?
- Is it the most sensible and urgent use of the machine?

Computers, of course, can be misused, just like other tools. You would not, for example, use a garden spade to eat an apple pie, or a spoon to dig a garden. Nor would you use a washing machine to wash a single handkerchief.

Most primary schools will have in their collection of software some programs which drill children by presenting practice exercises, with amazing animated and often tuneful rewards for correct responses. Is the use of a computer with this kind of practice material ever justified?

Teachers who have used such programs claim that the immediate feedback about the correctness of the answer, rather than waiting for a teacher to check the work done, is of benefit to many children. Some infant teachers argue that practice programs in which children count the number of objects on the screen, or identify a pair of matching shapes, have a place. A reception class teacher can only work with one group of children at any one time, and children who have been learning to count by handling and arranging real objects sometimes follow this activity by colouring in and numbering stamped outlines of animals or vehicles, so that the teacher can work with the next group. But the use of a computer program which presents pictures of objects to be counted could be a more meaningful follow-up activity, since colouring in three camels stamped on a page, although it might be justified on some grounds, can hardly be described as 'doing mathematics'.

When all children have their own portable computers, the arguments in favour of practice programs might be more persuasive. But at the moment, when the class machine must be shared between thirty, to spend any computer time in school using repetitive drill programs, no matter how much fun they are, seems questionable. Practice exercises for older infants and junior aged children are so easy for teachers to produce in worksheet or work-card form. Ideas for cheap and simple board games can be found in books or magazines and are easily reproduced. Gadgets like the Little Professor can provide randomly generated sums at various levels of difficulty. It is so much more difficult for teachers to create classroom situations which involve children in genuine problem solving, yet much of the software described in the various chapters of this book encourages logical thinking and the development of strategy. Surely a scarce resource should be used for things which are otherwise difficult to provide, not for activities which can easily be done in other ways?

There is a new kind of computer application called an Integrated Learning System (ILS). This may, at first sight, appear to be a kind of practice program but it is in fact something very different. Very few primary schools currently have Integrated Learning Systems because they are enormously expensive. Their nature and potential are explored in Chapter 11.

Some types of software

There are several different ways in which you can use computers effectively, whether you are a beginner with a computer in the classroom or whether you are more experienced.

In those primary schools which have established computer use in at least part of the school, it is evident that computers can:

- support the curriculum which is already being offered;
- enhance that curriculum so that what we offer children is rather better than what was offered previously;
- extend or even change that curriculum.

Many schools are already familiar with the ways in which the computer can support well-recognised teaching points; some schools will have reached the point where they want to enhance their curriculum by broadening the use which they make of the machine; a few schools will have changed their curriculum in order to exploit the possibilities which the technology offers.

A number of programs for primary schools can be used in specific ways to support the existing curriculum. Most primary schools will have a library of small programs of this type, selected with their own children in mind. Some of these programs are capable of being used as an animated blackboard to illustrate particular teaching points, or to promote whole class discussion; others may well involve the children in problem solving or help them to develop a mathematical investigation; some will, through a puzzle or a strategic game, encourage children to apply skills which they have acquired away from the computer.

Joanne, a top infant, described how she used one such program.

The computer helps you to do sums and number games today me and Toni had a game of counters I won 13 games and Toni won 10 games. how you play is there is nine squares and you have to try and make 15 with three squares and I have to try and stop Toni from winning like if Toni has 9 and 4 I have to press 2 because Toni will win if I dont. the program makes me think a lot.

Joanne Burchell

FIGURE 0.2

One advantage of small programs is that they are easy to operate since the instructions about which keys to press are provided on the screen. It is possible for a teacher to become familiar with the content reasonably easily, and for a group of children to use the program while their teacher works elsewhere in the classroom.

Small programs are generally intended to be used for short periods only, anything from five minutes to a maximum of half an hour. The most effective use of them can therefore be made when they have been catalogued and linked to the school's curriculum guidelines, so that they can be chosen to support selected activities.

Programs which can enhance the curriculum are sometimes more complex, but they can sustain work both at the keyboard and away from it over a period of weeks. Such programs often come with packs of linked resource materials and may be supplied on disc, or on CD-ROM. A simulation which is concerned with the management of a car-racing team or an adventure game which takes you into an enchanted land of magic and mystery in your search for six lost children, are both examples of programs of this type. They can stimulate a wide variety of tasks: craft activities (Figure 0.3), scientific experiments, creative writing, mathematical investigation (Figure 0.4), historical research, drama, music, or even PE. Like other cross-curricular topic work, their effectiveness is promoted if their use is related to the use of books, visits, pictures and artefacts.

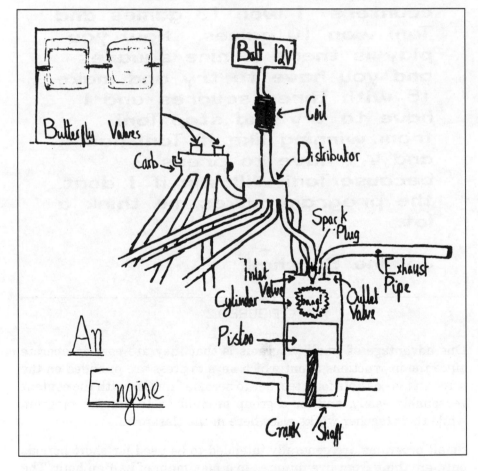

FIGURE 0.3

HMI, in their report *Aspects of the work of the Microelectronics Education Programme*, described how two schools had used a simulation program for the finding and raising of a Tudor warship.

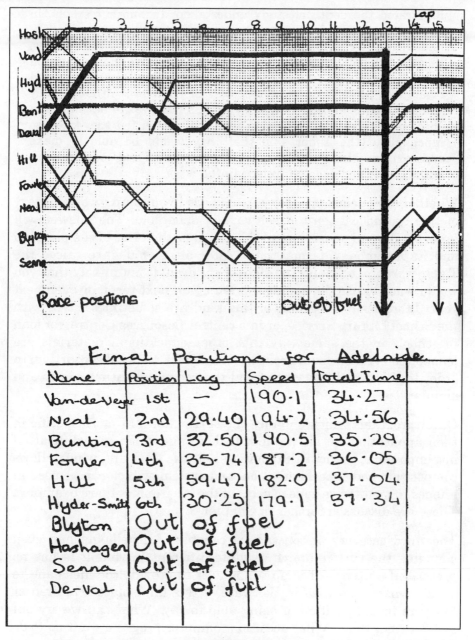

FIGURE 0.4

In one class children had plotted their finds on three dimensional grids; had gained a sound knowledge of the problems of working under the sea; and had researched the period in great detail. Their written work was lively and often established for the reader the excitement of diving or finding treasure, reflecting the computer simulation. Art work and model making added to the displays and illustrated the depth of study undertaken. In another school, in another region, work in mathematics, based on the same program, had included compass bearings, shape, co-ordinates and angles, these topics being reinforced by the computer work. Some children (having carefully researched the background) had recorded interviews pretending to be members of the crew. Although they were unable to visit the real *Mary Rose*, a visit was to be made to a ship built in the 1860s at Hartlepool; the teacher felt they knew so much about the Tudor ship that they would be able to make comparisons. In both schools the teachers and pupils were enthusiastic and deeply involved in the work.

Whether or not each primary school needs to build up its own library of this second category of software is debatable. The answer will probably depend on the size of the school or the price of the program and its accompanying materials. After all, if you have raised the Tudor warship, or found the six lost children, it is unlikely that you would want to use the same program again next term, or even next year! Libraries of programs of this kind are sometimes based with the School Library Service, or in a central Resources Centre, for loan to schools in the same way that other educational materials are loaned. Sometimes small groups of schools form a local consortium in order to share both the cost of and the use of adventure games and simulations.

Other programs which enhance the curriculum are more specific in their application but allow pupils to do things which were difficult, if not impossible, without the computer. Music software, which allows composition and experimentation, and systems which can be used in science to monitor various aspects of the environment, are examples. These are discussed further in Chapter 6.

The third category of software is capable of developing and even changing the curriculum. It is quite different in that it is has no prescribed content – it is up to the user to provide the ideas and to decide what to do with it. Software of this kind places children or teachers in the position of being able to say, 'What can we try out next?' rather than, 'What does this computer program want us to do now?'

Content-free software provides a flexible tool for children and teachers to explore new fields. It can be a fast retriever and sorter of information, allowing young children to carry out research, to pose and to test hypotheses, using a far greater collection of data than they would otherwise have been able to manage. It can be a means of drawing patterns or pictures (Figure 0.5), or of controlling the movements of a floor robot, so that the world of mathematical precision and logical procedures can be explored through trial and adjustment approaches. It can become a word processor, so that drafts and redrafts of writing – so often advocated but very time consuming in practice – can be refined and published. The most up-to-date computers can also be used for more sophisticated presentations, desk-top-published news sheets or on screen multimedia magazines, for example.

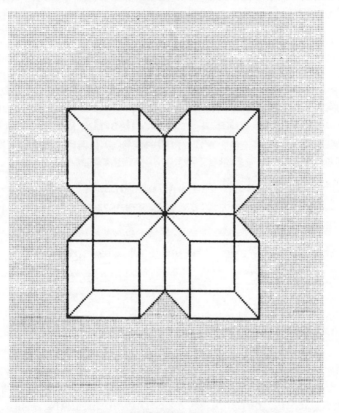

FIGURE 0.5

Donna and Cheryl, both aged nine, used a word processor for the first time in January when it was snowing. Their teacher encouraged them to type in some words about snow:

**snowflake snowman cold sky white soft shining
twist twirl float ground melt slush water puddle**

The next stage was for the children to move the words about, combining them with each other, adding more words where necessary, and deleting those that they decided not to use.

I am a snowflake. I come from the cloudy sky. I am as white as paper and soft as silk. I twirl and twist and jump about just like a butterfly. Then I start to slow down. I go down towards the ground. I land with a bump. Children pick me up and pat me into something. I roll round and round. I grow into a snowman. The sun starts to shine. Now I start to melt into slush.

More talk between the children, and with their teacher, eventually resulted in this:

**The story of a snowflake
by Donna Kelly and Cheryl Martin**

I am a snowflake from the cold grey sky. I am as white as a snow fox and soft as pure silk. I twirl and twist and jump about just like a little butterfly fluttering from flower to flower. Slowly, the ground gets nearer and nearer and I land gently on a snowy rock.

Children pick me up and pat me into a large wet ball. I roll round and round, growing, growing, growing. I am a snowman!

Now the snow stops. The sun shines softly, and I melt slowly into slush.

Skill development

A skill is an ability to carry out a task. At a simple level, skills include specific actions or movements which are carried out more or less automatically: for example, catching a ball, using a saw, reading and spelling common words, adding small numbers together, fingering notes on a recorder.

The use of content-free software demands skills of a much higher order, skills which have more general application, and which often draw upon complex thought processes: for example, devising strategies for problem solving, organising information, weighing and interpreting evidence, generalising by seeing common, underlying features in superficially different circumstances, recognising the relationship of action and consequence, and evaluating the outcomes of making changes.

Skills such as these cannot be acquired by practising them in isolation. Isolated practice does little to help learners to know when and how to use the skill, which after all is the point of the learning. The advice which is offered in *The curriculum from 5 to 16* (page 39) is: 'Skills are best acquired in the course of activities that are seen as worthwhile in themselves by children and teachers alike, and in contexts which ensure that the children are able to apply them as well as to master them.'

The book goes on to group skills under a variety of different headings. How can work with computers contribute to the development of these skills?

Communication skills. Computers can provide a focus for children's talk. They also offer children ways of representing and manipulating words, numbers, symbols, shapes or sounds, in the form of text, in a picture or diagram, in a pattern, or in a table or graph.

Study skills and observation skills. A computer can offer children opportunities to select and extract information, and to arrange and rearrange data, so that they can more readily recognise similarities and differences, or patterns and relationships, and draw conclusions from the evidence.

Problem-solving skills. Since many of the activities which children might undertake with computers are of a problem-solving nature, a whole range of problem-solving skills can be further developed through computer use: an ability to identify problems, to plan, choose and compare strategies, then carry the strategies out.

Physical and practical skills. A computer in a classroom, like a calculator, a tape measure or a hammer, extends the range of practical tools which children can choose to use when it is appropriate to do so.

Creative and imaginative skills. Simulations offer children opportunities to envisage and empathise with life at other times, or in other places (either fictitious or real), while design packages or music-making software add to the creative media which children might use.

Numerical skills. In a number of simulations or adventure games, in the use of information retrieval software, and in programming activities, there are many opportunities to make use of numerical and spatial relationships, or of graphical and statistical data.

Personal and social skills. In their use of computers, particularly where there is a responsibility for combined decision making, children are required to consider the views of others, to contribute, to cooperate or to take the lead as appropriate.

Helping children to appreciate the potential of powerful and versatile software packages, and to develop skills in using them, is not an easy task. Teachers need time to learn, time to plan, and time to reflect. Like children, they absorb new ideas at different rates and in different ways. Some will use a small number of selected and easily handled programs which support and fit comfortably into good primary practice; some will use bigger packages which provide enhanced opportunities for cross-curricular topics; some will integrate into their work the use of content-free tools, and will be thinking about the ways in which these are likely to change both how teachers teach and how children learn. In 1980 few primary school teachers had ever seen a computer. If teachers are now becoming aware of some of the different ways of using computers in primary schools, then in the words of the Greek poet Constandinos Kavifis: 'To have reached this point is no small achievement'.

In the themes which form the earlier chapters of this book, the uses of different kinds of software are described in detail, as well as the skills which are associated with them. Chapters 1 and 2, which are about information and communication, consider databases and presentation packages such as word processors and desktop publishing. Chapters 3, 4 and 5, which are all concerned with problem solving, discuss the use of puzzles, simulations, and programming. Chapters 6 and 7 describe how software can be used to stimulate or to support work in different areas of experience – language, mathematics, science and technology, social studies, and creative arts – and in cross-curricular topic work.

The later chapters of the book are concerned with the overall management of computers in the primary school curriculum. Chapter 8 deals with planning and organisation both in the school as a whole and in the classroom while Chapter 9 considers the teacher's role in learning, the need to encourage girls, and the support which is available from home. Chapter 10 is concerned with the whole question of evaluation. The last chapter looks ahead to what might be coming next, and debates whether or not in the future there will still be schools as we know them today.

1 Children using information

There has always been debate, within education and among the general public, about what is meant by good teaching practice. In thinking about good practice most people consider two aspects: first, the suitability of the curriculum content – the ideas, skills and knowledge to be acquired; second, the ways in which learning and teaching might take place. These two aspects are of course not separate from each other, but linked together. Information imparted in isolation is neither memorable nor useful; the processes of learning need content to give them substance.

Factual content has sometimes been dismissed by writers on primary education: anything will do as long as it interests the children. On the other hand, some regard the learning of factual content as the main purpose of primary education. Neither of these stand-points can really be justified. Factual content should be information that is as up to date and as accurate as possible and that will continue to be useful. It should relate to the children's personal experiences, and extend those experiences. At the same time, children should be helped to recognise that 'facts' are open to both personal and cultural interpretation.

Consider, for example, how history might be taught to young children. Before the advent of computers in classrooms only a few primary schools managed to draw together and examine for themselves historical data from their own locality. Most schools used books as sources of information about the past; the books were labelled 'The Vikings' or 'The Tudors' and the alleged information about the lives of people who lived in those times were the views of the author at the time the book was written, not those of the children today.

Contrast this approach with one in which children experience history through their own examination of first-hand sources of information. They look at parish registers and compare these with contemporary newspaper reports or census records. They observe the town or village or city street in which they live to see what buildings remain.

Railways may be a focus of interest, or clothes or kitchen utensils. Older people may have memories to recount or artefacts to lend for a class museum. Relevant books and pictures, as well as real places and people, help the children as they assemble for themselves facts which they can then arrange and interpret in their own way.

As they do so they find examples of conflict of evidence. They start to appreciate that 'facts' are what we make of them and what we do with them, not fixed and unchangeable items which can be neatly classified as true or false. It is the act of discovering and verifying information for themselves, solving problems as an historian would solve them, weighing evidence, making judgements, that kindles children's understanding of history and makes it come alive.

The nature of information

Children's perceptions about information are worth exploring. Pat d'Arcy, working with some 7-year-olds at Crockerton Primary School in Warminster, asked them to jot down what they knew about blood. Amongst their notes were the following statements:

> **keeps you alive**
> **Mum skreems at it**
> **a red liquid that vampires and Dracular likes**
> **underneath our skin**
> **dead blood turns into a wart**
> **it is different shades of red**
> **clots**
> **warm**

In the discussion about the validity of these remembered pieces of information, some questions arose which highlighted some of the gaps in the children's knowledge.

- Do insects have blood?
- How much blood have we got inside us?
- Why is blood red?
- Why does blood come out when you fall over?

The children considered how they could find out answers to these questions, and so add more information to that which they already knew. Where would the information be kept? Who would know about it?

I would look in books about blood and encyclopaedia
I would go to a hospital
I would go to the nature history museum
I would look in an animal dictionary
I would go to a special doctor to see if he new

When primary children are asked what they think information is they tend to suggest that it is something which somebody tells you, or which you read in a book or hear on the news. Another view is that information is something which you need to know and which you can find out. These are all attempts at definitions, without any description of the different circumstances in which information might be required or used. But the attempted definitions make it clear that children generally see information as something that comes from elsewhere; they do not usually see themselves as producers or creators of information.

Consider this discussion which took place with some 10-year-olds at Manor Way Primary School in Sussex.

Teacher: Information, now who has any ideas about what it means. What is information?
Child: Well, it's like instructions.
Child: It's like news.
Child: It tells you something about a subject.
Child: If you wanted to buy a house you would go to an estate agent.
Teacher: I think that might be telling me where I could get information from, not what it is.
Child: It's something you need to know to do something.
Child: It's like ideas.

And the sources of information? In children's eyes information comes from the Football Association, the church, the BBC, the railway station, or from people like a policeman, the Prime Minister, the weather man on television, or from teachers or parents.

Teacher: OK. Spencer said where you could get some information. He said that if you wanted to buy a house that you could get information from an estate agent. Can you name some other places you can get information? Where can we go for information, any sort of information at all?
Child: Police station.
Child: Building society. Bank.
Child: Garage.
Child: Airport.

Teacher: Right. Now you have told me some places. Now it's no good just going to an airport. What would you actually do to get the information you wanted?

Child: Ask.

Teacher: Ask?

Child: Ask someone who knows.

Group: Yes, ask someone.

Teacher: Perhaps that's the most usual way that we get information. We ask someone for it.

The children will probably recognise that information can be found in a variety of printed sources: newspapers, dictionaries, catalogues, reference books, or Yellow Pages. It can also be heard on the radio or shown on TV.

Teacher: What other ways could you find out information?

Child: The news.

Teacher: Where do you find out about the news?

Child: The telly. On the radio.

Child: The paper. You can look in the paper.

Teacher: Do all newspapers tell you the same news?

Child: No. Some have more sport.

Child: And some have more pictures.

Teacher: If the same story is in all the different newspapers, do they all give the same information about it?

Group: Yes.

Teacher: We could check that, couldn't we? How do you find out information at school when you want to know something?

Child: You could use a calculator to get an answer to a sum.

Child: You look on the clock to know the time.

Child: Or you can look in books.

Teacher: Books. There's a lot of information in books, isn't there? Information about what? What sort of information can be found in books?

Child: You can find out about history and all of that.

Child: About animals and birds.

Child: In the Bible. You can look in a Bible to find out about Jesus.

Child: You can look in a dictionary and learn how to spell words.

Teacher: What else is in the dictionary besides how to spell words?

Child: It shows you what the words mean.

Child: Shall I get one?

Teacher: Yes, if you would like to. What can we do with the dictionary?

Child: Look up some words.

Teacher:	How do we do that?
Child:	The words are in order. They're in order of the alphabet.
Teacher:	Which particular word could we look up?
Child:	Information.
Teacher:	Information! Yes, because we didn't really come to a good conclusion about what information is, did we?
Child:	I've got the dictionary here.
Teacher:	What does it say?
Child:	Giving facts, knowledge.

Information takes many different forms: words, numbers, signs and symbols, codes, maps, diagrams, tables, graphs, shapes and textures, sounds, smells, and tastes. Most primary children will appreciate very readily that information may be provided in the form of words, either spoken or written, but they are generally less aware that information may take other forms.

Teacher:	What do you think information looks like? What form does it take?
Child:	Words. Words on a page. Or a picture – like in an advertisement.
Child:	Words that someone says to you.
Child:	It could be a number. A number on a bus or a telephone number.
Teacher:	What information can you see in this room?
Child:	[*Pause*] Numbers. The numbers on my watch tell me the time.
Child:	The graph shows how far we live from the school.
Child:	The map shows our houses.
Child:	You can tell it's daytime because the light isn't on.
Teacher:	What about signs and symbols? Do they give information?
Child:	[*After a pause*] The arrows point the way to the office.
Child:	A plus sign tells you to add up.
Child:	[*Pause*] There are symbols on the TV switches.
Child:	And on the toilet doors.
Teacher:	Apart from people telling you something, do you think that sounds can give you information?
Child:	[*Pause*] The telephone when it rings.
Child:	When you clap your hands we know we have to stop what we are doing.
Child:	When you hear the sound of a car, you know a car is coming.

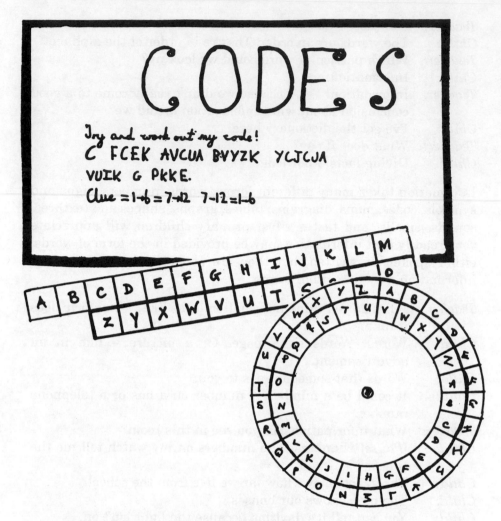

FIGURE 1.1

There are a number of different ways of sending or transmitting information. For example, people with a speech or hearing disability sometimes use sign language instead of words; blind people might use Braille. When the distance is greater, we have to find other means of communicating. People living in mountainous regions might use fire beacons or smoke signals to send messages to each other. Semaphore messages are signalled by using flags. Morse code can be sent by flashing lights or by tapping out sounds using telegraph or radio links.

To aid their understanding of the newer ways of communicating information children can devise their own means of sending messages, perhaps making a 'telephone' from two tin cans and a long taut string, and comparing the distance over which it can be used with, say, that of a home-made megaphone. It then becomes easier for them to appreciate modern information technology, and the part played by telephones, radio and television, by satellites, laser beams, and optical fibres – special glass tubes, thin as a human hair, along which flashes of light can be transmitted.

Information processing

There are many different ways of **processing information**, depending on what questions have been asked. For example, if you collect recipes and stick them in a scrap book, then from time to time you might want to:

- **search** through your scrap book in order to find a particular recipe;
- **sort** the recipes into alphabetical order, according to their title, so that you can find one easily when you want it;
- **select** particular recipes: for example, those cakes that use less than 150 grams of butter;
- **group** or **classify** your recipes by putting together all the recipes for, say, puddings;
- **count** your recipes to see how many you have;
- **calculate** the quantities needed to feed four people, rather than the six people for whom the recipe was designed;
- **rearrange** the layout or order of your recipes so that you can fit more of them into your scrap book.

Given a range of different problems, it can be interesting for children to consider first what information they would need to collect, and then how they would process it, in order to solve the problems. For example, what information, and what information processing, are needed to find out:

- if red is the most popular colour in the class;
- which was the hottest day last year;
- if the number 73 bus is late;
- where to position the computer in the classroom;
- if it is safe to cross the road;
- whether or not to buy a pair of shoes;
- what to choose from the menu for a school lunch;
- how to find a particular book in the library;
- who was absent from school on the most days last term?

Although people can and do process information every day entirely on their own, it sometimes becomes necessary to use a machine to help. Computers will not process any kind of information; they are designed to process data which can be coded as a set of numbers: for example, words, sounds, electrical signals, pictures, and numbers themselves. The advantages of a computer are the speed at which it can process data, and the size of its memory, so it can handle a lot of information very quickly – far more than the human brain can manage. But only occasionally will children mention a computer as having anything to do with the storage and retrieval of information, and few appreciate that even the small microcomputer in a primary school can be linked via a telephone or cable to the massive, world-wide, information system – the Internet.

Teacher: Now there is another way to get information that you use every day. What is it?

Child: Ask a teacher?

Teacher: Yes, of course you could ask a teacher. But are there other ways besides asking people?

Child: A computer. Or a CD-ROM.

Teacher: How can you ask a computer?

Child: By typing it in.

Teacher: If you wanted to get an answer, could you ask your computer anything you wanted.

Child: No.

Teacher: What sort of questions could you ask it?

Child: Like what is ten add ten.

Child: To print your name or to draw something.

Child: What creepy crawlies can kill you?

Teacher: Now in your homes I think that there are probably other ways of finding out information. Maybe in some of your homes. At home most of you have got a television set. Do any of you use it to find information?

Child: Ceefax.

Teacher: Yes, Ceefax. And the other one?

Child: Teletext.

Teacher: Mmm. So we can use our television sets if we have the right equipment to look at special things called Ceefax and Teletext. One or two of you might find information through your telephone.

Child: The time.

Child: My mum finds out the cricket score.

Child: My mum finds out recipes.

Child: The operator.

Teacher:	What might you ask the operator?
Child:	A number, what number you wanted.
Child:	You can use the telephone to get information from the AA. You can ring them up to find out the way to go a journey.
Child:	Or the RAC.
Teacher:	Have any of you heard of a thing called the Internet?
Group:	No.

It is only when time is found for the development of children's perceptions about information that the deeper issues start to emerge. Some information is thrust upon you (at school, on TV), but some you have to make an effort to get for yourself; some is visible and is easily verified; some is consequential or related to the circumstances in which it is found; some is a reflection of attitudes or opinions and is open to dispute. These issues are not often discussed with primary children, and yet the increasing use of information technology both inside and outside school makes them very relevant.

One of the most interesting conversations I have ever had with third-year juniors was with a group of confident children who were inventing a monster (incidentally as part of a computer activity). The children had reached a point of the program where some information about a monster (in this case Werewolf) was provided, and they were asked to consider whether or not the monster was real or imaginary. Their first reaction was that Werewolf was 'real because we've seen it on the television'. The planned lesson was abandoned. Instead, a long discussion took place about the kind of evidence presented in different TV programmes, with the children for the first time questioning the validity of photographs, the selection of material, and the possible vested interests of television producers or advertisers.

Information-handling skills

The increasing use of information-handling software and large collections of data on CD-ROM is creating a growing demand for more highly developed information-handling skills than have been generally encouraged in the past. Often the only experiences which children have had to draw upon were those involved in completing worksheets where the key words, the research strategies, and even the materials to be consulted were already identified. 'Use your atlas to find out ... and then complete the following paragraph.'

Any fact-finding enquiry which children carry our involves a number of different **information-handling skills:**

- establishing the purpose for which information is required;
- deciding what information is needed, and how accurate it needs to be or can be;
- deciding where information can be found;
- collecting information through research, by observation or experiment, by counting or measuring, or by sounding opinion;
- organising and storing or recording the collected information;
- sifting through information for evidence to support hypotheses;
- interpreting information, drawing inferences, thinking of explanations;
- building up and presenting findings through written or spoken reports, supported by tables of results, graphs and charts, sketches, models, photographs, maps, and so on.

When they are carrying out an investigation, conducting some research, or solving a problem, children can be helped to develop these information-handling skills if they are encouraged to ask themselves a set of questions, and to consider the part that the computer might play.

- What do I want to find out? Why?
- What information do I need? How much do I need?
- How accurate does the information need to be, or can it be?
- Where can I get it from?
- How shall I collect it?
- What questions do I need to ask so that I get the information that I really want? Are my questions fair?
- How shall I organise my collection of information? How shall I record it?
- How can I process the information in order to find answers?
- What exactly have I found out? Is it what I wanted or what I expected? What is the reason for it? What is its significance?
- What would be the best way to record or to display my findings?
- Who needs to know about my results? How shall I let them know?

A class of 11-year-olds at St Joseph's RC Primary School in London carried out a survey to see whether or not the school should change the things that were sold in their school tuck shop. They discussed many different issues before they began their survey.

- Whose opinion should be asked (children, staff, parents, anyone else)?

- What questions should they be asked?
- How many people in each group needed to be asked? All of them, or just some of them?
- If only a sample from each group were surveyed, how should the sample be chosen to make sure that it was representative?
- What should be done about absentees on the day of the survey?
- How should the people in the survey make their suggestions? Should they have a free choice, or should they choose from a given list?
- Should the information be collected by questionnaire or by interview?
- How should the collected information be organised?
- What kind of vote or result would be needed for a new item of food to be sold at the tuck shop, or for an existing item to be discontinued? Should the people in the survey be told this beforehand, or not?

After the children's first attempt to collect some information, their teacher discussed with them some of the issues that had arisen.

Teacher: I think some of you had problems, didn't you, getting the information that you wanted?

Child: Yes.

Teacher: Let's hear about your problems.

Child: We didn't get enough information. We only asked seven people.

Teacher: Did they fill everything in for you?

Child: No, we filled it in. We asked them all the questions.

Child: The young ones, when we'd started interviewing them, some of them went away.

Child: Some of them started mucking about.

Child: And my sister.

Child: We went round to the little ones and they weren't really interested.

Child: When me and Gifty asked them the questions while I wrote them down they went off and played.

Child: Some of them were getting impatient.

Child: Some of them though it was stupid.

Teacher: Now can anybody suggest, if we do this again on Monday, a better way of collecting the information that we need? What could we do to make it easier or better and to make sure that we get the answers that we really want?

Child: Go to the classes after tuck.

Child: When they are quiet and listening.

Teacher: So you want to change the time when you ask them and the place where you ask them? What about the lay-out of your form? Did that help or could it be designed better?

Child: It could be shorter.

Child: We didn't need all the questions.

Teacher: Which questions shall we miss out?

Child: We don't need to ask them the cost.

Child: We can find that out.

Child: Yes, and we shouldn't ask what they would most like to buy because they don't have enough money to buy what they say anyway. One of them said pineapple.

Child: We should give them a list to choose from, with things they could afford.

Further discussion took place after the children's second attempt to collect the information that they wanted.

Teacher: What did you think about the gathering of information today as against the way you collected it last Friday?

Child: It was better. We asked more people.

Child: It was much easier.

Teacher: Why was that?

Child: They weren't all moving about. They weren't playing so they didn't run off to the games.

Child: They were sitting down.

Child: They were listening to what we said.

Child: They were concentrating.

Teacher: What about filling in your forms, was that easier?

Child: Yes. We didn't ask so many questions.

Teacher: What about the way that you set out your forms? Was it better?

Child: Yes.

Teacher: Why?

Child: Last time we got mixed up with all the lines. In this one it was much easier. We drew the lines down and across with the ruler.

Child: And we got them to choose the kinds of things they would like from a list, so they said more sensible things.

Child: The things that they chose were things they could afford.

Child: It was more accurate.

Helping children to think about information

Teachers who are interested in developing children's awareness about information might like to try some of the ideas listed below.

- Discuss with the children what information looks like.
- Collect and display some examples of different kinds of information.
- Devise some ways of sending information.
- Encourage the children to pose some questions. Discuss what kind of information would be needed in order to answer those questions, and how that information might be collected.
- Discuss and experiment with different ways of processing information: ordering, classifying, selecting, counting, calculating ...
- Consider different sources of information. How do we know the information from those sources is reliable, accurate, up to date and complete?

Further reading

Diamond, D. 1983. *Pre-computer activities*. Hulton.
  ISBN 0 7175 1154 5.

Neale, G. (ed.) 2nd edition 1984. *Computers, information and you*.
  Acorn CES. ISBN 0 903885 31 X.

2 Some information-handling software

It has never been easy to give children access to first hand, up-to-date information. Managing the information and sifting through it have usually been impossible with anything other than very small collections of data, especially when each new finding has required an adjustment to be made to a table of results, a graph, or a written report. The school's computer is a tool which can make the management and presentation of information a realistic possibility. For even the youngest children in the infant school there are different kinds of software which will store and retrieve information, programs which present information graphically or which allow children to create their own diagrams or pictures, and simple word processors to aid all kinds of writing.

Databases and graph-drawing packages

Software which is used to store information is called a **database**. One sort of database works a bit like a card index system, with a large number of **records** all set out in the same sort of way. Each record has the same headings, called **fields**, under which information can be entered. For example, if children had collected some data about the weather over a period of a month, then each record might have eight fields: the date, the day number, the hours of sunshine, the wind direction and force, the temperature, the cloud type, and the rainfall (Figure 2.1).

If all the database could do were to store information, it would be of little help. But there are ways of processing the information by sorting the records into alphabetical or numerical order, or by asking questions to pick out particular records with properties in common. For example, with the weather database, you could find out which day was the wettest, or you could check if sunny days were the warmest, or if rain came when the wind was from the west.

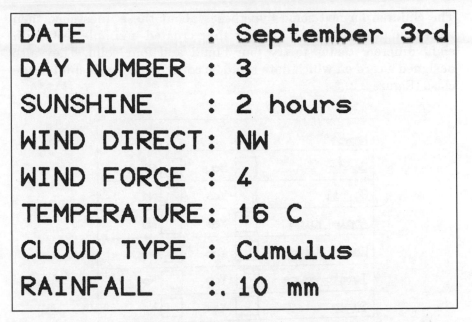

```
DATE         : September 3rd
DAY NUMBER   : 3
SUNSHINE     : 2 hours
WIND DIRECT  : NW
WIND FORCE   : 4
TEMPERATURE  : 16 C
CLOUD TYPE   : Cumulus
RAINFALL     :. 10 mm
```

FIGURE 2.1

Using a database enables children to deal with large amounts of information. They can hypothesise, ask questions, and test their conjectures out against what is stored in the database. The computer helps the children to explore the information in a way that would have been virtually impossible before schools had computers, since they do not have to check or to count every single detail themselves.

Any work with a database needs careful planning. Once the purpose of the investigation has been established, children need to consider what questions they want to ask about the subject, and what information needs to be collected in order to answer the questions. It is worth making a list of the questions at the initial discussion stage: they can be used as they are, or in a modified form, when it comes to interrogating the database later on.

Some top infants in London investigated what it felt like to have a sensory disability. Some of the questions which they listed about the sense of taste were:

- Which tastes are the easiest to pick out if you cannot see?
- Why are these tastes easy to pick out?
- Are liquids easier to identify than solids?
- Are some liquids easier than others?
- Are some solids easier than others?
- Are savoury tastes easier than sweet tastes?
- Which is the favourite taste, and why?

The children formed some hypotheses about these questions, then
with guidance from their teacher they created a simple test, with
eight different tastes to try: four liquid and four solid. They also
designed a card on which data could be collected for each child in the
class (Figure 2.2).

Name	....
Gender	☐ Boy ☐ Girl
Bovril	☐ Yes ☐ No
Apple juice	☐ Yes ☐ No
Lemon juice	☐ Yes ☐ No
Tomato sauce	☐ Yes ☐ No
Sugar	☐ Yes ☐ No
Salt	☐ Yes ☐ No
Mint polo	☐ Yes ☐ No
Cheese	☐ Yes ☐ No
Favourite	☐ Bovril ☐ Apple
	☐ Lemon ☐ Tomato ☐ Sugar
	☐ Cheese ☐ Salt ☐ Mint

FIGURE 2.2

Seven-year-old children have a strong sense of what is fair. The
children discussed whether it would be possible to tell which food
they were tasting by its texture or shape. They decided that the
sugar should be granulated, the mint should be crushed, and that the
cheese should be grated Parmesan rather than cubes of Cheddar.

They also made decisions early on about the way that they would
enter the information on their cards. From their previous
experiences they knew that consistency in a database is important:
for example, it is no use putting 135 cm in one place and 1.35 m in
another – the computer regards these as different. They also
remembered their difficulties in picking out a single record if it has
the same name as another one.

On this occasion, the children decided that NAME would mean first name only, but that the two boys called Paul in the class could put Paul S or Paul W so that their records would not get muddled up. Under GENDER, they would put BOY or GIRL rather than B or G, or MALE or FEMALE, and the other entries would be YES or NO, depending on whether or not the taste was correctly identified. Under the entry for FAVOURITE they would choose from a list in shortened form: BOVRIL, LEMON, APPLE, TOMATO, SUGAR, SALT, MINT, CHEESE.

The children worked in pairs on the tests, with each child taking a turn as the tester, offering a teaspoon of food to the blindfolded partner. The tester filled in the card for the other child as the test progressed, and was careful not to give away any clues in the process.

After the cards had been completed and checked by the children, their teacher checked them again to make sure that all the entries were filled in, and that spellings were consistent. She then helped the children to set up the database ready for each child to enter the information from his or her card. Different databases have different conventions about the number of characters which can be used in a field name: some will allow spaces and punctuation marks, some will not. In this case, the whole collection of data was kept in a file called TASTE, and each record was similar to Hannah's (Figure 2.3).

All the children involved were given an opportunity to type in some data. On this occasion, each pair of children typed in two records, but if there is a lot of data to enter, there is little to be gained by insisting that the children type it all in themselves. When all the children have entered a few records, a teacher or volunteer parent could finish the job much faster and more accurately.

The children needed to discover and be reassured that mistakes could always be corrected, but at the same time they started to appreciate that information in a database is only as reliable as the people who enter it. After school, their teacher printed out the complete file so that he could check the data and be forewarned about any mistakes that the children had made. An entry in the wrong place, or some small typing error, makes a lot of difference at later stages.

Information typed into a database is retained only while the computer is switched on. The data needs to be saved on disc at regular intervals, perhaps after every five or six records. It saves a lot of disappointment and retyping if the computer happens to be switched off by accident. It is also useful to keep two copies of each file on two separate discs, in case of accidental loss.

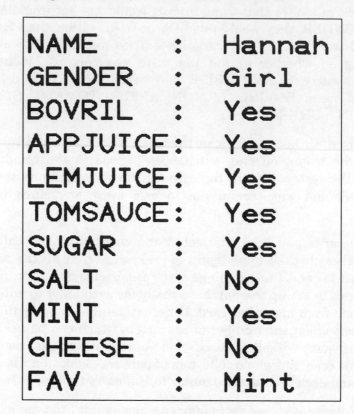

```
NAME       : Hannah
GENDER     : Girl
BOVRIL     : Yes
APPJUICE   : Yes
LEMJUICE   : Yes
TOMSAUCE   : Yes
SUGAR      : Yes
SALT       : No
MINT       : Yes
CHEESE     : No
FAV        : Mint
```

FIGURE 2.3

Once typing had been completed, the database was ready to be searched. The teacher worked with the children in groups of six, helping them to formulate and to refine their questions. It was possible, for example, to find out how many children had correctly identified cheese by counting how many entries for CHEESE were the same as YES. To find out whether more boys or girls had correctly identified SALT, it was necessary first to pick out records which had GENDER the same as GIRL, and SALT the same as YES, followed by an equivalent search for boys. The answers to these questions were printed in the form of a table.

All the information which was contained in the database under any one selected heading could be displayed graphically in a bar chart or a pie chart. It was also possible to look at the information under any two of the headings by looking at a scattergram. The children checked their tabulated results by looking at simple scattergrams relating the information under SALT and GENDER to see the same information displayed in a different way, and then again on a Venn diagram. The most popular choices of taste were identified by looking at a bar chart for the field called FAV, and then again on a pie chart. This led to further questions: did more girls or more boys opt for this favourite choice?

After each group had become confident in using the database to answer simple enquiries, their teacher discussed with the children more sophisticated questions, but left them on their own at the computer to try and find answers. Were the results for apple juice and lemon juice similar? Did most children who identified tomato sauce correctly also identify vinegar? Did anyone correctly identify all the tastes? Were savoury tastes or sweet tastes preferred? Were more liquids identified correctly or more solids? The children were disappointed to find that, in answer to these last questions, it was not possible for the computer to show them a graph. The information that they wanted was contained under eight different headings. They needed to take the separate pieces of information that they had acquired about each of the eight headings, and produce their own graph.

Having made their enquiries, and looked at their results, the children needed to decide what conclusions they could draw, and what reasons they could offer. Did the evidence support their original ideas? What possible explanations were there for what they had found out? Would their conclusions be true for older children? What about adults? Lastly, the class assembled reports on their general findings and mounted a large display along a corridor.

Children often need considerable support throughout the later stages of searching a database and deciding what inferences can be drawn. The teacher plays a vital part in pulling things together from time to time in discussion with the whole class, encouraging the children to share ideas, teasing out further lines of enquiry by asking questions, and drawing attention to relevant suggestions which are worth pursuing. The kinds of questions which can be asked are:

- How many ... are there?
- When they are in order, which is the smallest?
- Which one appears the most often?
- What is the difference between the number of ... and the number of ... ?
- How many of those that are ... are also ... ?
- Which of them are either ... or ... ?
- Is there a connection between the number of ... and the number of ... ?

- What is the average value?
- How are the ... distributed? What are the maximum and minimum values? Which is the middle value? Which is the most common value?
- Is it more likely that ... ?
- Is there a general trend?
- Would the results be different if the size of the sample were increased, or if the information had been collected at a different time or place?

It is best to use the children's own ideas for questions: they need to learn that some lines of enquiry are more pertinent and fruitful than others. The main aims are to nurture their curiosity so that they are stimulated to investigate, and to give them confidence that they can find out answers and identify possible connections for themselves.

It is important for children to develop an awareness of the range of ways in which the computer can show them the results of their queries. Most databases are able to display the information which they contain either set out in a table, or in the form of a graph or in a diagram. Children also need to realise that the same results can be presented in different forms of graphs or charts, and that one form can be more helpful than another in a particular situation. In the past children frequently have spent so much time drawing graphs and colouring them in that little time was left for looking at the graphs to see what they revealed. Where comments were made, they often simply repeated the details which were shown on the graph. Being able to deduce information from a graphical display, to interpret what it means, and to offer some explanation for it, are skills which are becoming increasingly important across the whole curriculum.

The teacher can help the children to appreciate that:

Pictograms (Figure 2.4) are useful for showing the results of a count when a single symbol can be used to represent each of the objects counted.

Block graphs (Figure 2.5) are useful for seeing that two values are the same, or for picking out which of a set of values is the greatest and which is the least.

Histograms (Figure 2.6) help to show how, for example, measurements are distributed, and what an average value might be.

Pie charts (Figure 2.7) are useful for making comparisons with a total, using simple fractions like a half, a third and a quarter.

Scattergrams (Figures 2.8 and 2.9) help you to see connections between things; for example, that taller people tend to have larger feet, or that on sunny days the temperature is higher.

Venn diagrams (Figure 2.10) are an effective way of showing how many things belong to one set or to another, or how many belong to both sets at the same time.

Tables (Figure 2.11) are useful for seeing how things are ordered, and also for spotting patterns.

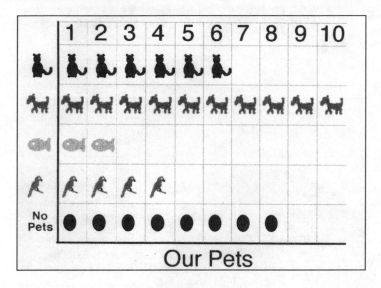

FIGURE 2.4

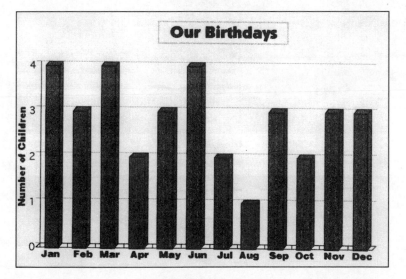

FIGURE 2.5

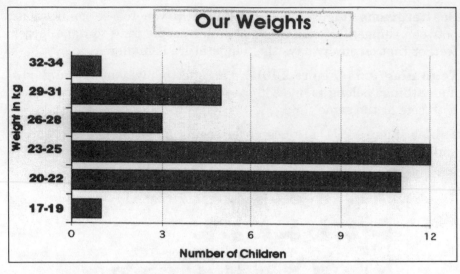

FIGURE 2.6

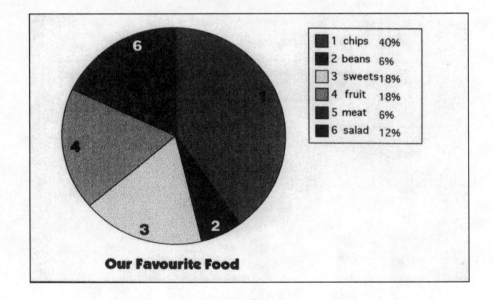

FIGURE 2.7

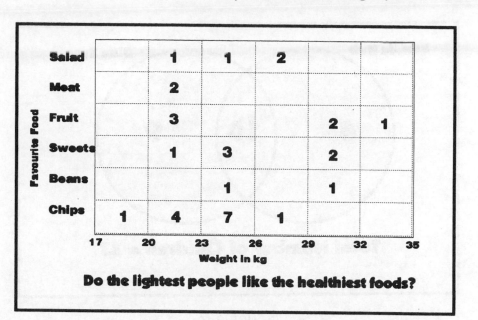

FIGURE 2.8

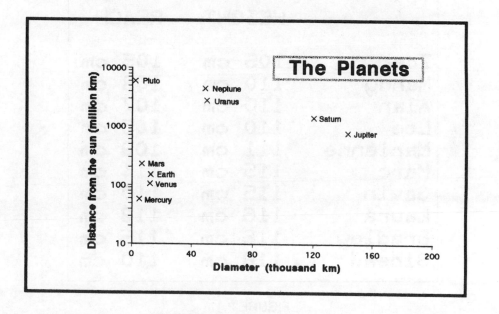

FIGURE 2.9

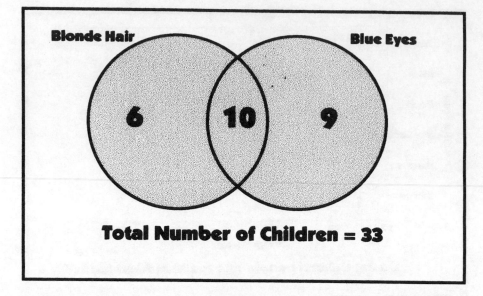

FIGURE 2.10

	HEIGHT	REACH
Zoe	105 cm	105 cm
Mandy	110 cm	103 cm
Alan	110 cm	107 cm
Lee	110 cm	105 cm
Marianne	111 cm	109 cm
Marc	115 cm	114 cm
Gavin	115 cm	110 cm
Laura	116 cm	112 cm
Bradley	116 cm	115 cm
Sinead	118 cm	110 cm

FIGURE 2.11

The projects which primary children have researched with the help of a database have been very varied. They have included, for example:

scientific investigations, using evidence gained by observing, counting, measuring, magnifying and testing specimens in many different ways, both out of doors and in the classroom:

* Do people who run faster have longer legs? Do their hearts beat faster?
* What makes a good conker?
* What factors affect the kinds of birds which visit the bird table?
* What is the best design for a paper aeroplane?
* Do caterpillars eat the same amount of food each day? At what times do they eat? Do they grow at an even rate?

social study opinion polls, using evidence gained from people in the school, from parents and the community, through interviews and questionnaires:

* What do people enjoy doing with a computer? Do women and girls enjoy and use them as much as men and boys? If not, why not?
* Does the school need a parents' room? What times of day should it be used? What facilities will be needed for it?
* How could local road safety be improved?
* In what ways could local banking arrangements be changed for the better?

historical topic work, using evidence collected from census returns, from parish records, school log books, street directories, and gravestones, from old newspapers or memories of local people, and from collections (like, for example, Robert Opie's old packets and tins at Gloucester docks, or the old pillar boxes and stamps at the National Postal Museum):

* What kind of jobs did local people have in the nineteenth century? Did many women have jobs? What about children?
* Did people tend to live and work close to where they were born? How did people travel and keep in touch with each other?
* On average, how large was a family? How many people lived in one house?
* Did people live longer in the late nineteenth century, or the early twentieth century?

Helping children to use a database

Teachers who are using a database for the first time might find the following checklist useful.

- Decide upon a list of questions. Decide what information will need to be collected to help to answer the questions.
- Plan and get ready some sheets on which information can be collected.
- Decide what vocabulary to use and any abbreviations.
- Check the completed sheets for consistency, and to make sure that spellings or abbreviations are accurate.
- Keep all the data sheets together, perhaps in a ring binder. Encourage the children to enter a few records into the database. Ask an adult helper to complete the entries if there are too many for the children to manage.
- Save the datafile at regular intervals, perhaps after every ten records.
- Check each record in the datafile for typing errors.
- Using the initial list of questions, discuss with the children how the database can help to provide answers.
- Decide whether there are further questions which have been thrown up, and which further enquiries might help to answer.
- Decide how to record results: perhaps in a class book, or in a wall display which includes graphs and written work, or in a verbal presentation to another class, and so on.

CD-ROMs

So far in this chapter it has been assumed that children will be handling information that they have collected for themselves, but it is also possible to buy collections of data on disc or CD-ROM. Ready-made databases may be purchased for the same computer programs that children use when they enter their own data. For example, census records for the local area or details of deaths from the plague during the seventeenth century are available on disc. These can be sorted, searched and graphed in just the same way, allowing children to explore much larger data files and to engage with information that is perhaps more remote than that which they have gathered for themselves.

CD-ROM machines, now increasingly found in homes and schools, take this much further. CD-ROMs are capable of holding vast amounts of information in a wide variety of forms including text, pictures, sounds, animation and video. They can be very entertaining and may seem to offer a beguiling panacea for education. But in order to use CD-ROMs effectively children need the same information handling skills that we set out in Chapter 1. They need to:

establish a purpose and decide what information is needed – Aimless browsing through a CD-ROM is as unproductive as aimless browsing through a book. Children will learn more about the topic under study, and about the information technology they are using to study it with, if they are clear about the purpose of their enquiry and have specific questions to answer. However, free exploration of any CD-ROM may be a necessary first step, to acquaint children with the options, rather like flicking through the pages of a book to see what is on offer.

decide where information can be found and find it – This involves both selecting an appropriate CD-ROM and learning how to navigate around it using the various systems of menus or searches available.

organise the information and sort through it to answer the enquiry – This may not be a simple matter. Few CD-ROMs have the same sorting and searching facilities as a typical database and the classificatory structure built in to the software may not be helpful to each line of enquiry. For example a CD-ROM on dinosaurs may contain a very comprehensive collection of information but it may not provide a search engine which would allow children to ask whether the larger dinosaurs came later by producing a scattergram of size against period.

interpret the information – Interpretation is a skill which is independent of the media used to gather the information but CD-ROMs may provide support for this. For example, a group of children who had decided that the oldest paintings in the National Gallery collection lacked realism were able to click on the word "perspective" and discover that it was not used effectively in art until the fifteenth century.

and present the findings – An ever present danger when children use books to collect information is that they will simply copy out long passages of text with little understanding or analysis of what they are reading and writing. This danger is magnified when CD-ROM is the source as chunks of text and pictures can be cut and pasted directly into pupils' own work. This, of course, can be a wonderful resource, allowing children to produce high quality reports without the process of rewriting or redrawing. But the process of thinking must not be left out.

An example of this process at work happened when one class of nine year olds set out to learn something about mammals with the aid of a CD-ROM on the subject. They began with free exploration of the disc, looking at the classificatory systems, searching out their favourite animals and watching some of the video clips of their movements. The teacher then established a clear purpose for the activity by asking a single challenging question, "What can you learn about a mammal by looking at its face?"

Some of the more obvious answers were very quickly noted. The teeth indicate diet; the length of nose shows the power and importance of the sense of smell; the position and manoeuvrability of the ears tells us about hearing, large eyes often indicate a nocturnal lifestyle. The teacher then drew the children's attention to the position of the eyes on the face. Some animals have their eyes at the front of their heads whilst others have them at the sides. She challenged the children to try to find out the significance of these differences.

They started by exploring, looking again at some of their favourite animals. The cheetah's eyes point forwards and the cheetah is famous for being the fastest animal in the world. Perhaps, someone suggested, animals with forward facing eyes are fast and those with side facing eyes are slow. But this idea was soon rejected because animals such as horses and deer are almost as fast as the cheetah. They have to be, in order to run away from their predators. Aha, maybe that is the answer! The hunters have eyes at the front and the hunted have eyes at the side.

This hypothesis was borne out by looking at lots of examples and the next step was to find an explanation. It seemed fairly obvious that the animals that might get eaten need side-facing eyes so that they can keep a good look out all around but the children did not find it so easy to explain why the predators should have eyes at the front. To help them, the teacher suggested a few experiments on binocular vision, in particular the difficulty of judging distances or seeing stereoscopic pictures with only one eye at a time. Several video clips on the CD-ROM showed predators making a kill, and the importance of being able to gauge distance with pinpoint accuracy could be clearly seen.

Helping children to use reference materials on CD-ROM

The following checklist provides

'a variety of techniques to encourage children to make information their own; to be selective in what they use; to understand that there might be much that is irrelevant to their task; and to choose appropriate information to answer the questions that they have identified.' (*Finding Out – Using Reference Materials on CD-ROM* page 1)

- Ask a challenging question or questions. Sometimes these might be questions with single right answers but there will be other occasions when open-ended questions will be appropriate.
- Encourage pupils to think about what kind of information will be needed to answer the questions (text, sounds, pictures, diagrams or video, for example).
- Give children time to play and explore freely, so that they can discover how the information is organised on the CD-ROM and find out how best to access it.
- Offer some advice to help children to select the information they want. For example, use of sub-headings or rapid scanning for key words may be good strategies for getting information from text, a picture may be worth a thousand words, and a video clip may be studied more carefully if the stop/start or freeze frame options are used.
- Plan ahead how children will record the information they have found. They might write down key words, sub-headings or rough notes. They might draw and label pictures or diagrams. They might produce charts or tables or fill in worksheets.
- Before starting get children to think about what the outcome will be. Will they present their findings as an on-screen multimedia magazine, a word-processed or desk top published report, a hand written essay in an exercise book? As they conduct their research they will then be able to plan what text or pictures from the CD-ROM they wish to import directly into their project or print for incorporation into hand-written work.

Word processors

Word processors are another kind of software which help with the management of information. In this case the data is in the form of continuous text, rather than being tabulated.

The author of a short story has many different concerns, requiring a hierarchy of skills connected with each different part of the composition:

STORY	determining the intention, audience, plot, overall plan and sequence
PARAGRAPH	elucidating one main idea (perhaps a description of a scene or character, or a conversation)
SENTENCE	connecting with what comes before or after, determining structure, checking grammar, punctuation
PHRASE	connecting with what comes before or after, checking grammar, punctuation
WORD	refining vocabulary choice, spelling
LETTER	spelling, handwriting, selecting letter style
PEN STROKE	forming letters, checking grip, choosing size and type of nib

Primary school children spend a lot of time writing short stories or reports, and have often been expected to get all these concerns pretty well right at their first attempt. The models which they see for written work, and the published works which they read, are often word-perfect lavish productions. One class of children were amazed to see a copy of a Roald Dahl manuscript with all the amendments which had been made to it. Some of them had assumed that he wrote his books in one go and sent them off to be printed!

Even where more than one draft has been encouraged, it has often been with the purpose of making work more presentable; any revision usually concentrated on perfecting spelling, grammar and handwriting. Important though these skills are, especially at the end of a piece of work when the final draft for others to read is being prepared, it is equally important that children should be learning to write in styles that are appropriate to their purpose. They need to express their thoughts accurately, in a way that interests the reader, and as succinctly as the occasion requires. They need to consider alternative words and phrases. Their arguments, where they are used, should follow sequentially one from the other. It is not easy to get all these things right first time, yet it can be tedious and time consuming to re-write each draft by hand.

The teacher's guiding principle in helping children to progress as writers is to start with what they want or need to say and then to help them to say it more effectively. Few adult writers are satisfied with the first drafts they produce: they redraft to ensure that they have said as well as possible what they mean. The same principle should apply to children's writing. (*English from 5 to 16* page 15)

Word processors are tools which help children to compose and refine their writing, focusing on just a few skills at a time, until they are completely satisfied with their work. To use the word processor merely for publishing purpose – to print a tidy copy of a piece of work which has already been written and corrected away from the computer – does not make use of the power of the word processor.

When a word processor is to be used for a particular piece of writing a preliminary group discussion may generate the main ideas which can then be ordered into an appropriate sequence. Paragraphs can be written at the keyboard, sentences arranged and rearranged, and word choice considered, without worrying about spelling or grammar in the first place. Children might take a printed draft home with them to share with their parents and to work on in the manner of Roald Dahl (Figure 2.12). The resulting piece of paper becomes a stage on the journey towards a published piece of work. In the final draft, grammar and punctuation can be corrected, and word choice refined, perhaps with the help of a dictionary or thesaurus, either in book form or incorporated into the software.

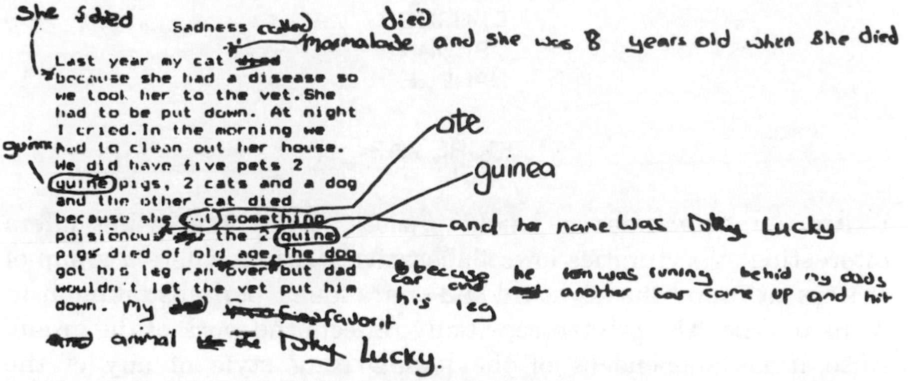

FIGURE 2.12

Minor editing of text usually takes place as it is typed in, by using the delete key and the keys which control the position of the cursor or pointer on the screen. Words or phrases can be inserted at any position, and major editing can be achieved by marking and moving large chunks of text, or by deleting them altogether. Changes can be made to the width of the margins, to the spacing between the lines, and to the number of lines on a page. Ten-year-old Ozia, who made several drafts of her firework poem, finally presented it like this (Figure 2.13).

```
                A shower

            of red hot sparks

        shining, golden in the night,

          threw out an eerie orange light.

It strengthened slowly, like the flowing tide.

    The smoke was choking, thick and white.

  Last, there was a burst of crimson light,

            which quickly dimmed

                and died.

                    .ROMAN
                    CANDLE
                    .ROMAN
                    CANDLE
                    .ROMAN
                    CANDLE
                    .ROMAN
                    CANDLE
```

FIGURE 2.13

Writing is sometimes a lonely process. Word processing offers interesting opportunities for collaborative writing, where a group of writers sit round the keyboard and share ideas, perhaps taking it in turns to type. The printed copy truly reflects the work of the group, since it is independent of the handwriting style of any of the individuals. The discussion and interaction which occur between the children while they are creating their text on the screen allows their written language to draw naturally upon their spoken language. Exactly the same principles apply when a word processor is used to support the work of bilingual children writing and talking in their heritage language (Figure 2.14).

ਪਰਮਾਣੂ ਸ਼ਕਤੀ

ਸਾਡੇ ਵਿੱਚੋਂ ਬਹੁਤ ਸਾਰੇ, ਪਰਮਾਣੂ ਸ਼ਕਤੀ ਨੂੰ ਇਕ **ਵਿਨਾਸ਼ਕਾਰੀ** ਸ਼ਕਤੀ ਹੀ ਸਮਝਦੇ ਹਾਂ। ਇਸ ਦਾ ਕਾਰਨ ਇਹ ਹੈ ਕਿ ਪਰਮਾਣੂ ਸ਼ਕਤੀ, ਦੂਸਰੇ ਵਿਸ਼ਵ-ਯੁੱਧ ਦੇ ਦੌਰਾਨ ਲੱਭੀ ਸੀ। ਸ਼ਿਕਾਗੋ ਯੂਨੀਵਰਸਿਟੀ ਵਿਖੇ ਵਿਗਿਆਨੀਆਂ ਦੀ ਇਕ ਅੰਤਰ-ਰਾਸ਼ਟਰੀ ਟੋਲੀ ਨੇ, ਜਿਸ ਦੇ ਆਗੂ ਐਨਰਿਕੋ ਫਰਮੀ ਸਨ; ਪਹਿਲੀ ਵਾਰ ੨ ਦਸੰਬਰ ੧੯੪੨ ਨੂੰ ਸਫਲਤਾ ਸਹਿਤ ਇਕ ਲੜੀ ਬੱਧ ਨਿਯੁੰਕਲੀ ਪ੍ਰਤਿਕ੍ਰਿਆ ਪ੍ਰਾਪਤ ਕੀਤੀ। ਸਾਇੰਸ ਦਾ ਇਕ ਬਹੁਤ ਵੱਡਾ ਦੁਖਾਂਤ ਹੈ ਕਿ ਸ਼ਕਤੀ ਦਾ ਉਹ

FIGURE 2.14

A teacher in a primary school in an inner city area, some of which is scheduled for redevelopment, set up collaborative activities with the word processor in order to support particular individuals in her class. One group of five children (three boys and two girls, all aged 8) included a boy, Michael, who generally needed special help with reading and writing activities. His teacher hoped that, by working with the other children with the word processor, Michael would feel that he could make a positive contribution. A task was suggested in which the group would comment on a story which had been read to the whole class. Michael had clearly enjoyed the story, and the teacher felt that by undertaking a book review the children would have a common core of knowledge upon which to draw.

During their first session at the computer the children produced a rough draft. It took them about twenty minutes to become familiar with the order of the letters on the keyboard, and to remember to put spaces between the words.

The Silver Sword
There was a man called Josph, and he was captured by Jermans.He was taken to a prison camp.He knocked him out and stole a Jerman uniform and he put it on. He walked across a hill,soon he saw a drunken Jerman, came after him.He started to run away from the Jerman soldier.
Then he go on a cablecar and ... ?

One of the group, Janine, who started as the typist, kept consulting the others about what to say – 'Is this what you want?' Their first debate was about the spelling of German – a word which for many young children is more commonly heard than read. The children thought of other words which started with the same phonetic sound, and came up with 'jump' and 'jelly' and 'jerk', and so decided to use J.

Michael played a very active part in the general discussion about the story and what really happened in it – the children were very concerned about the accuracy of the detail. There was some query about who was being knocked out by whom, and whether this was being relayed accurately to the audience. The children also began to focus on style, and the kind of information that a reader of their review would want. Michael had lots of information about the story and some awareness of shades of meaning: for example, 'Why not write "Nazi" instead of "German"?' For the first time ever, he expressed an interest in participating in the writing. He became the typist and typed in 'Solider' for 'soldier' – all the correct letters were there although two were reversed.

At the end of the session, each child made a printed copy of the review. Michael was very proud of his piece of writing, and after showing it to some of his friends, he put it away carefully in his work folder. On the following day the children discussed their review around a table, away from the computer. Their teacher asked them to look at their work and to see if what they had written actually said what they wanted it to say, and if it didn't, to reshape the meaning of the text so that it did. The children referred to the copy of the book which they were reviewing, and with help from their teacher in locating passages they re-read small pieces to each other. Michael did no reading, but made a number of sensible suggestions about the kind of detail which they should check, and whether a certain incident had happened before or after another in the book. Eventually the children came to a consensus about the changes and extensions they would make to their review.

The Silver Sword
There was a man called Joseph, and he was captured by Germans.He was taken to a prison camp.He knocked a German out and stole a German uniform and he put it on.He walked out of the camp with some of the Germans. He walked across a hill,soon he saw a drunken German coming after him.He started to run away from the German Soldier. Then he got on a cablecar and went across to the other side and met a farmer. He stayed until the summer,one day two German patrol guards come to the farm house.The farmers wife told Joseph to hide up the chimney.The Germans began to search the house.They looked all over the house.Then they fired a bullet up the chimney and soot fell down.This is a good book.It is very exciting so read it.

Before he had even sat down, Michael was saying, 'We've got to change something.' He was keen to take part and to do some of the corrections. Looking at the phrase 'he knocked him out', Janine commented, 'That's wrong – it still doesn't say who did it', but the group did not pursue this. Noah wanted to put 'he stayed in his house until' but Michael insisted it should only be 'he stayed until'. The others agreed.

There was a lot of debate about the spelling of 'chimney' amongst them and after several attempts on the screen they got it right. Michael participated in the discussion. 'Search' was originally typed in as 'surch', and there was more debate as soon as 'sur ... ' appeared on the screen. After printing out the unamended version, the children moved on to making further changes. This time, corrections to the text were made with the help of a dictionary, in a systematic way one line at a time, by reading back the text and looking critically at it. Michael, who by this stage had become very familiar with the typed text, took his turn to read a line along with the other children. When the final draft was produced, Michael asked if he could take his printed copy home.

For children who have difficulty with using a pencil, a word processor offers relief from the physical task of handwriting. Once acquainted with the layout of the keyboard, it is far easier and quicker to press the key labelled A than to scribe it with a pen or pencil. Teachers who have less experience of using computers sometimes worry that because the keyboard shows upper-case letters the children will be unable to cope. In fact, the whole world is full of messages written in capitals, and most children are blissfully unaware that this poses problems for them! Recently, I watched 3-year-old Sharon using a computer for the first time, confidently tapping upper-case keys, and saying the correct names for individual letters, as her name appeared in lower case letters on the screen: ess, aitch, ay, are, oh, en.

One device which can be used if children are likely to have difficulty with typing is a different kind of keyboard which can be attached to the computer and used instead of, or in conjunction with, the normal keyboard. One kind of alternative keyboard has extra large keys for children who have difficulty in operating the usual ones. Another kind is flat, and is sensitive to slight pressure, so that different overlays can be placed upon it (Figure 2.15a–c).

An overlay with a selection of whole words can be used by the youngest writers in much the same way that Breakthrough to Literacy cards have been used. Some reception class children, with the help of their teacher, made a class story book from pages which were first produced in this manner, and then printed out and illustrated. Once the book had been stuck together, it was covered with wrapping paper, fitted into a zip-up bag, and the children took turns to take it home to read with their parents.

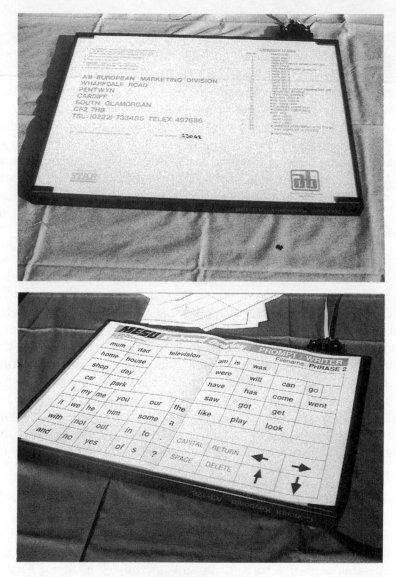

FIGURE 2.15a

FIGURE 2.15b

home	mum	dad	television		bed	nan	baby	am	is	are	was	were	be	will	can
brother	sister	boy	girl	friend	mate	day		have	has	come	go	play	came	went	watch
birthday		present		shop	car	park	a	see	saw	want	got	get	like	help	walk
the	and	some	all	this	my	you	me	yes	no	what	there	when	with	after	but
it	we	our	he	him	I	they	for	to	in	out	of	happy	sad		
his	her	she	good	bad	all	lot		es	s	ed	ing	?		not	n't
autumn	winter	Christmas	cold	dark	wet	frosty	foggy					CAPITAL	RETURN	↓	↑
												SPACE	DELETE	←	→

Overlay file developed by Jean Ashcroft (Sefton)

M.E.S.U. Primary Project.
M.E.S.U. Special Needs Software Centre

FIGURE 2.15c

Sometimes a word list is provided with the word processor, so that children can look up and check the spelling of a particular word; sometimes there is a thesaurus which offers alternative words with the same meaning. Automatic spelling correctors are becoming quite common – helpful for teachers who want to produce a word-perfect copy of a letter or a report. A spelling corrector can sometimes be switched on as the copy is typed; alternatively, and more commonly, it can be applied after the whole passage has been entered. For classroom use, most teachers would find it more helpful if a different spelling check program could be devised – one which would pick out the two or three most commonly misspelt words which should be the next for the writer to learn how to spell.

When decisions are being made about the final style of presentation of a piece of writing, there are a number of possible options. For example, word processed text can easily be printed in narrow columns in order to assemble a newspaper page using a cut and stick technique with scissors and paste. The problem of making a passage of text fit in the space allowed provides the motivation for finding ways of making work more concise without losing any of the meaning. For children who prefer to undertake the composition of the page at the keyboard, there are newspaper publishing programs available for primary schools which allow the whole page to be set up on the computer before it is printed out (Figure 2.16).

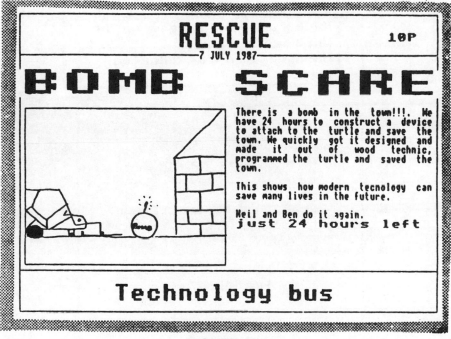

FIGURE 2.16

A desk top publishing package takes this much further by allowing children to experiment with layout at the computer. Desk top publishing is all about presentation and design, and only really became a viable proposition when computers were developed which could be controlled by a mouse as well as a keyboard. With this type of software, each item, whether it be a piece of text, a picture or a graphic such as a line or a box, can be treated as a separate object and moved around the screen by dragging with the mouse. This gives total flexibility and means that primary school children can produce very professional looking magazines, newspapers or project reports.

A huge variety of different letter fonts and sizes is available, perhaps Gothic characters or a script that looks like handwriting, or you can even design your own characters. Clip-art collections, sets of ready made pictures or graphics, may be used to enhance the work, as any picture can be pasted into a document, resized to fit the available space and transformed in various ways such as by rotation or stretching.

For children in the early years there are precursor programs which allow pictures to be built up from sets of ready made objects, such as birds, trees and teddy bears, much like an on-screen fuzzy-felt kit. Text may be added to many of these so that they can be used to design items such as posters or greetings cards or to write illustrated stories (Figure 2.17).

FIGURE 2.17

Children readily take to these various new facilities for the management of text: it is we adults who find them difficult. Some 6-year-olds in Somerset, who had made only limited use of a word processor, wrote about it with enthusiasm:

> **I like useing the computer because it has got a delete presser if you use pencil and you rub it out it is dirty.**

> **I think I would like to do that all the time becuase when youve done it rong you dont have to go round looking for a roubber All the time so I think it is easyer than writing with pensole and I think a dicshanary is a good Idea**

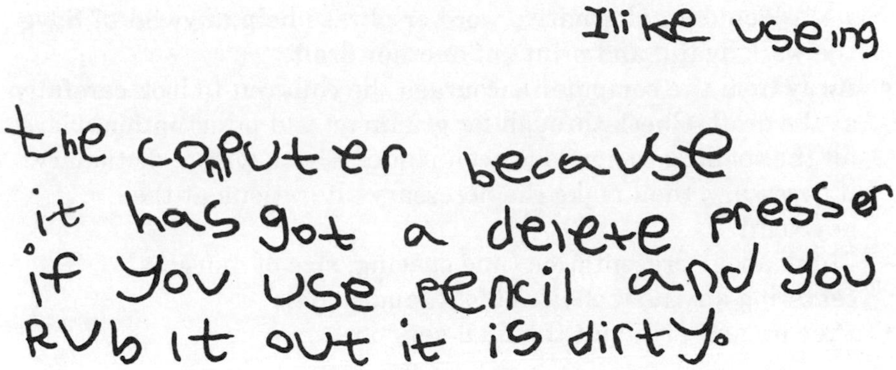

I like useing
the coputer because it has got a delete presser if you use pencil and you Rub it out it is dirty.

FIGURE 2.18

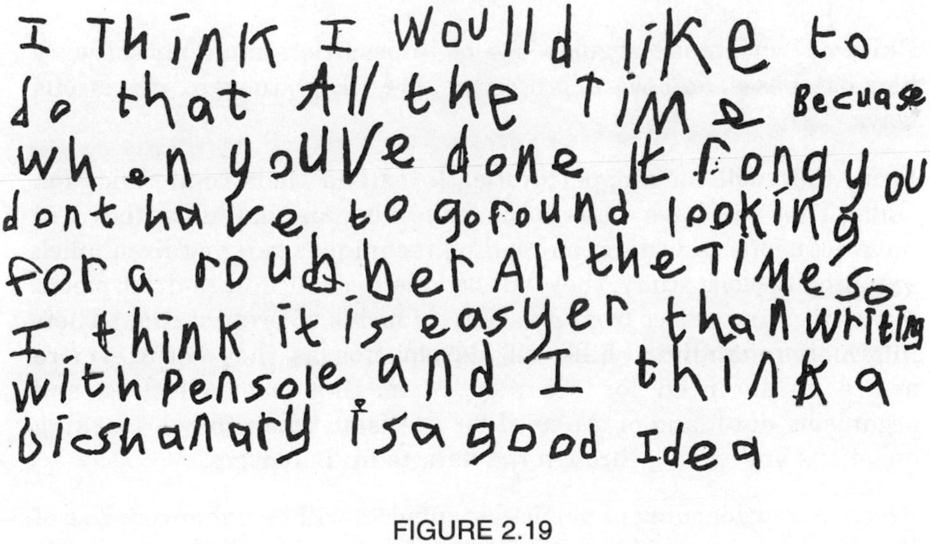

I think I woulld like to do that All the time Becuase when youVe done it rong you dont have to gofound looking for a roubber All the Time so I think it is easyer than writing with pensole and I think a bicshanary isa good Idea

FIGURE 2.19

Helping children to use a word processor

Teachers who are encouraging children to use a word processor for writing may find it helpful to work in the following way.

- Carry out preliminary planning and discussion with the children before they go to the computer.
- Encourage the children to write freely, without worrying too much about spelling and punctuation in the first instance.
- Save the work, and print out a draft for them to consider away from the computer. Are the ideas in the right order? What needs to be added? Should anything be deleted?
- Re-structure the writing using the word processor. Does it read well? Would an alternative word or phrase help anywhere? Save the work again, and print out another draft.
- Away from the computer encourage the children to look carefully at the draft. Check through for grammar and punctuation. Have all the spelling corrections been made? Check with a dictionary if necessary, then make the necessary alterations at the keyboard.
- Think about presentation (line spacing, size of margins, centering any text, choice of font, and so on).
- Prepare and print out the final version.

What do children gain from using information-handling software?

Children who make regular use of information-handling software like databases and word processors are likely to gain in various ways.

First, they will have opportunities to extend their communication skills. They will have a new focus for talking and listening; they will have occasions to use screen-reading techniques ranging from quick scanning to close study; they will be able to draft and re-draft pieces of writing, and select from a variety of forms of presentation. Their information-handling skills will develop too as they become more aware of the need for accuracy when they are collecting and organising data, and of the need for precision when they are asking questions and sifting through the data to find answers.

Second, their learning of particular subjects will be enhanced. Use of the word processor helps children to focus on particular language skills ranging from a sense of audience and an awareness of style to spelling and punctuating correctly. Use of the database helps to extend mathematical skills of ordering and classifying, of estimating and approximating, and of choosing and interpreting graphical displays.

In addition, as they work with information-handling software children will develop an appreciation of the manner in which computers handle quantities of information, and of the speed at which this is managed.

Further reading

Ross, A. 1984. *Making connections*. MEP Case Studies 5. Council for Educational Technology. ISBN 0 86184 122 0.

Daines, D.R. 1984. *Databases in the classroom*. Castle House. ISBN 0 7194 0099 6.

Finding Out! Using Reference Materials on CD-ROM. NCET 1996 ISBN 1 85379 343 4

Making Sense of Information NCET 1995 ISBN 1 85379 319 1

Getting Started with Information Handling NCET 1994 ISBN 1 85379 293 4

3 Problem solving and investigation with a computer

A problem exists when either an individual or a group of people wants to achieve something that is not immediately attainable. The problem and its solution will generally have three basic features: some given information which describes the circumstances or the setting of the problem, a sequence of actions or procedures which the problem solver can use to try and reach a solution, and a goal which describes the required outcome.

The process of solving the problem is usually defined with an active verb:

- **to find** a path through a maze;
- **to decipher** a passage of coded text;
- **to detect** the culprit when some goods are stolen from a country house;
- **to identify** a fossil found in the chalk quarry near the school;
- **to investigate** the connection between the number of edges and the number of diagonals of a regular polygon;
- **to discover** the greatest capacity of an open box made from an A4 piece of card by cutting a square out of each corner and folding up the flaps.

In each of these problems the solution will be a single clear-cut outcome, although the routes taken to arrive at the 'answer' may be very varied. But not all problems have a single, unique solution. Some may have no solution; some might have a solution if more information were available; some have many possible solutions. In more open-ended investigations children can be encouraged to pursue alternative strategies, to seek evidence to support their conjectures, to compare their different results, and to ask what would happen if, or what would happen if not. This time the goal might be:

- **to create** a repeating wallpaper pattern for a doll's house;
- **to design and build** a bird table so that you know (without constantly watching) when a bird has landed;

- **to decide** where to go locally to buy the best potato crisps;
- **to find out** why several of the shops in the town in the census year of 1881 were connected with rope making;
- **to discover** which factors are important when choosing the strongest conker for a game;
- **to investigate** the different shapes and patterns which can be made with spirals.

These examples are very varied, but what they all have in common is that each of them has been tackled by primary school children, and in every case the problem-solving process was aided by making use of the school's computer. Some of these problems would never have been attempted if the computer had not been available, while in other cases the investigation would not have been so thorough, because the amount of data involved would have been too cumbersome to manage.

Some types of problem-solving software

Real problem solving, the sort that is part of everyday reality in our society, the sort that helps children to make discoveries about themselves and about their relationships with other people, is like cooking: it is learned by doing it yourself. If children are to become confident problem solvers, then they need to meet problems and explore solutions to them on a regular basis.

In the past, teachers who have been committed to the provision of problem-solving activities for children have had little to support them in the way of materials. However, research is now giving some insights into the ways in which children develop problem-solving strategies, and materials to help teachers are being produced.

Software is one of the resources which teachers can use to foster and support problem-solving activities. Its versatile nature means that it can play different roles in different circumstances.

- It can **suggest** problems to be solved by including them in the program itself, perhaps in the form of a puzzle or a game of strategy.
- It can **support** problem solving with databases, graph plotters, design programs, and so on, all of which can help with the management and presentation of information, both essential parts of the problem-solving process.

- It can **stimulate** problem solving, in the sense that the availability of, say, a database with graph-drawing facilities, or of a programming language like Logo, is an invitation to think of things to do with it.

Richard Harrison worked with Tracey, Jamila and Jo-Ann, aged 10, in Peckham Rye Primary School in South East London. They evaluated a puzzle in which 'rays' are directed into a square grid containing some 'atoms' (Figure 3.1). The rays are deflected, reflected or absorbed, depending on how they strike the atoms. The results are shown at the side of the grid; the same letter at each end of a deflected ray and symbols for a reflection (↕) or an absorbtion (↓).

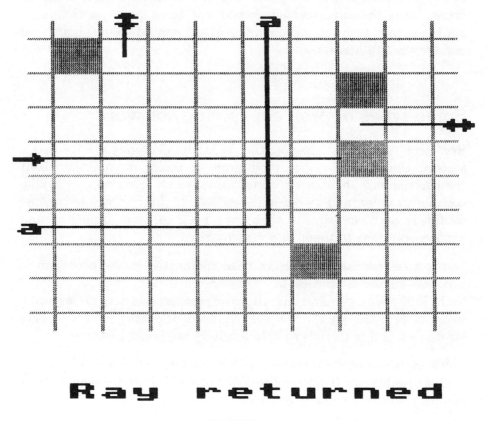

FIGURE 3.1

Before the girls came in from playtime, Richard placed four atoms in the grid in such a way that all the rules could be discovered. He explained that there were some atoms in the box (but not that they affected the rays), then showed the girls the firing button and asked them to try it.

The girls' first attempt to fire a ray from a particular position produced a deflection. They then explored a few other positions. It was clear from the conversation that they were curious.

Tracey: Perhaps you have to fire from a different angle.
Jo-Ann: Sometimes letters light up.
Jamila: [*Looking quizzical*] This is nutty.

The girls asked if they could try again. This time, they chose their own problem by selecting the positions for the atoms, choosing two each.

Jamila: What shall we do?
Teacher: Try and find the rules. See what different kinds of rays you can produce. Perhaps you could try to make a 'bender'.

Much discussion followed. Jo-Ann suggested that it was the atoms that made the ray bend, Jamila traced out predictions on the screen. Eventually, they began to realise what was happening, and they succeeded in making 'benders'.

Tracey: Oh yeah. It's got a force field round it.

The girls then asked if they could try a problem with six atoms, placed in random positions by the computer. This time the positions of the atoms and the ray paths were not shown on the screen and the girls' task was to use the behaviour of the rays to work out where each atom was concealed. They spent a lot of time in theorising and in purposeful discussion. Two rays enabled them to find the first atom, and they went on to locate all six atoms, without using all the possible firing positions.

After they had completed the game, they tried a challenge. They were shown how some atoms could be placed to produce a four-bend pathway; the problem was to investigate the maximum number of bends that could be produced. Tracey tried first, and there was great amusement when her ray went straight through the raybox without any deflections at all.

Jo-Ann: I'm going to try and make a rectangle loop.
Jamila: Mine's going to be the bendiest ray in the whole wide world.

She eventually managed six bends, clapping her hands as she saw the rectangular loop made by the ray (Figure 3.2).

Away from the computer, the girls used squared paper so that they could design possible pathways for a ray. There was an obvious enthusiasm in the way that they approached the problem, and over a period of a week they built up a hypothesis about the maximum number of bends which they could produce with one, two, three, four or five atoms. About six, they were not so sure. It was becoming difficult for them to check all the possible variations in the positions, so the problem was left for the time being to be returned to at a later date.

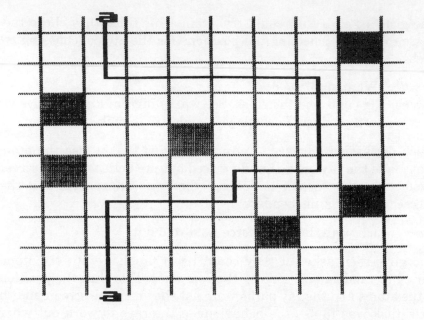

FIGURE 3.2
Jo-Ann and Jamila's first response to the 'bendiest ray' challenge

At Springcroft Primary School in Staffordshire, David Brown's Year 5 class turned to the computer to support some problem solving of a different kind. This time it was not suggested by any particular program; it grew out of two sessions of dance and drama based on the music from *Cats*.

The original objective was to extend the mime skills of the children by observing real cats and then to develop and interpret their movements and mannerisms against a musical setting. It was the poor quality of the recording that started the rot ...

Child: What are they singing about?
Child: I can't hear the words!

The class were given copies of the 'Song of the Jellicles' – thinly disguised as a comprehension exercise.

Child: Who's this T. S. Eliot?

Child: What does 'Jellicle' mean? It's not in the dictionary.
Child: What do you mean – it's not a real word?

In their further study of battered copes of *Old Possum's Book of Practical Cats* the children were delighted to discover that they had already met Macavity in the first year of the junior school.

Child: ... but if Jellicle names are secret, special ...
Child: ... like a password ...
Child: ... and only other special cats are allowed to know ...
Child: ... it must be like a secret society!

The children were intrigued. David asked them all to make up a Jellicle name for themselves.

Teacher: I'd like you to describe yourself – tell me what colour your eyes are – any special distinguishing features you may have. But don't tell anyone – *anyone* – your Jellicle name.
Child: [*After half an hour*] Can I draw a picture of myself now I've finished the description?
Child: I've only got three legs – I lost the other in a trap!

David then set up a database with eleven fields, and each child completed the first four fields using the information from their descriptions. The computer screen was hidden from the rest of the class, and a helpful parent supervised to make sure that no peeping at previous records took place. The whole process of entering the data took just over an hour.

JNAME	:	The Jellicle name
COLOUR	:	Skin colour
EYES	:	Eye colour
FEATURE	:	Distinguishing feature
AGE	:	Age
DHAUNT	:	Daytime haunt
NHAUNT	:	Nighttime haunt
FRIENDS	:	Two Jellicle friends
CRIME	:	Major sin
HATE	:	Thing most hated
FOOD	:	Favourite food

The first four fields were printed out, duplicated forty times, and distributed to the class.

Child: Look at Jessary – he's only got one eye!
Child: There are two with pink eyes and black fur.

Child: I wonder who Mr Wipston Cream is? I bet it's one of the twins!

Teacher: Now I want a cat record for each one of you. Name, age, where you spend your time during the day and at night, what you like most, what you have most, the worst 'cat crime' that you ever committed, and finally two cats from the list that you think that you would be best friends with – oh, and if you get time a 'photograph' of you and a pawprint!

There was lots of discussion about what would make good cat crimes, but then silence as the cat records were completed. This time the parent helper typed the information into the data file. A few graphs were printed out, and a list of NAMEs and CRIMEs. Eight copies of each were made and allocated to eight friendship groups, together with four questions.

Teacher: It says here – 'Foo Wong, the owner of the local Chinese restaurant, has complained to the cat police about a group of cats knocking over his dustbins at night. He chased them and says that he thinks one had red eyes and another was limping. Which of the cats do you think were responsible, and what evidence can you find to support you?'

Child: How can we work that out? We need to know all their night time haunts.

Child: No! We need a list of who's friends with who.

Child: ... or which of them like Chinese food.

A long discussion took place about the information that would be required. David gave an explanation of what information the computer now held, and reminded the children of the ways in which it could be displayed, either in tables or in graphs. He showed them, as an example, how to find the most popular cat by displaying all the information in the FRIENDS field. He also laid down some rules. On this occasion, the detective work had to be done with a list of names and two other fields for all the Jellicles, and full information on five cats only.

The following day, the search began. There was a great deal of cooperation, plenty of 'work noise', movement, excitement, requests for relevant information, correct usage of computer terms ... and gradually the solutions emerged.

Problem posing is an important adjunct to problem solving. One way to stimulate children to pose problems is to take them out and to encourage them to observe closely and to ask questions about what they see.

- Why does it look like that? Could we draw one, or make a model of it?
- How does it work? Could we design and make one?
- What happened when … ? Does it always happen? How often does it happen? What factors affect the frequency? What would happen if one of the factors were changed?
- Why has it been placed there? Could we find a better place for it?
- Why are they arranged like that? What other ways of arranging them would be possible?
- Why do so many of these things have this in common? What would explain it? Which of the various explanations is the best one?

After going out to look at a windmill in Lincolnshire, and studying the locations of various mills on ordnance survey maps, a group of Year 6 children asked: 'Why did they put that mill there?' In trying to find out, they used a simulation program in which they posed themselves the problem of locating six windmills on the best sites. Their aim was to find positions that would give the lowest running costs for the windmills by maximising production and minimising transport costs. Their first attempts helped them to identify the kind of position which would catch enough wind for the sails of a mill to turn, but proved to be very expensive. They then grappled with the problem of finding the best compromise between placing the mills near the farms that grew the wheat (which cut down the cost of getting the grain to the mills but increased the cost of getting the flour to the market), or near the town (which had the opposite effect). Another factor which they had to consider was spreading the mills out around the wheat growing area so that each mill could work to maximum capacity. And then there were ground rents to think about: sites are expensive in towns, but cheap in woodland – but there is no wind in woodland.

Rory:	Which one is the cheapest?
Sam:	That one just next to the river.
Jenny:	[*Pointing at the screen*] Look, listen. Perhaps we could try and put them all round here.
Mandy:	That's silly. The wheat has to go too far to get there.
Sam:	And it costs more to carry wheat than to carry flour.
Rory:	I don't think we should put any of them there. It would be better if we could solve the problem of getting them all in windy places first.
Jenny:	Yes, perhaps that's right.
Mandy:	Why don't we keep these four the same?

Sam: Just change two.

Rory: Yeah. Just change two.

Sam: Do you think we should try to put one down here, although it's not near the wheat land and it's not near the station.

Rory: Let's go back to ... Where's the map?

Mandy: If that's windy land, what about here, in the middle, although it's quite far away ...

Rory: [*Pointing to the map*] Have we got one in this area?

The children's conversation was stumbling and rather hesitant as they groped their way towards an understanding of the complicated factors that govern the location of industrial sites. But they gained some insight into the difficulties of decision making and the need to accept compromise solutions. Their teacher also discussed with them the part that they as individuals had played in the discussion. Was one of them dominant? Who took the most decisions? Did personalities influence which mill sites were kept and which were changed? And do these factors affect the way that problems are solved in the real world?

Another way to stimulate children's own questions is to make collections and then to think of things to ask about them, to do to them or with them. Menus, maps, travel brochures, advertisements, newspaper headlines, and so on, might all suggest a problem to be explored. So might collections of pebbles, patterned fabrics, old packets, twigs, cheeses, or powders. Historical information from parish registers, census records, or old newspaper reports, or present-day data like weather statistics, football results, time-tables, and tables of heights and weights all offer good starting points for investigations. Constructional materials such as card, dowel rod, wheels, string and wire, or Lego and Meccano, can act as another stimulus. These resources need only be coupled with suggestions to build, assemble, plan, produce, create, discover, compare, come to a decision about ... and there is a problem to be solved.

The computer may or may not play a part in problem solving which starts in this way. Rachel, aged 11, built a flashing beacon to send SOS messages (Figure 3.3), using a battery to power a circuit with a switch which she built from drawing pins and a paper clip. Later, she connected her circuit to the computer, and incorporated a light sensor, so that the light would flash automatically every night when it got dark.

If questions and possible lines of enquiry come from the children themselves, so much the better. HMI, in their booklet *Mathematics from 5 to 16* (page 41), put this very clearly.

... a classroom where a range of activities is taking place and in which pupils express interests and ask questions can also provide on-the-spot problems. Teachers need to exploit these situations because there is greater motivation to solve problems which have been posed by the pupils themselves.

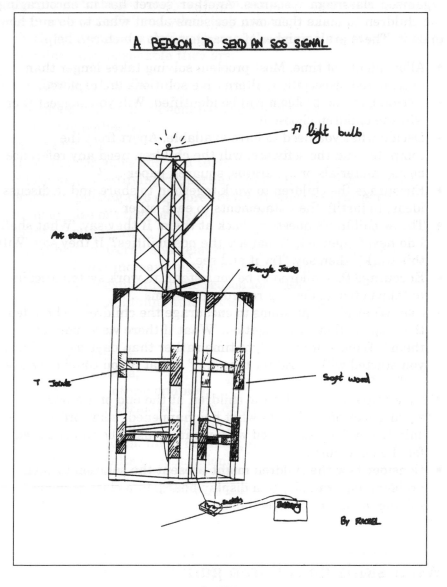

FIGURE 3.3

- When they are **collecting and organising information** they must decide what to collect, how to find it, how to collect it, how to organise it, which of it is relevant and how to use it, and so on.
- When they are **classifying a collection** of, say, leaves children have to choose what properties to consider, what sort of arrangement or set diagram is helpful, which leaf goes into which set, and whether they need to find other ways of classifying the leaves using different criteria.
- When they are **evaluating solutions to problems** children have to decide whether a solution is accurate enough or even if it is too accurate, how efficient or effective or justified it is, whether it solves the original problem completely or partially, and even whether or not it is correct.

When children are developing these skills, whether by using their computer or by using other resources, it might be worth stressing to them that in real life the best solution to a particular problem may not be practicable: it may be too expensive, it may spoil the environment, or it may be anti-social. For example, one group of children may want to observe the feeding habits of birds without keeping a constant look-out. To solve the problem, they could construct a tilting bird-tale which rings a warning bell in the classroom when a bird has landed, but frequent bell ringing might be quite unacceptable to the rest of the class who would be disturbed by the noise.

In the classroom, as well as in the adult world, many problems (and their eventual solutions) can appear to be simple or even trivial. Yet the intervening process between the posing of the problem and arriving at the solution may be very complex. It is the process of reaching a solution, combining choice and decision making with creative thinking, which is the essence of learning.

Some Year 4 juniors in Lambeth made the following comments about their problem-solving activities:

May: It gives you a chance to find out for yourself.
Sarah: I like working with others. You get better ideas.
Amin: You can try things out and it doesn't matter if it all goes wrong.
Njero: You don't have to write everything. You can draw and make things.
Dwain: It makes you think.
Anna: Sometimes it's hard.
Gary: You can decide your own way of doing it.

Further reading

Fisher, R. (ed.) 1987. *Problem solving in primary schools*.
  Stanely Thornes.

4 Programming: a creative activity

Young children begin 'to program' as soon as they start to find ways of recording things like a sequence of moves in a game, the commands to give to a robot, or the shapes which are needed to make up a picture (Figures 4.1, 4.2).

FIGURE 4.1

1. get ○	17. colour
2. make bigger	18. get —
3. move ↓	19 move ↓
4. colour	20 turn
5 get ◐	21 make bigger
6. Make bigger	22 Colour
7. turn	23 repeat last 4
8. Move ↓←	24 get △
9 colour	25 Move ↓←
10. get ◢	26 Colour
11. Move ↓←	27 repeat last 3
12. colour	28 label
13. get □	29
14. Move →↑	30
15. get ⊙	31
16 Move ↑←	32

FIGURE 4.2

A **computer program**, like a sheet of music or a knitting pattern, is simply a set of coded instructions arranged in an appropriate order, and programming is another way in which children can use the computer as a tool to explore their ideas.

The point of introducing young children to programming is to allow them to feel in control, to give them a way of clarifying their ideas, and to encourage them to order their thoughts in a logical sequence. Although the children will need to be taught some simple programming techniques, the emphasis should not be on learning the techniques, but on the ideas that can be explored through programming as a creative activity.

Sequencing activities

Most infants can identify the stages in ordinary processes like coming to school, getting dressed, laying the table for a meal, using the library to borrow a book to read. The stages can be illustrated by an ordered sequence of mimed actions, a set of pictures (Figure 4.3), or a list of simple sentences, and the illustrations can be given to other children to describe or to carry out. Some of these procedures are cyclical – and children will invent their own way of indicating that once the process is finished it should be repeated (Figure 4.4).

FIGURE 4.3

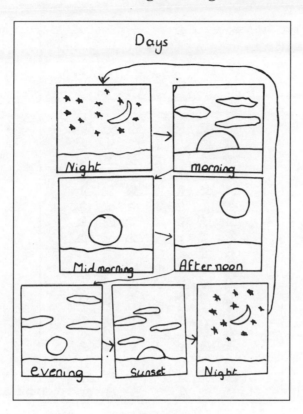

FIGURE 4.4

In their PE lessons children learn body movements or simple dances making use of instructions like forward, backward, left, right, turn, roll, and hop, often with numbers attached to them: go forward three steps. In mathematics, they are accustomed to following sets of instructions to make patterns with beads, with felt shapes, or with pegs on pegboard. Making up coded sets of instructions for other children to carry out could be their first experience of writing a program: 3R, 2B, 1R, 2G for three red beads, followed by two blue, one red, two green. They can then invent their own ways of showing that the pattern should be repeated a number of times.

Older children need to be encouraged to look for examples of 'programs', to modify them, and to make up their own: rules for games; recipes for cooking; or instructions for making models, for controlling traffic lights, or for ringing peals of bells. Some of these procedures may have branching statements in them, or loops or repeats; and some, like knitting patterns, country dances, or musical scores, are coded. One group of children played the pegboard game of Frogs (Figure 4.5), and then when they had found out how to do it, they recorded a procedure which gave instructions for the solution.

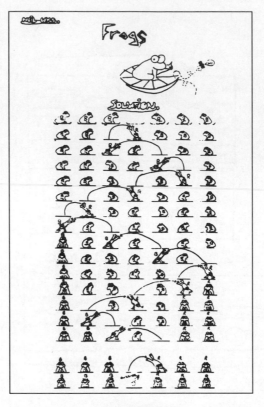

FIGURE 4.5

As they carry out these various sequencing tasks, and devise ways of recording them, the children start to develop their own form of coded language – something a bit like a programming language, but much more loosely defined. The vocabulary is likely to include words like first, last, after that, next, start, stop, do again, once more, repeat, continue, until, if, then, otherwise, jump back, jump on, and finish.

Battery-driven robots

Activities with programmable toys and battery-driven robots extend the opportunities for sequencing. Programmable toys can be operated so that they carry out one action at a time, but they can also store a complete sequence of instructions to be carried out continuously.

Ideas for what a battery-driven robot might be made to do can of course be suggested by the teacher, but the best suggestions have come from the children themselves. 'How can we teach the robot to …

- go to the top of the slope and stop;
- move in a circle;
- go all round the table and back to us again;
- zig-zag through the bean bags;
- make the waves on the sea;
- do a dance with the other robot?'

A visitor in one teacher's classroom listened to a group of 6-year-olds working unsupervised with a toy moon buggy called BigTrak (now, alas, no longer being manufactured) (Figures 4.6 and 4.7), and recorded snippets of their spontaneous conversation:

Go left a bit more.
Try 45 and see.
First go forward, then right.
Next, we'll have to work out the difference.
If BigTrak is going to do that, then it will have to start from here.
Let's see what happens if we start in the middle.
How many more times shall we do it?
Try a bigger number.
Try a smaller number.
Try twice as much.
Let's try changing the turn.
Yes! we've done it!
Let's do it again!
Come and see what we've done.
How did you do that?
Can I try that?
Will you show me?

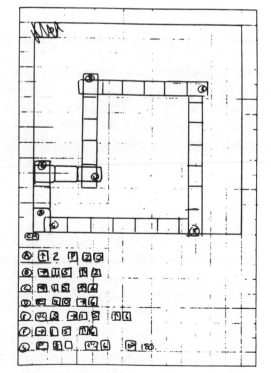

FIGURE 4.6

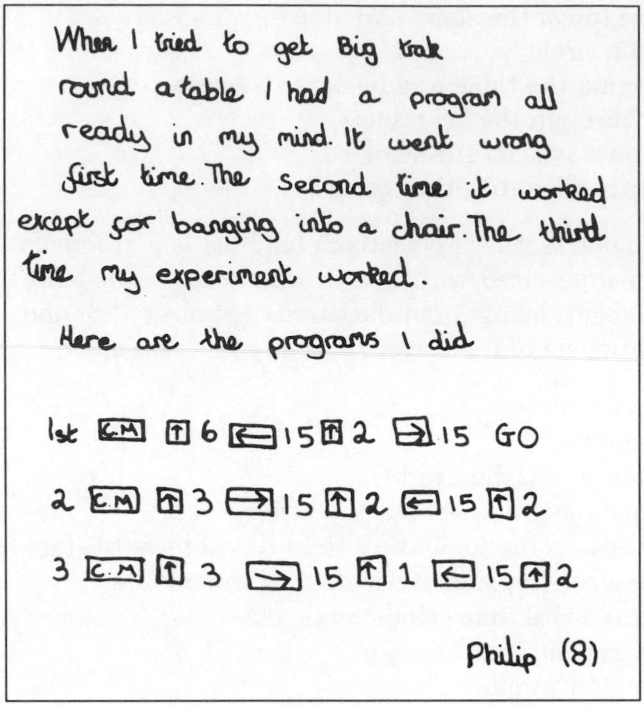

When I tried to get Big trak
round a table I had a program all
ready in my mind. It went wrong
first time. The second time it worked
except for banging into a chair. The third
time my experiment worked.

Here are the programs I did

1st [C.M] [↑]6 [←]15 [↑]2 [→]15 GO

2 [E.M] [↑]3 [→]15 [↑]2 [←]15 [↑]2

3 [C.M] [↑]3 [→]15 [↑]1 [←]15 [↑]2

Philip (8)

FIGURE 4.7

Developing and recording algorithms

An **algorithm** is a method or procedure – or even a recipe – for carrying out a particular task. A sequence of instructions for creating a bead pattern could be described as an informal algorithm. A more formal definition of the word would be a finite sequence of steps which will bring about a required result; each step must be a simple, unambiguous instruction which can be carried out in a mechanical way.

Algorithms can be devised with particular tools in mind: perhaps pegs and pegboard, or pencil and paper, or a set of drawing instruments; perhaps an abacus, or a calculator, or a computer. It is the existence of calculators and computers, which are very efficient machines for carrying out algorithms, that has increased the importance of children being able to design procedures and algorithms for themselves.

The word 'algorithm' is derived from the name of the Arabian mathematician Al-Khowarismi, who was the keeper of the treasures of Haroun-al-Raschid, the Caliph of Bagdhad, around the year 800. It was Al-Khowarismi who invented the four most well-known algorithms: the vertical methods for pencil and paper arithmetic. However, today's school children will be adults in a world equipped with a multitude of technological aids for calculating. For them mental algorithms for calculations involving small numbers, and calculator algorithms for calculations involving larger numbers, need to replace these traditional pencil and paper methods.

Many infants already use a simple yet fundamental calculator algorithm to add two small numbers together: enter a number, press '+', enter another number, press '='. This is a very powerful algorithm; it is not only simple and easy to remember, but it works for any numbers, large or small. There is no need to worry about rules like 'line up the decimal points underneath each other' or 'put down 7, carry 1'.

Calculator algorithms are not just concerned with 'the four rules'. Seven-year-old Waleed invented an algorithm for getting from 6 to 52 using only the $\boxed{2}$ and $\boxed{4}$ and $\boxed{+}$ keys (Figure 4.8).

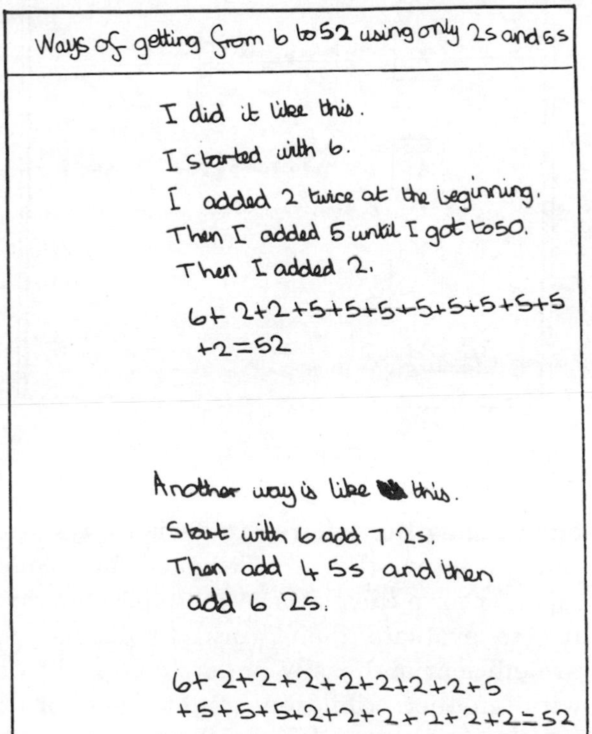

Ways of getting from 6 to 52 using only 2s and 6s

I did it like this.
I started with 6.
I added 2 twice at the beginning.
Then I added 5 until I got to 50.
Then I added 2.

$6+ 2+2+5+5+5+5+5+5+5+5$
$+2=52$

Another way is like this.
Start with 6 add 7 2s.
Then add 4 5s and then
add 6 2s.

$6+ 2+2+2+2+2+2+5$
$+5+5+5+2+2+2+2+2+2=52$

FIGURE 4.8

Older children have explored algorithms which make use of the constant for repeated addition or multiplication, rules to generate the sequences of square or triangular numbers, or the Fibonacci sequence 1, 1, 2, 3, 5, 8, 13, ... in which each number in the sequence is the sum of the previous two numbers. Some children have enjoyed being given an algorithm to experiment with, perhaps for finding a square root, a cube root, or the highest common factor of two numbers, with the challenge of trying to puzzle out why the algorithm works.

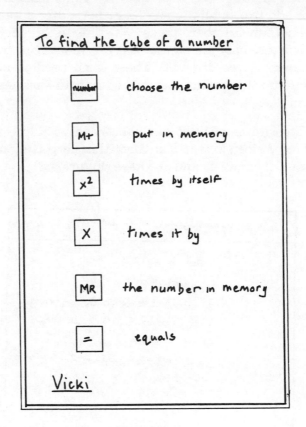

FIGURE 4.9

It is worth encouraging the children to devise ways of representing their algorithms, whether they are designed for coloured rods, for pencil and paper, or for a calculator. A more permanent record often helps children to evaluate their work, to decide whether their procedures are efficient and easily understood, and to compare one procedure with another. Children might use various forms of representation: a set of pictorial instructions, a list of written or of coded instructions (Figure 4.9), a flow chart, or – perhaps more appropriately in a primary school – a structure diagram (Figure

4.10), which shows how an algorithm can be broken down into smaller and smaller parts until it is described in elementary instructions.

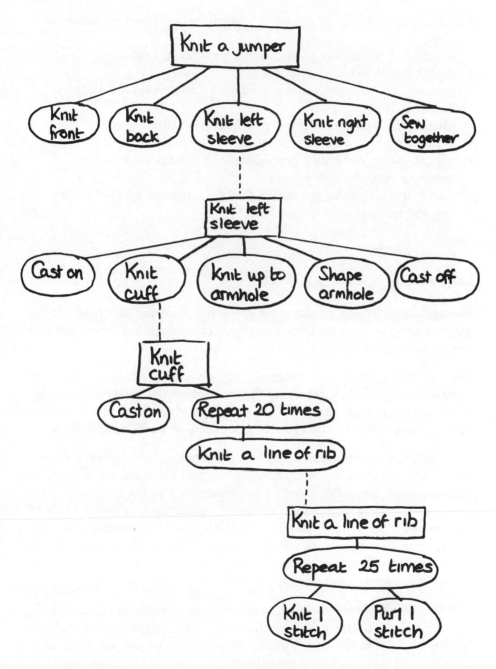

FIGURE 4.10

The **algorithmic skills** which children need to develop and use throughout the primary years are likely to include those listed below, although there is no specific order to their development:

- following or using an informal procedure described by someone else;
- describing a familiar procedure in an informal way;
- making up their own procedure;
- making modifications to a procedure so that it does a slightly different task;
- identifying and correcting errors in a procedure;
- explaining how a procedure works;
- describing or defining a procedure in a precise way so that someone else can carry it out;
- modifying a specific procedure so that it can be applied to the general case.

Logo and turtle graphics

The computer is one of the most powerful tools for carrying out an algorithm once the algorithm has been transcribed into the code of a programming language.

Logo is a programming language which young children can use almost as soon as they can count and recognise simple written words. Logo offers, amongst other things, a method of drawing lines to make pictures or patterns called **turtle graphics** or **turtle geometry**.

The lines are drawn on the screen by a small arrow, called a screen turtle, or on a large sheet of paper by a small robot on wheels, called a floor turtle. Some floor turtles are connected to the computer by a long cable; others receive an infra-red signal from a small piece of equipment which is plugged into the computer. Between the turtle's wheels is a pen holder, which can either be up or down. When it is down, then the turtle will trace a line as it moves.

The turtle can be moved using four simple commands: FORWARD and BACKWARD (to make it move in those directions), and LEFT and RIGHT (to make it turn on the spot). Each command needs to be followed by a number to determine the amount which the turtle is to be moved or turned. Using just these four commands, together with the commands to put the pen up or down, a great deal is possible.

FIGURE 4.11

stephen

The Turtle.
The Turtle is a Small
Machine Shaped like a
turtle It is worked off
the computer. It can
go forwards a 105 centi
Metres and back wards
the Same and right and
left It has pretending
feet.
I played against Neill.
cand Samuel and Christopher
We had to Make the
turtle touch a box
I won

FIGURE 4.12

Children are often introduced to work with Logo in PE activities, in which they explore space through body movements of left and right, or forward and backwards. They also play at being a turtle using a pencil and squared paper; one child gives instructions, and another tries to make a line drawing, or to trace a path through a maze. The work with the 'real' turtle usually starts by the children designing target games or maze games on the floor.

- Starting from here, how close can I get the turtle to the skittle? Can I do it in just one move?
- Can I get the turtle to go away from me and then turn round and come back again?
- How quickly can the turtle knock down the skittles in this obstacle course?
- Is it possible to get the turtle round the maze without touching the sides?
- Starting from its house, can we make the turtle go to the police station, the supermarket and the shoeshop on this street plan? What is the least number of moves needed?

One group of 6-year-olds from Westbury Laverton Infants' School in Wiltshire wanted to make the turtle draw them a map of their school. They paced round the outside of the building, carefully recording when they turned left and when they turned right. Their first attempt was lop-sided, and the starting and finishing points did not meet. The children looked again at the shape of the school, noting the lengths that ought to be the same, and pacing them out again to make sure. The turtle then drew a second map which they were very satisfied with (Figures 4.13-4.15).

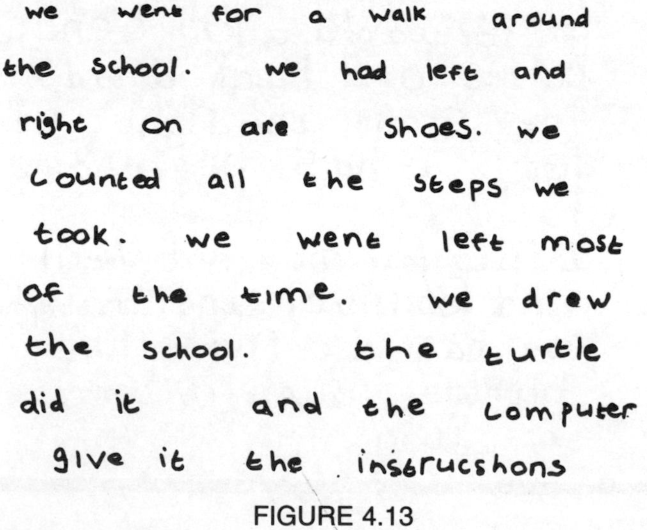

we went for a walk around the school. we had left and right on are shoes. we counted all the steps we took. we went left most of the time. we drew the school. the turtle did it and the computer give it the instrucshons

FIGURE 4.13

forward 7

turn left

forward 21

turn left

forward 27

turn right

forward 24

turn left

forward 7

turn left

forward 24

turn right

forward 12

turn left

forward 10

turn right

forward 13

turn left

forward 18

turn left

forward 11

turn right

FIGURE 4.14

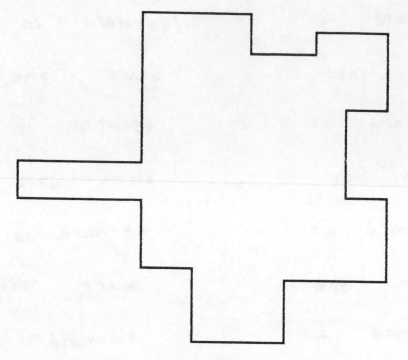

FIGURE 4.15

Children generally enjoy making the turtle draw simple pictures or patterns. Sometimes they want to use the turtle to reproduce a shape that they have already drawn for some other purpose, as did a group of 6-year-olds at Chater Infants' School in Watford. Using felt pens, the children had drawn a snowman made up of a large hexagon for the body, a smaller hexagon for the head, and a top hat made from a square (Figure 4.16). They were keen to use the floor turtle to draw a similar snowman.

Zena McNiven, their teacher, had some reservations about whether it might be too difficult because of the angles involved, but with the knowledge that they could abandon the project if it proved too hard, they went ahead.

The children looked at the large hexagon in the drawing first.

Teacher: How many sides are there?
Children: Six.
Teacher: Are all the sides the same length?
Children: No. Perhaps they are. Not sure.
Teacher: How can you find out?
Children: We could … um … we could get some string and measure.

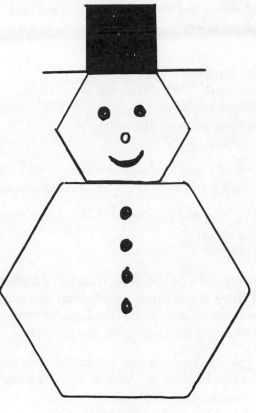

FIGURE 4.16

The children tried this and confidently said that the sides of the large hexagon in their felt pen drawing were all the same length. Zena then asked them what number they wanted to choose for the length of the hexagon's edge. The first number that they chose (17) made the turtle draw a fairly long line on the paper on the floor.

Teacher: If all the sides are the same length what number will you choose for the next line?

Children: Seventeen.

Teacher: Before you draw that line what have you got to do?

Children: Turn left.

Teacher: What number will you use for the turn?

The children chose a random number for the turn. They then proceeded to draw their second side, again using 17 turtle steps. They realised they had to turn left again, but this time they chose a different number for the second angle. They kept on using different numbers for the angles but were consistent in using 17 for the sides. They drew a shape with six sides, and knew that they had drawn the right number of sides, but the shape looked nothing like the one in their original plan. There was a look of total bewilderment on their faces.

Teacher: What happened?
Child: [*Indignantly*] We did it. We did it right.
Child: We drew six lines.
Child: And they were all the same.
Child: They were all 17.

All the children could think of was the lines which they had drawn, and they knew they had made them all the same length.

Teacher: What else did you have to do, apart from drawing the straight lines?
Children: Turning.

So far the children were of the view that the number they used for turning was of little importance apart from allowing the turtle to turn. At this point another child, Rhoda, who was not part of the original group, came up and surveyed the situation.

Rhoda: I think it's because you haven't drawn the sides exactly the same size as the one in the drawing [*the children's original felt pen drawing*].

Zena stood back while the children found the piece of string which they had used previously, and stuck it on to the paper on the floor. Using trial and error, they found the number of turtle steps that matched the length of the string. They then followed the same procedure as before, but using the new number for the sides. Once again, the children kept using random numbers for the angles so the end product still did not look like a hexagon.

Zena decided on this occasion to give them the number 60 for the turn, so that they could produce their hexagon. The children were delighted with it, and were able to find their way to the top of the hexagon to begin drawing the smaller hexagon for the head. They realised they would have to use a shorter length for the straight sides, and they continued to use 60 for the turns.

To draw the square for the hat the children had to investigate the nature of the square – that it had four sides which were all the same length, and four equal angles. Again they realised they would have to use the same number for each side. They also realised that one side of the square was going to be the same length as the edge of the hexagon because it was sitting on top of it.

Then it came to the turn. Someone suggested a turn of 10 units.

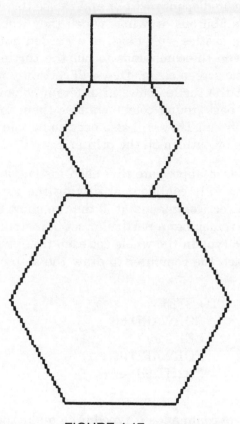

FIGURE 4.17

Zena immediately seized on the idea and suggested that they turn 10 each time until they thought that they were pointing in the right direction. She suggested that they should write down each LEFT 10 as they used it. They used nine instructions altogether before they were satisfied that they had drawn a square corner. They were not confident about adding nine 10s together in their heads, so they paused and used Unifix cubes to confirm the total of 90. When it came to the second corner of the square, they used LEFT 90 without any hesitation, 'because nine lots of LEFT 10 is LEFT 90 altogether'. There was great excitement as the snowman shape was completed.

Like the children at Chater Infants' School, most middle infants who work with Logo start to use much larger numbers than teachers would normally expect for children of that age. They also show that they are capable of adding or subtracting these numbers in their heads. Numbers in the hundreds are commonplace, and in one infant classroom which we have visited a number line up to 3000 extended right round the walls!

After children have worked with the floor turtle for a while, they will probably want to dispense with it and to use the faster screen turtle for the more ambitious drawings which they would like to produce: anything from castles with flags, to a garden with trees. They will need to be given the commands to put the turtle back to the start, and to wipe the screen clean. They will certainly want to set the pen colour so that the turtle draws in different colours; setting the pen colour to the background colour enables them to 'rub out' lines by drawing over them. They will also need to be told how to print their screen picture or pattern on the printer.

Once the children appreciate that each instruction has a particular effect, and are fully confident at driving the turtle around with a sequence of direct commands, it is time to show them how to make the computer remember a particular set of instructions, so that they do not need to type in the whole set each time. For example, if they wanted to teach the computer to draw the step of a staircase, they could type

```
TO STEP
    FORWARD 30
    LEFT 90
    FORWARD 30
    RIGHT 90
END
```

While the list of commands is typed in to make the short program or procedure called STEP, the turtle will not do any drawing. But once the children have finished defining their procedure, all they have to do is to type in STEP and the computer will carry out all the commands without pausing. If the children wish, the procedure called STEP can then be used in another procedure:

```
TO STAIRS
    REPEAT 6 [STEP]
END
```

The children may well decide that the steps that they have drawn are the wrong size. They could, of course, edit their procedure for the step, using FORWARD 40, instead of FORWARD 30. But a better way is to make a procedure which will draw steps of any size.

```
TO STEP :size
    FORWARD :size
    LEFT 90
    FORWARD :size
    RIGHT 90
END
```

In this procedure, :size is standing in the place of a number. Its value will vary, depending on what you type, so it is called a **variable**. If you type

STEP 100

the turtle will draw a big step with a rise and a tread of 100 turtle units. If you type

STEP 10

the turtle will draw a very tiny step using lengths of 10 turtle units.

It is much better if, at the outset, the children themselves decide what they would like to draw. Later on, when they are more familiar with turtle geometry, there may be times when it is appropriate for a teacher to suggest a challenge, and for the children to suggest challenges for each other. But for most of the time it is best if the decision making about what to try to do is left to each group – the children then feel that the problem 'belongs' to them, and are very motivated to solve it.

Two 9-year-olds made their first attempt to get the turtle to draw a circle after about 12 hours using Logo spread over six months. They had learned to use abbreviations for the FORWARD and RIGHT commands, and they had tried using combinations of these in a sequence like FD 10, RT 45, FD 20, RT 10 ... They were about to give up. Their teacher intervened, and suggested that they should walk around a circle pretending to be a turtle, and thinking about the movements that they were making. The activity convinced them that what was needed was 'forward a bit and right a bit and forward a bit and right a bit'.

Teacher: How many turtle steps do you want the turtle to draw?
Lena: [*Pause*] Eight.
Ashley: Yes.
Teacher: OK. On your rough paper draw me a circle with eight turtle steps around it.
Lena: [*After drawing an octagon*] That's not nearly circle enough. We want littler steps.
Ashley: Oh, I know. We'll need 360 tiny little steps to make a circle and if our steps are so little we'll only have to turn right one turtle turn.

Convinced that they had a solution, they started t type FD 1, RT 1, FD 1, RT 1, FD 1, RT 1 ...

Lena: Oh no! This is going to take ages.
Ashley: We could use that REPEAT thing.

They used the REPEAT command to produce the circle, and when it was drawn Ashley suggested that by using left instead of right the circle would go the other way, and they would get a 'pair of glasses'. Their next project was to put a pair of eyes behind the glasses, which they eventually managed by using REPEAT 90 [FD 1 RT 4].

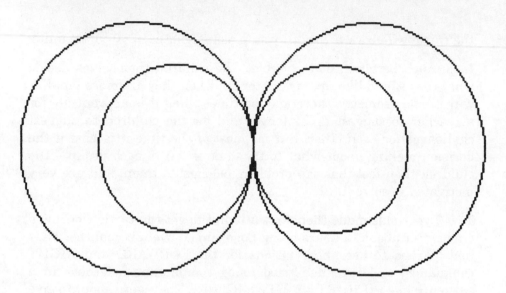

FIGURE 4.18

Logo offers almost endless opportunities for exploring mathematical ideas through projects which the children suggest for the turtle. In one school, some middle juniors produced a long wall frieze from turtle shapes drawn by the class: it had flowers and plants, a hedgehog, some snails, several butterflies, and in the sky a sun and some clouds. In another school, some Year 6 juniors used Logo to illustrate their own written stories about a chase across a roof. They used concepts of distance, time and speed in order to program **sprites** (small symbols which can be designed by the children and made to move across the computer screen, Figure 4.19).

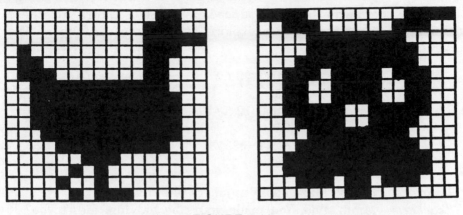

FIGURE 4.19

Using Logo for number work

Many of the activities which children do on a calculator can also be carried out, and often extended, by using a computer. After they have learned how to add two numbers together on their calculator they can type in

PRINT 6 + 9

to see the result on the computer screen. They can try a group of operations:

PRINT 7 + 5 − 3 + 17

or even

PRINT 83 / 42 + 45 ∗ (82 − 37)

(the asterisk is used for multiplication).

PRINT 3 ∗ 4 compared with PRINT 4 ∗ 3

or

PRINT 4 + 5 ∗ 2 with PRINT (4 + 5) ∗ 2 and with PRINT 4 + (5 ∗ 2)

One teacher who had introduced 7-year-old Laura to these commands found that she was exploring the halving of numbers. The screen displayed:

PRINT 25 / 2
12.5
PRINT 12.5 / 2
6.25
PRINT 6.25 / 2
3.125

Laura: Do you know about numbers like that?
Teacher: Mmm, I do. You made yours by halving, didn't you? It was like sharing between two. Perhaps we could try doing it again with Unifix cubes?

Laura took 25, and gave out 12 each, but couldn't halve the one left over.

Teacher: Let's make a Plasticine cube, and then we can cut it in two. ... [*After Laura had made and cut the cube*] So what have we got?
Laura: Twelve and a half.
Teacher: [*Pointing to 12.5 on the screen*] What about the computer? Do you think that might be how it writes twelve and a half?

They went on to make six and a quarter, and consulted the screen once more. Laura was quite happy to accept the evidence of her Plasticine and the naming of a quarter as explaining the 6.25. They went on. Six and a quarter halved gave them each three whole cubes and an eighth (the word was supplied by 7-year-old James who was watching the whole process). They checked again on the screen.

Laura: [*Pointing to 3.125*] That must be how the computer writes three and one eighth.

Laura insisted on doing one more – even though her pieces of Plasticine were now very tiny. She was fascinated by the numbers, and commented that they seemed to be getting longer. She went off to see if she could make her calculator 'write' these numbers in the same way.

Older children have experimented with operations involving large numbers or decimals in just the same way as they have done on their calculators. They have found that watching the result of a pair of commands like FORWARD –30 BACKWARD –50 gives them an admirable introduction to operations on negative numbers. They have tried simple investigations: for example, finding different pairs of numbers with a product of 1440, or the largest number which can be made by using the digits 1, 2, 3, 4 and 5 and any operations. The advantage of using the computer is that, unlike the calculator, it is possible to see the entire sequence of keys which have been pressed since they remain on the screen – a useful facility if an unexpected result appears!

When the children can define a procedure which uses a variable they can make up small programs which carry out calculations. For example,

```
TO SQUARE :number
    PRINT :number * :number
END
```

Typing SQUARE 5 should produce the result 25, SQUARE .3 should produce .09, and SQUARE –11 should produce 121. What numbers are needed to produce the results 256, or 10.24, or 0.11111111? Some children who defined a procedure which worked like a function machine:

```
TO TRY :number
    PRINT 2 :number – 3
END
```

then asked their friends to try it, to see if they could guess the 'rule' contained in their procedure.

Other ideas which some children have experimented with have included programs to help to find the factors of a number like 1988, procedures to add up three numbers, or to print the area and perimeter of a rectangle.

```
TO TEST :factor
    PRINT 1988 / :factor
END
TO ADDUP :number1 :number2 :number3
    PRINT (:number1 + :number2 + :number3)
END
TO RECTANGLE :length :breadth
    PRINT [THE AREA IS]
    PRINT :length * :breadth
    PRINT [THE PERIMETER IS]
    PRINT 2 * (:length + :breadth)
END
```

One favourite idea is the use of the random number generator. A command like

PRINT RANDOM 10

will print a random number between 0 and 9. Experiments with this command can lead to questions like, 'What number will appear next?' or, 'What number is the most likely to appear?' or even, 'How many times do we need to try it before we can be sure?' Tyrone and Dean, both aged 11, got fed up rolling a real die to find out how often a six would appear. They wrote a procedure to simulate ten throws.

```
TO DICE
    REPEAT 10 [PRINT 1 + RANDOM 6]
END
```

They then sat at the computer with their tally chart, and by typing DICE they could collect information about ten throws at a time.

By creating number programs like these, children can explore many different properties of numbers, as well as number patterns. But as with turtle graphics, it is best if they suggest their own ideas.

Using Logo to print words

Logo is capable of printing words as well as numbers. The words to be printed need to be enclosed in square brackets. Making a quiz is a fairly straightforward matter if the questions have simple alternatives as answers.

```
TO QUESTION1
    PRINT [Is a banana RED or YELLOW?]
    PRINT [Type RED or YELLOW.]
END

TO QUESTION2
    PRINT [Is a cabbage GREEN or BLUE?]
    PRINT [Type GREEN or BLUE.]
END

TO YELLOW
    PRINT [Well done. Now try this.]
    QUESTION2
END
```

```
TO GREEN
   PRINT [You were right. Next question.]
   QUESTION3
END

TO RED
   PRINT [If a banana is red then you are a monkey!]
   QUESTION1
END

TO BLUE
   PRINT [Whoever heard of a blue cabbage!]
   QUESTION2
END
```

With a little more effort and some careful planning it is possible to make a simple adventure game. It is best to work on the text screen (TS) if the scene description takes more than four lines, but otherwise the adventure can incorporate some turtle graphics.

```
TO START
   TS
   PRINT [You are in the witch's house.]
   PRINT [She has cast a spell on you.]
   PRINT [Can you escape?]
   PRINT [Stairs go up to the LANDING.]
   PRINT [The KITCHEN is left and the HALL is right.]
   PRINT [Type LANDING or KITCHEN or HALL.]
END

TO LANDING
   TS
   PRINT [On the landing you can see a CHEST.]
   PRINT [To see what is in it type CHEST.]
   PRINT [A BEDROOM is ahead of you.]
   PRINT [To go inside type BEDROOM.]
END

TO CHEST
   REPEAT 2 [FORWARD 100 RIGHT 90
     FORWARD 200 RIGHT 90]
   PRINT [There is a BOOK inside the chest.]
   PRINT [To read it type BOOK or LANDING to
     go back there.]
END
```

and so on.

Helping children with Logo

Logo has endless possibilities for problem solving and creative work. When you are working with the children it is worth keeping some of the following things in mind.

- Encourage the children to make their own suggestions for things to do.
- Allow plenty of time to explore what can be done. Introduce new commands as children express a need for them.
- Be prepared for most children wanting to dispense with the floor turtle before too long. The screen turtle works faster, and can be made to 'rub out' its mistakes!
- Although most middle infants deal readily with large numbers, a very few children of this age, including some with special needs, may need to use some adapted procedures which will reduce the numerical demands made upon them. For example, a procedure called F can be written for them, so that each time they type F, the turtle will move forward 20 steps.

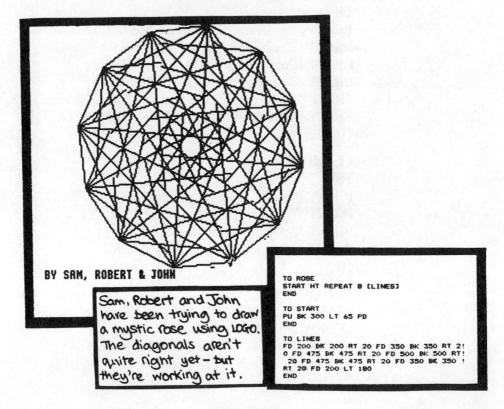

FIGURE 4.20

Very often when children are working with Logo things will go wrong with their plans, and something unexpected will happen: the turtle may go too far or not far enough, it may move in the wrong direction, or carry out moves in an unanticipated order. 'Bugs' like these are not 'mistakes', but are a step on the way to further discoveries. It is important that children sort out any bugs for themselves as far as possible. It is through thinking and talking about what might be wrong, and experimenting to put it right, that deeper understanding of the underlying ideas is achieved.

To help the children to minimise bugs in their programs you could use some of the following strategies.

- Encourage the children to make plans on paper (Figures 4.21 – 4.23) before they start at the keyboard. Often, they will combine commands together when they are typing in their written record (for example, FORWARD 50 FORWARD 30 into FORWARD 80), which will make their procedure more elegant and easier to follow.
- Plans on paper also help the children to look for structure. For example, they may notice that they have used the same sequence of commands in two different places, and will realise that it would be more efficient to turn the set of commands into a procedure.
- If a procedure using turtle graphics is not working properly, encourage the children to play turtle: to walk and turn through their sequence of commands in order to test them out.
- Again, if a procedure does not work satisfactorily it is worth trying out each of the commands in the procedure one at a time. Watching the effect of each command separately helps to identify which one is producing the unanticipated effect.
- When children start to use a sequence of turtle graphic procedures, suggest that they think carefully about the position of the turtle and the direction in which it is pointing, at both the beginning and the end of each procedure.
- Children who are more experienced with Logo can be shown the TRACE command, so that as a program is carried out it can be followed through step by step.

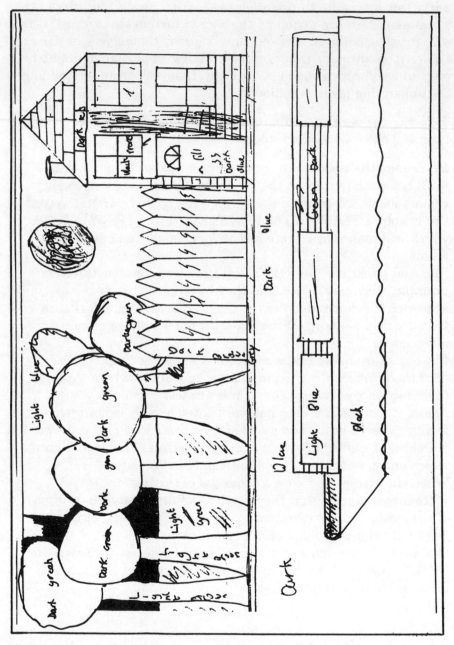

FIGURE 4.21

```
tree
setpc 6
trunk
lt 70
setpc 12
arcr 20 360
lift
rt 90
fd 20
fill 1 3
lt 20
lift
bk 30
setpc 6
fill 1 2
```

```
wall
setpc 15
repeat 6 [panel]
```

```
house :side
square :side
fd :side
rt 45
fd :side / 2.8
rt 45
fd :side / 2
rt 45
fd :side / 2.8
```

FIGURE 4.22

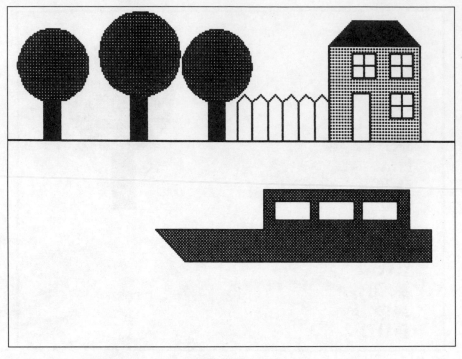

FIGURE 4.23

What can children gain by working with Logo?

There are three different but related aspects of the use of Logo with young children that make it worthwhile:

- it can encourage discovery learning;
- it can help children to develop mathematical concepts;
- it can provide insight into the power of programming.

The first aspect, discovery learning, has been recommended in reports on primary education for more than half a century. In the Hadow Report of 1931 there is the statement, 'The curriculum of the primary school should be thought of in terms of activity and discovery, rather than of knowledge to be acquired and facts to be stored.'

Helping children to become active, independent learners is perhaps easier said than done. A balance needs to be found between free activity and play on the one hand, and progression and development on the other. Encouraging children to explore ideas of their own, to try things out and to make adjustments according to what happens, does not mean that they should be left entirely to their own devices. Skilfully used, Logo can provide a situation in which it is easier for teachers to provide the balance between free expression and structure.

The second aspect of Logo is its support for the development of mathematical skills and concepts. Amongst the varied mathematical ideas which Logo draws upon are:

- big numbers and small numbers
- positive numbers and negative numbers
- number operations and the laws of arithmetic
- distance measured in turtle steps
- directions of left and right, clockwise and anti-clockwise
- angles measured in degrees
- estimates of distances and angles
- properties of two-dimensional shapes

Depending on the kind of picture or pattern which the children select as a goal, and the kind of procedure which they adopt, they may meet or use:

- line and rotational symmetry
- translation
- tessellation
- spirals
- coordinates
- bearings
- enlargements using ratio and scale
- letters standing for numbers (variables)
- passage of time using a WAIT instruction
- speed

The challenge for teachers is to capitalise on the possibilities for mathematical learning which Logo offers. Often, the mathematics in the school's scheme of work, and in the published textbooks which support it, are out of step with the ideas which children can and do use when they are working with Logo. If children are to gain mathematical understanding from their experiences with Logo, a better match between the use of Logo and the use of other resources for mathematics will need to be found.

The third aspect of Logo is its power as a programming language. Richard Noss, in the September 1983 issue of *Mathematics Teaching*, draws an analogy between problem solving and programming.

Problem solving	Programming
understand problem	analyse problem
devise plan	write program
execute plan	run program
review plan	debug and modify program

The essential difference between problem solving and programming is that when they are programming children must work with exact precision. The computer will make no allowance for hazy semantics or hesitant syntax. When their program or procedure is working to their satisfaction, children gain in their understanding that the computer is a machine which will carry out their instructions in the precise order in which they have been specified. They also grow to understand that in order to make modifications to a program or procedure, it needs to be well structured and easy for them and other people to follow.

Logo can never be 'finished' in the way that an adventure game can be completed. There is always more to try out, more to explore. There is no need to move on to the next programming word or technique until the children have thoroughly explored what they can do with what they already know. Some 8- and 9-year-old children in Avon who had been working regularly with Logo for a year expressed their thoughts about it (Figure 4.24).

Further reading

Blythe, K. 1990. *Children Learning with Logo – a practical guide to working in the classroom*. NCET. ISBN 1 85379 097 4.

Goodyear, P. 1984. *Logo: a guide to learning through programming*. 1984. Horwood. ISBN 0 85312 711 5.

Papert, S. 1982. *Mindstorms: Children, computers and powerful ideas*. Harvester Press. ISBN 0 71080 472 5.

Many people say computers are stupid
(which they are) and I believe that.
Probably because that whatever you
tell the turtle do it will do it. So you
have to do the thinking.

Ellie

Pete

When I first tried Logo
1 thought it was quite boring but
when I went on it a few more times
it began to help in ways of angles,
measuring and learning.

At first I did not understand logo but
after a little while I started to draw squares
circles and rectangles and now I'm into more
complicated things.
.. and you can make
proseedyures and rub things out and edit your
proseedyures.

Jonathan

At first I found Logo boring but when I
saw what it could do I started doing simply
things like squares and boxes but I am
now trying to do things like windmills
with rotating sails and squares rolling across
the screen.

Alexandra   age 8

FIGURE 4.24

5 Using the computer for control

Since the very earliest times people around the world have attempted to tap sources of energy in order to help them to adapt their environment and to exercise control over it. Tools were first created to extend the power and efficiency of human muscles. Hunting equipment like traps or bows and arrows, and farming implements like the plough, all increased the control which people had over food supplies. The power of the wind has for centuries provided the driving force for windmills and sailing boats. The first mechanical clocks used the energy provided by a large weight; later they used the energy stored in a coiled spring, controlling its release with a device called an escapement mechanism so that the hands of the clock turned at the right speed.

With the invention of engines and machines powered by hot air or steam a new technology of mechanical control began. Leonardo da Vinci, for example, invented many ingenious control systems, including one which automatically rotated a cooking spit using the hot air rising from the fire. As new forms of energy have been discovered and put to use, more sophisticated and often complex developments have occurred, powered by oil, electricity or nuclear fission.

Once it has been connected to a source of power, the control of a system is carried out in two different ways:

1 **manually**, where human beings are needed to switch things on and off, as in the usual electric lighting system in a house;
2 **automatically**, where switching continues without any human action until a target is reached or until the power supply is turned off, as in the running of a gas fired central heating boiler.

An important characteristic of many automatic control systems is **feedback**. Feedback is the signal which tells the control system when the target has been reached and whether or not the energy supply should be switched on or off. For example, an immersion heater is set on the dial of the thermostat to run at particular temperature. If the water is too cold, or if it has reached the correct temperature, a signal is sent back automatically to the switch which turns the electricity supply on or off.

By making use of feedback more and more technological systems are able to work by themselves with little human intervention. Nowadays whole systems of machines and circuitry are controlled automatically.

Control technology – the kind that works automatically – exists all around us in so many different ways that we take them for granted. A discussion with the children about a 'technology trail' round the kitchen will reveal an oven which is turned down when the correct temperature is reached, a light inside the refrigerator which comes on when the door is opened, a washing machine which fills the wash tub, heats the water, washes, rinses and spins the clothes dry. In a trail round the town it is possible to see things like the level crossing barrier which comes down when a train is coming, the supermarket door which opens when someone approaches, the traffic lights which change in sequence at regular time intervals.

Introducing children to control technology

Children's first experience of 'computer' control is likely to be with programmable toys and robots, either at home or at school. It is quite common to find dolls which can be 'taught' to respond with particular actions when they hear certain sounds, and toy cranes or buggies which can be instructed to move in a particular direction, to pick things up or to put them down (Figure 5.1).

Children who have been using computers for either word processing or Logo will already have grown accustomed to the idea that the computer can control other devices like the monitor, the printer or the floor turtle. It will probably come as little surprise to them to find that they can link the computer to a model which they have designed and made, and that they can then control the model in some way. This is something which most children find very exciting.

Computer control in the primary classroom needs to grow out of other technological activities that have taken place. Right from the earliest days at school children will start to build with simple everyday materials, making something that interests them. In doing so they solve practical problems of construction and design, two processes which go hand in hand. Builders who put up a house working to an architect's design do a great deal of approximating and making things fit!

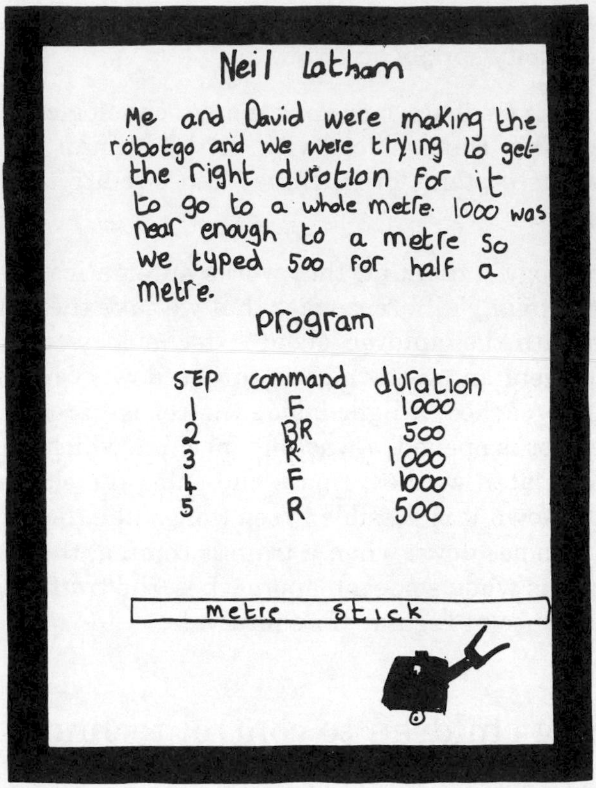

FIGURE 5.1

As children grow more confident with the techniques of designing and making, and as they increase the range of materials and tools which they use, they become more ambitious. They often want to make their models work in some way: perhaps because they have moving parts, like a windmill, a lift or a go-cart, or because they can be illuminated or made to make a sound. HMI explain this development in *The curriculum from 5 to 16* (page 35).

> Even at a very early age, pupils can begin to gain confidence in their ability to get to grips with the world about them; to be active participants as well as users and spectators. For example, the familiar primary school activity of making a model of a bridge, a crane or other vehicle ... can be readily extended to provide some involvement and insight into the process of technology; for example, designing a model crane that will actually lift, a bridge that will support a load, or a vehicle that will perform a specified task such as covering a set distance in a set time ... Technology at this stage has sometimes been called 'making things work better'.

With models that move in some way there is a new set of problems for children to think about.

- What source of power is possible?
- How can the energy be used to make things move?
- How is it possible to ensure that things will move in the right direction, and at an appropriate speed?
- How will things start and stop?
- How is it possible to slow them down or to speed them up?
- How can things be made to change direction, or to go backwards?
- Could things be connected in some way: for example, so that the train will only start when the signal is clear?

Some of these problems can be solved in quite straightforward ways. The power might be provided by a twisted rubber band, by the air being expelled from a rubber balloon, or by the wind created by a hair-dryer. It might be provided by a 4.5 volt battery, perhaps connected to an electric motor, with simple contact switches made from paper clips or drawing pins, to be operated by hand.

Speeds can be altered by systems of gear wheels or pulleys: first home-made using cotton reels and corrugated cardboard, then precision made using the pieces provided in a construction kit like Lego Technic, Fischertechnik or Robotix.

Robotix is a set of grey plastic parts: girders, wheels, walker legs, pincers, and so on. These parts fit together easily and firmly using octagonal-shaped connectors so that a wide variety of models can be built with them. Actuator motors, each fitted with an integral gear box and clutch, are also provided in the kit. The motors are powered by a battery box containing two pairs of batteries and are controlled from the rocker switches of a hand-operated controller. Pressing the switch in one direction results in the motor connected to it turning clockwise; reversing the switch reverses the direction of rotation.

Classroom projects with Robotix generally involve the children in finding solutions to practical problems. The first problems might relate to the parts included in the kit.

- Using just three pieces, how many different ways can they be fitted together?
- Can you build a model making use of at least one of each of the different parts?
- Can you make the grabber mechanism work?

When the children have familiarity with the parts, they can tackle the problem of making models that move or which carry out a task.

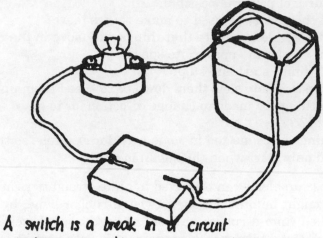

A switch is a break in a circuit
which you can join whenever you wish

children can make their own switches
from everyday materials to suit their
own particular needs

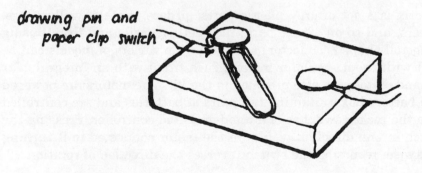

drawing pin and
paper clip switch

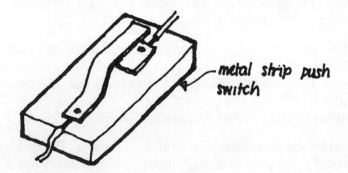

metal strip push
switch

FIGURE 5.2

The problems can of course be suggested by the teacher, but children themselves are never short of ideas.

- Can you design and build a windmill?
- Can you make a tracked vehicle which will move over snow?
- Can you build a machine which would be useful to a farmer?

Still later, the models which have been built with the Robotix kit can be used to conduct experiments.

- How much weight can your Robotix model lift?
- Can your model pull the same weight over different surfaces?
- How steep a slope will your model climb? What difference does the type of surface make?

The children at Lansdowne Primary School in South Glamorgan posed themselves the problem of designing a robot which would move half a metre to pick up a two centimetre block of wood and bring the block back to the starting place. Some children made tracked vehicles; some made machines which would 'walk'; Joanne and Michelle built a robot with wheels (Figure 5.3).

Sometimes the technological problems which children are tackling can be more easily solved by controlling their models, whatever materials they are built from, by using a computer. The computer as a 'controller' simply sets switches to an on or off position, or tests switches to see which of these two positions they are in.

Carol Wisely's class of 9-year-old children at Grafton Primary School in London constructed some lighthouses using everyday materials: softwood, cardboard rolls, lollipop sticks. Their designs were varied. Some were tall and thin, some were short and fat; some were round, some were square, and one was hexagonal. Three 1.5 volt batteries inside the lighthouses powered a simple circuit with a bulb. A contact switch was controlled manually. One group then wanted to make their light bulb flash, 'just like a real lighthouse'. The children painted a translucent bottle black on one side and inverted it over the top of the lighthouse. Their idea was to make the bottle turn and so create a rotating beam of light, but the mechanics of the problem proved to be too difficult for them. The best that they could achieve was flicking the manual switch from the off to the on position, and back again.

The children were then shown how a different circuit could be set up, drawing its power through an interface box which transformed the mains voltage to a safe level. The interface box could also be connected to the computer, receiving instructions from it and sending information to it along the connecting cable. Their particular interface box had eight output sockets into which things could be plugged, and the lighthouse light was connected into the socket numbered 8.

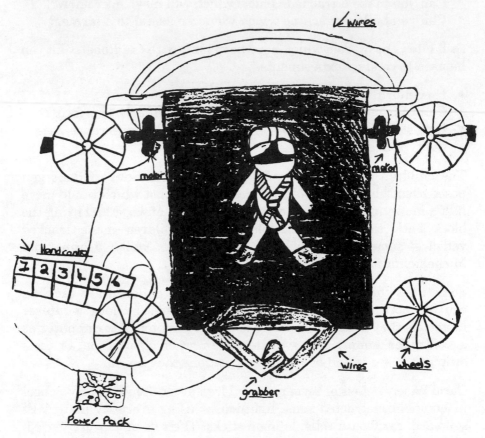

We had to make a machine to pick up a
block 2cm high. It had to move 50cm then
pick up a block, then take it 50cm back
to the paper and put it in the middle of
the paper.
We built a buggy with the Robotix kit.We
used three motors,a pair of grippers to
grab the block of wood,four wheels and
other bits and pieces.We fitted the
wires in and we controlled it with the
hand control.

Joanne and Michelle

FIGURE 5.3

Marlon thought we should make a light house. So we got some wood and started making the base. We went down to the nursery and got some nails and hammered a small piece of wood to a bigger piece of wood and then searched for a kitchen roll for the body and soon me and Marlon found one.

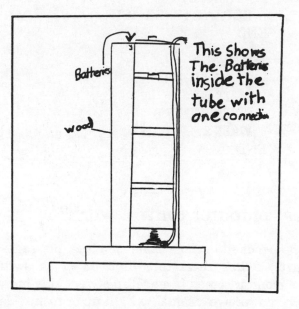

This shows The Batteris inside the tube with one connedu

Batteris

wood

We fixed on a spring and some wire Beacause a spring is a good contact for electricity. We put on the spring and held it down by drawing pins and we twisted on the wire and then put the tube on top. To hold the batteries in place

FIGURE 5.4

Using an extension to Logo which provides commands for switching things on and off, the children could then make the computer behave like an automatic switch for their model. By typing

SWITCHON 8

the lighthouse beam was turned on, while

SWITCHOFF 8

turned the beam off again.

The children were delighted. They went on to write a very simple program to control their lighthouse light automatically.

```
TO LIGHTUP
   REPEAT 100 [FLASH]
END

TO FLASH
   SWITCHON 8
   WAIT 2
   SWITCHOFF 8
   WAIT 2
END
```

How does computer control work?

A computer spends its whole time sending messages to all its different parts, telling them to switch on or to switch off. For example, the monitor screen is made up of very tiny individual dots, each of which can receive a signal to light up or to stay dark in order to form a picture.

A message to switch on is represented mathematically by the digit 1, and a message to switch off by the digit 0. These digits are known as **bits** (short for binary digits). The computers which were offered to primary schools under the Department of Trade and Industry's first hardware scheme were eight-bit machines. In these, the circuitry is designed to send or to receive eight on-off signals in one go. A Logo command like

SWITCHON [4 5 7]

indicates that, counting from the right, the 4th, 5th and 7th digits should be set to 1 in a binary number with eight digits:

8th	7th	6th	5th	4th	3rd	2nd	1st
0	1	0	1	1	0	0	0

Once this binary number has been transmitted to an interface box the corresponding switches in a row of eight would be switched on simultaneously. By sending different binary numbers it is possible to switch on or switch off all the possible different combinations of eight switches.

Similarly, by 'reading' the settings of a set of eight switches as a binary number, the computer can gain feedback, and know which of the switches are turned on and which of them are turned off.

The purpose of making models and controlling them

Every model made in the classroom is constructed with a particular purpose in mind. Sometimes the model helps to illustrate or to represent a particular idea; sometimes it is built with the purpose of exploring construction techniques and the properties of materials; sometimes it is made to solve a particular problem. Good model making is often part of an in-depth study, rather than being an isolated, uncoordinated exercise, and it results only when the time scale allowed for it is sufficient to promote quality and accuracy.

Children need to be encouraged to judge the success of their classroom models. There are various criteria which they can use: for example,

- Does it work?
- Does it perform reliably?
- Will it be durable?
- Is it efficient?
- Is the cost of building it and running it justified?
- Is it well finished, pleasing to look at and to handle?

The same criteria should apply to the models associated with control technology as they do to other models. In two different primary schools which we have visited recently we have seen models of castles. One was built in proportion, beautifully finished, with intricate detail both on the outside and the inside. The model had been wired discreetly for lighting, and different key presses on the computer illuminated different parts of the building. The children had clearly learned a great deal – about the castle itself, about wiring and circuits, and about the quality of construction and presentation. In the other school, the model of the castle was built of balsa wood, poorly cut, badly fastened, smothered in thick grey paint with no attention to detail. The wiring ran outside the building to some out-size light bulbs fastened to the top of the tower. It was difficult to see what the children had gained from this second exercise, apart from excitement through using the computer to make the lights flash on and off. The model making had clearly been rushed. No time had been set aside at the design stage to consider the quality of the finished product.

Equipment for control technology

If a decision is made to introduce control technology into a primary schools, then it will be necessary to ensure that there are sufficient resources for the children to work with.

First, some everyday materials are needed. The cost will have to be considered, since these are consumables, and 'junk' materials like tin cans and cardboard rolls, although useful, will not suffice. Lengths of 11 × 11 mm softwood, 4 mm dowelling rod, 5 mm plastic tubing, 16 mm wooden beads, pre-cut wheels with 4 mm holes, PVA washable glue and thin and thick card are all required. Models can be built using lengths of the square cut softwood joined together using card triangles and a PVA glue like Marvin or Alocryl (Figure 5.5). The quality of the glue is important – if it is too runny it will drip everywhere making everything more difficult to do.

Hand tools and jigs which fit the kinds of materials in use also need to be provided: for example, 4 mm and 4.5 mm drills to make tight- or loose-fitting holes for the dowel rod. Most schools start with a basic set of tools, choosing those which are most essential for the activities which they have in mind, adding to them as work progresses and as the children become more experienced. A basic set might consist of hacksaw, cutting block, scissors, metal ruler, and a jig which can make a perfect 90 degree or 45 degree cut, as well as guide the drilling of a perfectly centred hole.

Second, some commercial construction materials such as Robotix, Lego Technic or Fischertechnik are required. Although kits such as these are expensive, the materials can be used over and over again provided that care is taken of them. The construction process is also much quicker, particularly when motorised models are being made and gear wheels are being used to make things run at the right speed.

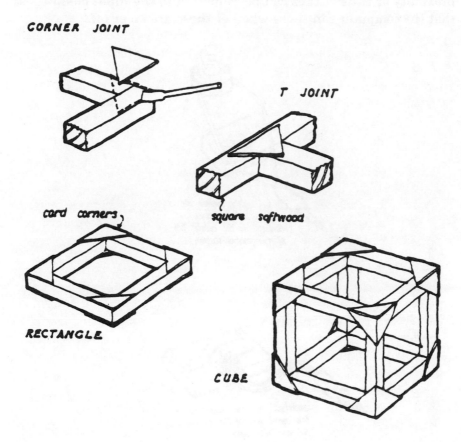

FIGURE 5.5

Whatever materials are used, some thought needs to be given to their storage. There is nothing worse than finding that the piece of Lego which you have been looking for has been lying on the floor all the time! Tools need to be kept in a way that gives children ready access to them. It is also helpful to arrange them in such a way that it is easy to check at the end of a session whether any of them are missing.

Once models have been built, sensors, switches and motors can be attached to them using Blu-tack or Sellotape. Although children can and should make their own switching devices using tin foil, springs, drawing pins, paper clips, and so on, it is helpful to have available a range of different devices which have been commercially produced. Light bulbs, buzzers, and motors can all be plugged into the output sockets of an interface box ready to receive a signal from the computer; pressure pads, light or heat sensors, and push button, proximity or tilt switches can be connected to the input channels so that the computer can sense whether these are on or off.

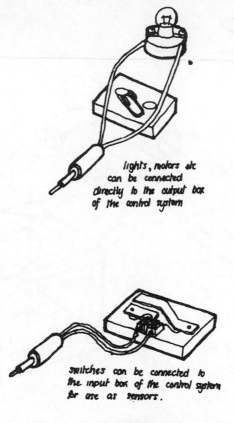

lights, motors etc
can be connected
directly to the output box
of the control system

switches can be connected to
the input box of the control system
for use as sensors.

FIGURE 5.6

Switches and sensors need to be stored and labelled so that children can easily find the one that they want. If you are buying sensors for primary school use, try to get some which are robust. Those produced by Deltronics, for example, are protected by a plastic casing and last much longer.

The choice of interface box to support control technology in your school is probably the most important decision to be made. The box should be robust, simple to use, pleasing to look at, and, above all, safe to use. Avoid offers of a cheap system which can be built in a few days by a friend! Try to buy a control system from a reputable company that will give an assurance about safety. Almost certainly,

your local authority advisory service will have a list of those which
are recommended.

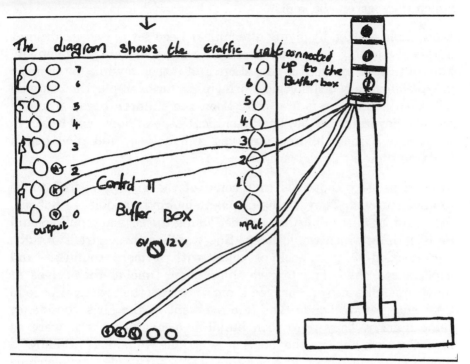

FIGURE 5.7

Finally, you need a piece of software which will allow the children to
program the control of their model. If you already use Logo for work
with turtle graphics, then it makes sense to use a ready-made set of
Logo procedures for control technology as well. If Logo is not
available in your school, then you may need to use some software
which simulates the way that Logo works. The most important thing
is that the presentation and commands are suitable for young
children, and that the editing facilities are easy to operate. The
software should support the children in what they want to do, not
impede them.

Getting started

One teacher, Linda Samson, became interested in what control
technology might offer to her class of 8-year-olds after she herself
had attended a one-week introductory course for teachers. Before she
began work with the children Linda reorganised her classroom,

making a space for two extra tables to use as a work bench. She also labelled all the tools and building materials, as well as the shelves on which they were to be kept.

Linda then started by giving a technical Lego set to two children at a time and letting them experiment. The children were not given any kind of task or problem at this stage and it took a while for them to grasp elementary technological principles: for example, that an axle will turn if the wheels are fixed. Soon the children began to make models. Several of the boys had technical Lego at home and began to build cars. Other children observed and helped, and then began building their own constructions.

Linda was very conscious that some of the girls appeared to be unadventurous. They built pleasant-looking models – houses, furniture, bridges – but they avoided using the cogs and pulleys and built nothing which would move. She watched these girls carefully, and decided to pair each of them with a more confident and experienced child, and to give them some time to themselves at lunchtime. She also encouraged them to borrow the technical Lego to take home at weekends. The improvement in the girls' confidence came quickly. They were soon building mechanisms that were as ingenious as any in the class: a whirligig to amuse a baby, a mushroom transporter with a pulley and a turntable, a wheelchair with a complex steering mechanism.

Linda made no suggestions to the children about what they might build; the ideas came from them. When the children had completed their model she would talk to them about it, asking them how it worked and whether they thought they could improve upon it in any way. Some pairs were satisfied with their work; others went away with renewed enthusiasm for modification and development of their idea.

After a term with the technical Lego, Linda introduced some wood construction techniques to four children at a time. The groups had some problems at first with the manipulation of the tools, but their skills improved rapidly. The children also found that they needed to pay far more heed than they had ever done previously to the accuracy of their measurements! Impatience was another difficulty at first – the children found it hard to wait for the glue to dry sufficiently to make a firm joint.

At the time, the school was researching a project about the jungle. Linda decided to ask the children to design and draw a machine that could lift a crated animal on to the back of a lorry so that the animal could be taken to a better part of the jungle and released. Most of the design drawings incorporated a pulley and a hook in the sketch. After discussion, the ideas were refined, and building began. Linda was always present to supervise and advise, but found that the children turned to her less and less as their confidence and ability grew.

In the third term the children were introduced to simple electrical circuits powered by batteries. They learned how to build a circuit, to make a switch, to connect in a light bulb and a buzzer. After they had designed and built some models of blocks of flats using everyday materials they were able to add a bell and a light to the front entrance, taking care that the wiring did not spoil the appearance of their models.

The following year Linda had the same class of children, who were by then building impressive battery-powered models. At that stage she had not touched upon the notion of computer control, but she felt that the children were ready, and that she was sufficiently confident, to embark upon a problem that would ultimately lead to control from the computer.

Once the interface box had been set up, she began as she had done the previous year, by organising the children to work in pairs. Each afternoon three of the pairs of children could fit in a forty-minute turn, so that by the end of the week everyone in the class had been given the same opportunity. Each pair was provided with a light bulb, a buzzer, a switch and some wire. Linda explained how to program the computer to operate these devices, and then encouraged the children to experiment freely. The following week she suggested simple problems for them to solve: for example, programming the computer to switch on first the light, then the buzzer, and then to switch off both the light and the buzzer simultaneously. Since the children were already accustomed to writing and editing Logo procedures for turtle graphics, the control commands were easy for them to use.

Linda watched the children, and listened to them, as they set about solving their particular problem. They all tackled it with enthusiasm, consulting each other about the strategies that they should use, and talking their way through the steps that they should take.

It was then time to give the children their heads, to let them suggest the models which they could build and then control from the computer. Linda offered a range of construction materials to the children, as well as a variety of switches and sensors. 'Can we make another whirligig, one with flashing lights on?' said one group of girls with a gleam in their eyes. The ideas flowed fast. 'We're going to make a bridge which goes up when a boat goes under.' 'We'll build a house so the lights come on when it gets dark.' 'Can we protect our computer at night by sounding a warning if anything gets too close to it?' Sally and Andrew, with memories of the jungle project, chose to make an animal trap which would not harm the animal in any way (Figure 5.8).

We decided to design an animal trap that will work using the computer and control box. To make the trap we made a wooden box and put a flap on the front with a block, which would stop the animal from escaping. Then we put a pressure pad inside connected to a light bulb, which would signal when the animal was caught. We were going to use a buzzer, but we thought it might scare the animal.
Here is the procedure we used.

```
TO TRAP
IF INPUTON? 1 [SWITCHOFF 1] [SWITCHON
WAIT 6
SWITCHOFF 1
TRAP
END
```

By
Sally and
Andrew

FIGURE 5.8

Helping children to build and control models

Some primary teachers who had already used control technology with the children in their classes devised this checklist for other teachers who are planning a start.

- Decide what equipment is needed. Allow time to become familiar with it yourself before embarking on work with the children.
- Decide how to organise the materials and equipment in the classroom. Where will the work bench go? How will the construction materials be organised? Will everything be easily accessible to both you and the children? Is everything labelled so that children will know where pieces are and where to put them away?
- Prepare any information or instruction sheets that are needed to help the children in their use of the tools or building materials.
- Give the children some guidance about how and when to take and return the things that they will use.
- Make sure that each child receives instruction in the safe use and general care of any tools and electrical equipment.
- Decide how the children will be grouped. Will they be friendship groups, groups with mixed experience, single-sex groups ... ? Will the groups remain the same or will they change?
- Plan the working time for each group. Make sure that each group has sufficient time for trying out ideas and for making modifications to their plans and prototypes.
- Allow plenty of time for skills to develop. There is little point in rushing to control a model which is poorly made!
- Encourage the children to build models that both look good and function well.
- Take special care to ensure that the girls are as involved and as confident as the boys.
- Decide how the children's models will be stored or displayed. Is there a suitable board on which to display sketches, diagrams and written work? Is there a suitable horizontal surface, perhaps a table, some shelving or the floor? If not, could some shelving be improvised using planks?

What do children gain by working with control technology?

Ten major aims of CDT are described on page 3 of the booklet *Craft, design and technology from 5 to 16*. Two of these aims are:

to give girls and boys the confidence and competence to identify, examine and solve practical problems involving the production of artefacts or systems using a variety of approaches, materials and methods;

to develop pupils' understanding of the ways in which products or systems might be controlled and how they might be made to work more effectively.

Activities involving control technology help both these aims to be realised. In addition, the activities help children to appreciate the variety of problems which can be solved through the application of a programming language.

Further reading

Blythe, K, 1996, *Children and technology*. Nash Pollock Publishing, ISBN 1 898255 10 5.

Williams, P.H.M. 1985. *Teaching craft, design and technology 5–13*. Croom Helm. ISBN 0 7099 2776 2.

6 The computer in particular areas of the curriculum

This chapter discusses the use of the computer in five different areas of the curriculum: language, mathematics, science, environmental studies and creative arts. Although software tools like word processors and databases, and programming languages like Logo, play an important part in these subjects, they are mentioned again only briefly; their applications have been considered in greater detail in the earlier parts of this book. This chapter focuses on other software tools, and also on some software with specific subject content.

Amongst those programs which are designed for use within particular subjects there are many which drill and test skills like adding two numbers together, spelling common words, using map references or recognising notes on a stave. Software like this can only be effective in helping a child with a specific difficulty if the child's problem has previously been identified as part of a well-developed diagnostic procedure. The program can then be selected with an individual child in mind and matched to that child's particular needs. Indeed, this may be one of those rare occasions when a computer is best used with a single child.

It would not be sensible to describe examples of drill and practice programs in this book: what may be useful for one child in one school on one particular occasion may not be useful for other children in other schools. In contrast to drill and practice software, the subject-related programs which are described in this chapter are sufficiently flexible to be used productively with many different children in many different circumstances.

Language

> With regard to English, it is clear that, far from reducing demands, IT may increase requirements for literacy ... However, aims and objectives for English are not made substantially different by IT, though they may be made more urgent ... It is already plain that IT offers important potential to the teacher for motivating pupils. It can also support individualised learning and permit access to ever increasing banks of information both within and outside the school. The technology is enormously flexible allowing information to be handled and displayed in a wide variety of ways, including through word processing. Thus, drafting and the associated positive teacher intervention can be assisted, 'real' acts of communication may be promoted by electronic means, individual research can be supported and a variety of cooperative teaching and learning approaches can also be assisted. (*English from 5 to 16*, second edition, page 41)

One of the most impressive aspects of the use of the computer in the primary classroom is the amount of talk which is generated. When three or four children are sitting around a computer they have a natural focus for their talk, which encourages listening, reflection and participation. This feature is common to many different programs although the kind of talk, and its quality, varies from one piece of software to another. In the best programs – those that require collective decision making – the children must think clearly, express themselves effectively, listen to each other and take into account alternative viewpoints. This generation of talk may be one of the greatest advantages of having computers in primary schools, but only if the computer is used by groups of children rather than by individuals, and occasionally by the teacher to promote whole class discussion.

The computer's ability to stimulate purposeful conversation applies equally to children for whom English is a second language. Bilingual children need opportunities to talk in their mother tongue, as well as in English. The use of a program such as a game of strategy provides a chance for those speaking the same heritage language to work with each other unimpeded in their thinking by any need to speak English. Alternatively, they can join an English-speaking group, and can use the visual evidence provided on the screen to help them to make sense of and if possible contribute to the group's discussion.

Another big stride forward which has been made in language work by the introduction of computers into schools is undoubtedly word processing. In the 'electronic office' a word processor is simply a sophisticated typewriter; in the classroom it has the potential to alter the whole way in which the business of writing is approached. Children can readily test out versions of what they want to say and refer back to what they have written without any difficulty. The word processor also offers unrivalled conditions for shared writing tasks – coming to a consensus about what needs to be said, developing and making changes to successive drafts, justifying to others what has been done – and being rewarded by visually attractive copy in the anonymous style of the printer.

Word processors encourage the development of reading skills as well as writing skills. One reception class teacher abandoned all her published reading scheme books as soon as she acquired a word processor in her classroom. She took time to sit with each child at the computer keyboard, then as the child related a story she typed it in. The active sharing of the story as it was being written had a profound effect. It was found that children who were unable to read from conventional early readers were able to read and reread their stories from the screen. They could also tell when their teacher had departed from their own words. 'I thought so,' said one 5-year-old. 'You've put witches. I didn't say that yet.' The children very much enjoyed reading their own books and, later, the books of the other children in their class.

Another teacher, working with three older children who were reluctant both to read and to write, skilfully combined the use of a tape recorder with the use of the word processor. First she ascertained that the children were prepared to write a story about a circus. She then questioned the children about their story. What happened at first? What did the ringmaster look like? Why were the clowns so funny? How did the acrobats feel when the people clapped? Why did the lion escape? And so on. While the children responded to these questions she recorded what they said on tape, but switched off when she herself was speaking. She then left the children to type a first draft of their story with the help of the recorded tape. Once the story had been refined and printed the teacher made a book from it, which the children read and re-read so avidly that it eventually fell to pieces!

Programs which not only allow simple editing but which respond to typed text with animated graphics are certainly great motivators for young children. One example is a program in which the actions of a tomato-like creature can be discovered by completing sentences which start, 'Podd can ... '; simple cartoon stories about Podd can be created by linking five of the actions together (Figure 6.1).

Podd can wink

FIGURE 6.1

Another example is a program which is concerned with moving into a house. The children type instructions like 'put a cooker in the kitchen' or 'make Jane have a bath'. They can 'make it snowy' or 'make Jim play the piano' (but not 'go to the toilet'!) A wall frieze with furniture cut out from catalogues and with captions added can be made to accompany use of the program; multiple outline drawings of the empty house can be printed so that the children can draw their own arrangements of furniture, write sentences to describe their houses, and so create a class 'Moving in' book.

The massive storage capacity of CD-ROM has allowed the development of 'talking books', multimedia programs which combine pictures, animation, words and sounds to form on-screen books. Many have a clear story line with the text printed in short sections on each page. Others are poetry collections. Clicking on the text causes it to be read aloud while clicking on certain active parts of the picture causes animated effects such as a squirrel peeping out of its hole and running away up a tree. These programs are highly motivating and can stimulate reluctant readers to engage willingly with text and to take a greater interest in stories or poems. Children who normally have a short attention span will spend long periods working on their own with these CDs or will take great pleasure in introducing peers to the sound and animation effects that they have discovered.

Another program which helps to develop both reading and writing strategies can be used with all age groups. Children will sit around the computer screen for lengthy periods, talking animatedly and trying to decipher the text on the screen. Very little happens. In this case there is no animated action or sound effects. A short poem or piece of prose gradually reveals itself as the children predict words or phrases (Figure 6.2).

```
--- fl--r w-- --ggy u---r --- k----,
--- w-ll- w-r- w-- --- ---cky, ---
p--c- ju-c- w-- -r-pp--g fr-m ---
c--l--g. J-m-- -p---- --- m-u-- ---
c-ug-- --m- -f -- -- --- ---gu-. --
------- --l-c--u-.
```

Use the ARROW keys to move.
Type your guess then press RETURN.

FIGURE 6.2

At the start of the program, there may be some letters in place, or even no letters at all. The text is then developed in much the same way that a negative comes into focus in a photographer's developing tray. The meaning is disclosed slowly; words or phrases give clues – occasionally misleading ones – and bit by bit the piece comes together as a coherent whole.

All the reading strategies used by mature readers can be brought into play as the text is deciphered, but in slow motion. Individual letters and words, and the ways that these fit together, give graphical and syntactic cues. The meanings of words and phrases provide semantic cues and the overall style of the piece of text can provide stylistic cues. The letter-by-letter build up of text allows plenty of time for a teacher to discuss with the children the various ways in which predictions can be made.

At any time the computer can be asked to provide all the occurrences of a particular letter or group of letters. The temptation to use this facility to work through the alphabet letter by letter needs to be resisted! The choice of timing for a new letter is important, too – not too early, since children need plenty of thinking time; not too late, or they will become frustrated.

The passage of text which is used in this program can be created in advance either by the teacher or by a group of children, or chosen from a library provided with the program. If children's own work is used then it is best to make sure that the spelling and punctuation is standard, in order to avoid confusion. For the program to work well, the text which is used needs to be fairly pointed, and likely to hold the children's interest. An unusual image, or even a cliché, can lead children to be more adventurous and less predictable in their own writing.

A quite different kind of language software draws on the computer's ability to substitute alternative words or phrases, or to rearrange them. A computer program can easily produce all the possible anagrams of a given word; it takes a far more complicated program to recognise any sensible anagrams. Nevertheless, programs which generate alternatives can provide talking points about language structures. One such program allows children to experiment with and discuss the joining of simple sentences with subordinating conjunctions. For example:

> **I put up my umbrella because it is raining.**
> **Because it is raining I put up my umbrella.**
> **It is raining because I put up my umbrella.**
> **Although it is raining I put up my umbrella.**
> **I put up my umbrella unless it is raining.**
> **It is raining unless I put up my umbrella.**
> **When it is raining I put up my umbrella.**
> **When I put up my umbrella it is raining.**

The children themselves must make judgements about the sense or nonsense of these different combinations. It requires a fair degree of insight to appreciate the difference between deduction and inference in the last of these sentences – after all, I might well put up my umbrella in order to ward off the sunshine on a hot Mediterranean beach!

A similar principle is used in programs which ask children to provide lists of nouns, adjectives, verbs or adverbs, and to specify phrase structures in terms of these categories. The computer will then generate a series of phrases, drawing randomly on the lists of words. After their school had made a visit to a nature conservancy, Emma and Franchesca, both aged 8, created some word lists:

Nouns	Adjectives	Verbs	Adverbs
trout	brown	sparkle	swiftly
fish	swirling	twist	quickly
	slippery	swim	sharply
	slimy	jump	hungrily
	rainbow	wriggle	greedily
	listening	dart	
	glistening	swerve	

They then created a single phrase form 'adjective, noun, verb, adverb' so that all the phrases generated would have a similar structure. After considering several of the variations produced by the computer, Emma and Franchesca selected the combination of phrases which they liked best and printed out their computer-aided 'poem'.

Brown trout sparkle sharply,
Swirling fish twist swiftly,
Slippery trout swim hungrily,
Slimy trout jump greedily,
Rainbow fish dart quickly,
Listening trout swerve sharply,
Glistening fish jump hungrily.

Maud, aged 9, had been impressed with a hawk at the conservancy, but in her session with the program she experimented with a greater variety of phrase structures.

Breathtaking wings, powerful eyes,
Talons tearing, bird swooping,
Grabbing talons, cruel beak,
Masterful eyes,
Masterful wings,
Powerful killing, viciously, greedily.

The point of a program like this is not of course to create great poetry – and it is a matter of debate whether text generated by a computer should even be referred to as poetry. The purpose is to get children to think carefully about how words fit together, and how different parts of speech function. Using the program may improve their own writing by encouraging them to consider alternative phrases. It should certainly convince them that human poems are better than those produced by a computer. Fiona, aged 10, looked at the phrases about hawks which she had generated on the screen, and went away to incorporate those that she liked into her own version.

> **Giant bird in the sky**
> **Swerving, soaring, flying high,**
> **Wings still, about to kill,**
> **Hovering cruelly, eye so bright.**
>
> **Giant bird swooping low**
> **Quickly swooping, plunging now,**
> **Eyes glaring, talons tearing,**
> **Prey eaten, out of sight.**

Mathematics

The ways in which the computer contributes to mathematics teaching and learning are described in *Mathematics from 5 to 16* (page 13).

> Microcomputers can be used in at least three ways which often overlap:
> (a) as a teaching aid;
> (b) as a learning resource for the pupils;
> (c) as a tool for the pupils to use in doing mathematical tasks.

It is not difficult to find examples of the computer being used as a learning resource for mathematics. Not very long ago I watched Philip and Emerson, both aged 6, playing a short computer game in which they took turns to pay a coin towards the cost of an item in a toyshop. The one who paid the last coin gained the toy, and the game had reached the stage where the outstanding amount on an 18p toy cat was 6p. It was Philip's turn to choose a coin, and he was looking glum.

Emerson: Six is a loser.
Me: [*Somewhat taken aback*] How's that?
Emerson: Well, if Philip pays 5p, then I pay 1p, and I win. If Philip pays 1p, then I pay 5p, and I win again.
Me: But what would happen if Philip pays 2p?
Philip: Emerson still wins. If I do pay 2p, then he'll be on 4p, and he can win on that.

Emerson: We know four's a winner cos if you're on four then all you
have to do is **pay a one**. Then there's three left to pay and
three always loses. We worked it out just now.

He showed me their record (Figure 6.3):

On 1 pay 1 Win

On 2 pay 2 Win

On 3 pay 1 2 left Lose

On 3 pay 2 1 left Lose

On 4 pay 1 3 left Win

On 4 pay 2 2 left Lose

On 5 pay 5 Win

FIGURE 6.3

Philip finished off the explanation: 'Pay one and you lose 'cos there's
only two left to pay. Pay two and you lose 'cos there's only one left to
pay.'

They left the computer to make way for another group, and went to
add their record to their computer work folder. It was time for lunch.
As they went, Emerson looked back over his shoulder. 'If six is a
loser, then seven can be a winner,' he said. 'And eight,' said Philip.

The toyshop game is just one example of a small mathematical
program in which children are encouraged to think logically and to
develop a strategy. There is a large selection of similarly easy-to-use
games, puzzles and simple investigations for children of all ages to
use on the computer. The problem for the teacher is not so much

knowing which of them to use, but which of them not to! If programming with Logo is playing a major part in the children's mathematical work, then there may be no time for the smaller packages like the toyshop program, useful though these might be for particular children on particular occasions.

Some teachers like to support more extended problem solving in mathematics through the use of an adventure game. In one such game, the players must find their way around a coastal fort and escape to the sea. Many of the rooms in the fort have a lock which takes the form of a mathematical puzzle, and inside the rooms are useful objects which can be picked up, carried around and used to aid the escape (Figure 6.4).

The children at the Augustus Smith Middle School at Berkhamstead worked in pairs on this program over a period of half a term. Taking turns, each pair of children was given about 30 minutes at the keyboard for exploration and note taking. They then moved away from the computer to think about the strategies that they needed to adopt in order to solve the problems that they had encountered. Some worksheets and further investigation sheets were made available to help them, as well as plenty of equipment: counting blocks, cards, scissors, needles, thread, coloured pencils, paper, buttons and so on.

Although a map was provided with the package, the children were encouraged to draw their own in order to keep track of their position, as they often needed to retrace their steps to get around the fort.

At first many groups used a trial and error approach to the problems, but they soon realised that more thought would be necessary if they were to make progress. The children encouraged each other and became so engrossed that many of them stayed in during the mid-morning and lunch-time breaks in order to carry on with the program. Several of the children tackled problems which were very difficult for them, simply because they were so motivated to find solutions.

Apart from providing many different mathematical puzzles to be solved, the program inspired a great deal of other work. The children made mystic roses, and drew scale plans and elevations for their own forts. One group invented their own board game on the same lines as the computer game. The history of Martello towers was researched, stories were written about escaping from castles, and pictures drawn as illustrations (Figure 6.5, 6.6).

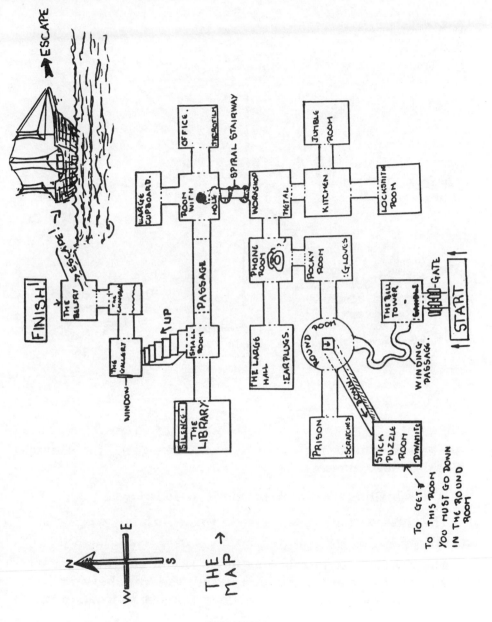

FIGURE 6.4

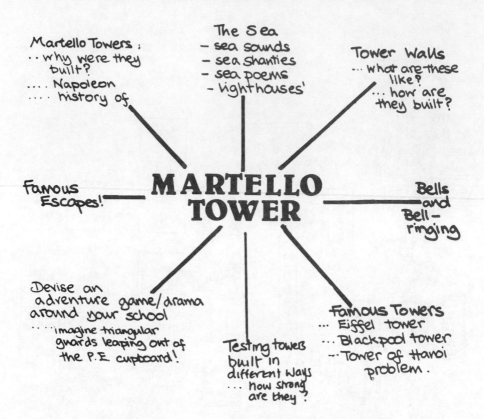

Martello Towers :
.. why were they
built?
.... Napoleon
.... history of

The Sea
- sea sounds
- sea shanties
- sea poems
- lighthouses'

Tower Walls
... what are these
like?
... how are
they built?

Famous
Escapes!

MARTELLO TOWER

Bells
and
Bell-
ringing

Devise an
adventure game/drama
around your school
...."imagine triangular
guards leaping out of
the P.E cupboard!

Testing towers
built in
different ways
... how strong
are they?

Famous Towers
... Eiffel tower
... Blackpool tower
... Tower of Hanoi
problem.

FIGURE 6.5

At the end of their work with the adventure game, the children recorded their comments.

It was brilliant. We were brilliant to do it.

The instructions were clear, the solutions were not always so clear.

The mystic rose puzzle was hard. If you got the answer wrong, the next time you tried the numbers were different so you had to have a good theory to work from.

The guards were a pest, they sent you right back to the beginning if you could not solve the problems on triangular numbers.

None of our group ever thought they would finish in 60 moves, but we did.

One particular problem that made me think hard was the one outside the library. It took me three days to think out how to do it.

Why couldn't you just go out of the front gate again and walk round the edge of the fort to the sea? But if you could, it wouldn't be so much fun.

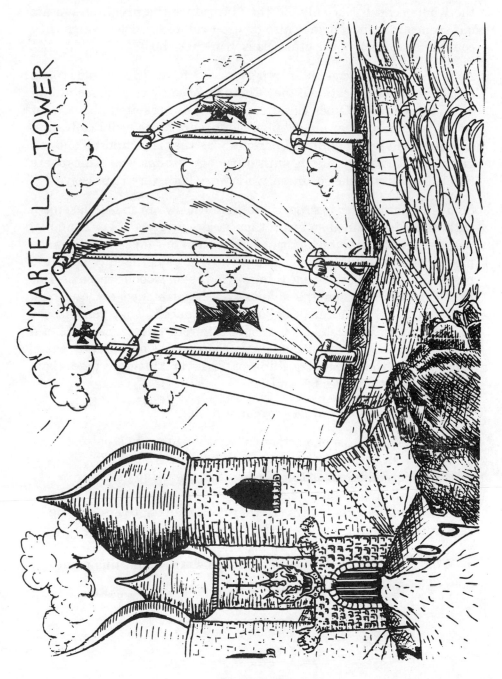

FIGURE 6.6

Another teacher who used the same adventure program was Chris Rowlatt, working with a mixed class of Years 4 and 5 juniors at The Lea JMI in Harpenden. After the children had completed their work with the program they decided to present an 'adventure' assembly for the whole school. Not only did they introduce the program and act out scenes from it, but they also devised related puzzles which they could offer to each of the other classes in the school.

Activities from a computer program for 9 to 13-year-olds need considerable modification if they are to be used by reception children or middle infants! Other class teachers were consulted about what would be appropriate, and detailed plans were made well in advance. The general view of staff and parents was that the children showed great sensitivity in working with other age groups; the atmosphere and the quality of the resultant work were both very impressive.

Some teachers prefer to support mathematical work in the classroom with more open-ended software than strategic games. For example, there are programs which provide a selection of shapes which can be moved about the screen to make a picture or pattern. Of course, it is possible to do much the same thing with a set of wooden mosaics. But in a computer version the shapes can be stretched or squashed, reflected in a line, rotated, enlarged or reduced. They can also be coloured in different shades to create different effects. Sections of a pattern can be moved about the screen using a 'cut and paste' technique so that repeating tiling patterns or kaleidoscope designs can be created (Figures 6.7 and 6.8).

Software like this encourages problem posing:

- Can we fit squares and octagons together to make a pattern?
- Can we cover the whole screen with scalene triangles?
- How many different patterns can we make using just four squares touching each other edge to edge?
- How many different ways are there of colouring this tile using just two colours?
- Can we make a pattern with six lines of symmetry?
- What would happen if we rotated this shape about this point?

FIGURE 6.7

It is possible that mathematics is the area of the curriculum which is most affected by new technology: every mathematical technique or routine which children have been accustomed to learning can now be carried out more quickly and more accurately by a machine. Mathematics lessons in the future may well emphasise learning how to make imaginative use of a programming language and a set of software tools in order to solve mathematical problems, rather than emphasising practice of the pencil and paper manipulative techniques which machines do so much better than people. This view is explained in *Mathematics from 5 to 16* (page 34).

FIGURE 6.8

Microcomputers are a powerful means of doing mathematics extremely quickly and sometimes in a visually dramatic way. If pupils are to use microcomputers in this way they will need to learn to program the machines. For mathematical purposes, such programming does not need to be highly sophisticated. It may be a form of Logo, or the early stages of a language such as BASIC, or indeed any form of computer control which enables pupils to carry out their own mathematical activities (Figure 6.9).

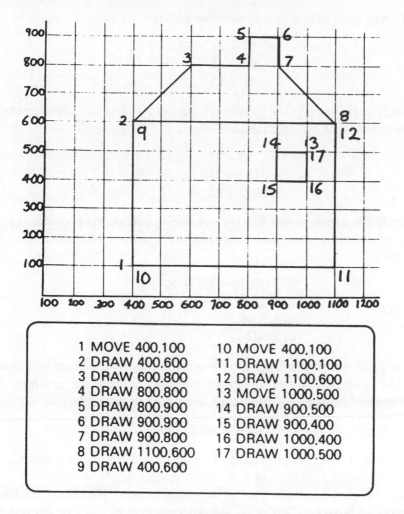

1 MOVE 400,100	10 MOVE 400,100
2 DRAW 400,600	11 DRAW 1100,100
3 DRAW 600,800	12 DRAW 1100,600
4 DRAW 800,800	13 MOVE 1000,500
5 DRAW 800,900	14 DRAW 900,500
6 DRAW 900,900	15 DRAW 900,400
7 DRAW 900,800	16 DRAW 1000,400
8 DRAW 1100,600	17 DRAW 1000,500
9 DRAW 400,600	

FIGURE 6.9

The obvious choice of a programming language for primary school use is Logo, so is it necessary for children to learn how to program in BASIC? Maybe not. But consider what one group of Year 6 juniors did using the knowledge of BASIC which they had gained on their home computers.

The children had discussed the patterns in the early part of the eleven times table. They were asked to use their calculators to work out

$$15 \times 11 = 165$$

and

$$27 \times 11 = 297$$

and were then asked to hypothesise about

$$17 \times 11$$
$$23 \times 11$$
$$54 \times 11$$

The children were quick to spot a rule, and were soon able to predict accurate results for calculations like

$$29 \times 11$$
$$154 \times 11$$
$$2672 \times 11$$

Some of the group wanted to try out their predictions on whole blocks of numbers, and after some trial and error they produced this BASIC program:

```
10 FOR N = 1 TO 10
20 PRINT 11 * N
30 NEXT N
40 END
```

Their program printed the first ten multiples of 11. Then by making simple changes to the program they were able to produce any sequence of multiples which they wanted: for example,

```
10 FOR N = 50 TO 65
```

This investigation of multiples of eleven could also have been tackled by using another software tool called a **spreadsheet**. In some ways a spreadsheet is a bit like a two-dimensional database. It has a number of boxes, called cells, set out in a grid of rows or columns. A number, or a short word, or a formula, can be entered into each cell, or it can be left blank. Part of a builder's spreadsheet for the cost of materials for a job might look like this, where R2C2 stands for row two, column two, R2C3 for row two, column three, and so on, and SUM(C4) stands for the sum of the numbers in column four.

Item	Number	Cost	Sub-total	VAT	Total
windows			R2C2*R2C3	17.5%*R2C4	R2C4 + R2C5
doors			R3C2*R3C3	17.5%*R3C4	R3C4 + R3C5
glass			R4C2*R4C3	17.5%*R4C4	R4C4 + R4C5
TOTAL			SUM (C4)	SUM (C5)	SUM (C6)

As soon as the numbers and prices are entered in the first two columns, everything else is calculated automatically.

Item	Number	Cost	Sub-total	VAT	Total
windows	4	35.00	140.00	24.50	164.50
doors	1	50.00	50.00	8.75	58.75
glass	5	20.00	100.00	17.50	117.50
TOTAL			290.00	50.75	340.75

If the cost, say, of a window frame changes, or if the customer wants one more door and one less window, all the builder has to do is enter a new number in the appropriate cell, and all the rest of the figures are recalculated instantly.

Spreadsheets are just beginning to be used in primary school projects by older juniors; it is possible that in the future more applications for them will be found. In those schools which have used them the children have, for example, kept running accounts for an imaginary bank, built up patterns of the eleven times table or of square numbers, or investigated the rectangular areas which can be enclosed by, say, 72 centimetres of string.

The National Working Group for Mathematics, in its *Mathematics from 5 to 16*, recognised the importance of work with calculators and computers. The accompanying letter, from the Chair of the Group to the Secretary of State, stated:

> In our report we emphasise at many points that mathematics is not static, and that of all subjects, it is perhaps the one that is most affected by technology. It is therefore of the utmost importance ... [to] keep the impact of new technology under continuing review.

Science and technology

> ... pupils need to grow accustomed from an early age to the scientific processes of observing, measuring, describing, investigating, predicting, experimenting and explaining. Appropriate work can and should begin in infant classes. Pupils

should also use their science in technological activities which pose realistic problems to be solved and involve designing and making.
(*Science 5–16: A statement of policy*, page 8)

First hand enquiry should lie at the heart of all scientific activities for young children, so any programs which simulate experiments, though commonly used in secondary schools, need considerable justification if they are to be used at the primary level. Without handling the materials themselves, young children have no real experience on which to base their observations and predictions. One experimental simulation supposedly for use in primary science starts with a demonstration of objects floating and sinking in a bath, then asks children to predict whether a particular object will float or sink, or whether it will sink faster or slower than another! There is really no need for such a program when experiments with sinking objects are so easy to set up in the classroom. There are similar programs, equally misjudged, which demonstrate the relationship between distance, time and speed, or the principles of shadows and reflections.

However, science can be messy and there are occasions when dealing with practicalities can obscure the scientific principles being explored. A program which simulates growing a plant is no substitute for the real thing but can be used alongside it to explore, for example, what would happen to a plant grown in a dark cupboard if we didn't keep forgetting to water it!

Perhaps the most useful piece of software to support primary science is the database. Experimental information collected by observing, counting or measuring can be stored in a data file and then interrogated in different ways so that patterns and trends are revealed. Children have used a database for varied science activities: to help them to monitor the life style of caterpillars, to analyse results of eye-sight tests, to assess the factors affecting the growth of plants, to investigate the best design for a paper aeroplane, and so on.

A class of children in a first school on the Isle of Wight set out to observe birds and to collect information about those which visited three bird tables sited on a bank by the classroom windows. The study started by talking about the birds which the children had seen.

Brian: When I was look ... leaning against the pole I saw the two ... three baby birds, and they put their wings out and tried to fly, and when I made a noise, the mother noise, they all put their heads up and flapped their wings and started to fight. And I saw the mother come back. She had a worm in her mouth ... and then she gave it to them. She sat on the bar for a little while and then she flew away to get some more food. The little birds ... they had all like stripes going down them ... and they were black, brown and white ... and they had only little wings about this big ... and on top of their heads they had all fur sticking up ...

Julie: I liked watching the swallow build its nest in the shed with mud all round it and it put straw and feathers inside it so that it wouldn't be rough for the baby birds ... and the swallow's tail is forked and it looks light ... and it glides in the sky and makes flying look easy ...

Unlike minibeasts, which can be brought into the classroom, the opportunities for watching birds, even on a bird table, are very brief. During their initial observations of the feeding birds the children made sketches and wrote descriptions so that they could more readily identify the birds which they saw (Figure 6.10).

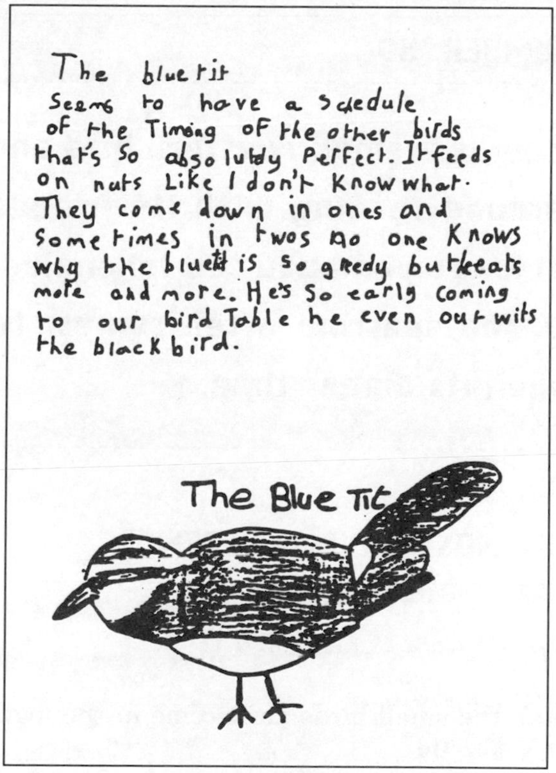

The blue tit
Seems to have a scedule
of the Timing of the other birds
that's so absolutly Perfect. It feeds
on nuts Like I don't Know what.
They come down in ones and
some times in twos no one Knows
whg the bluett is so greedy but eats
mote and more. He's so early coming
to our bird Table he even out wits
the blackbird.

The Blue Tit

FIGURE 6.10

Slowly the children began to get a feel for patterns of behaviour. Some birds were bossy, others were shy and flew away as soon as another bird arrived; some preferred to feed from the ground; some walked, others hopped. Particular questions arose. Did the birds feed at particular times? On the ground, or on the table? Did they feed alone or together with their friends? Were there special times when more birds seemed to feed?

The children's teacher decided that they would use a very simple form of database in which children could type a short description about a particular bird and its feeding habits. In addition, up to four key words could be specified which might help the children to identify behaviour patterns more clearly (Figure 6.11).

The records were created over a period of time until the children had more than seventy descriptions. They then searched the records looking for the key words which appeared most often. They consulted reference books for additional information about their hypotheses, and gradually came to some conclusions.

NOTICE NUMBER: 59

The sparrow is a small chattery bird and mostly it hops around feeding with its friends on the ground. It is grey and you can tell males by their black bib. The sparrow often comes. It always knows when its dinner time.

KEYWORDS:

SMALL, FRIENDS, GROUND, OFTEN.

FIGURE 6.11

Duncan: I think the small birds don't come in the fog because they can't see to fly.

Mandy: I think all the birds prefer the dry weather because their food is not always dry when it is raining and it is hard for them to fly if their wings are wet.

Kevin: If it is wet and muddy not many birds come because the birds could think that they would get stuck in the mud.

I don't know why but the small birds know precisely when it is their dinner time they seem to fly with a clock in their brain.

FIGURE 6.12

Scientists at work often need to identify things: substances, rocks, animals, plants, and so on. In the simple database which stored the children's information about birds it was possible to identify particular birds by selecting records with key features: for example, long tail and black and white plumage. They are other recognised ways of narrowing down a list of 'suspects' in order to eliminate them from an enquiry. For example, someone trying to identify a particular twig might ask the following questions:

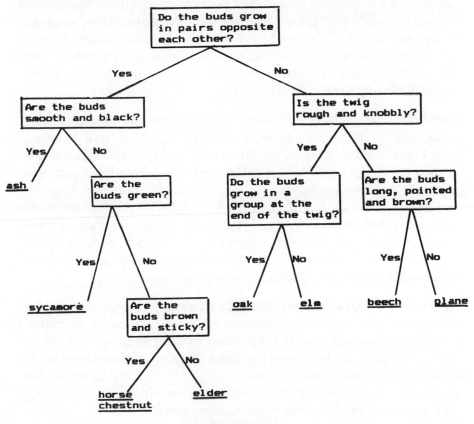

FIGURE 6.13

The same questions about the twigs can be arranged in a different format, in the form of a key.

QUESTION	YES	NO
1 Do the buds grow in pairs opposite each other?	2	3
2 Are the buds smooth and black?	ash	4
3 Is the twig rough and knobbly?	6	5
4 Are the buds green?	sycamore	7
5 Are the buds long, pointed and brown?	beech	plane
6 Do the buds grow in a group at the end of the twig?	elm	oak
7 Are the buds brown and sticky?	horse chestnut	elder

The two representations are equivalent to each other – any key can be displayed as a tree, and vice versa. Keys are more common in identification books, probably because the tree structure does not fit easily on a rectangular page. The tree structure, on the other hand, is easier to view and gives a better overall picture of the ways that things are classified. In tree structures where each question has just two possible answers (yes or no, as with the questions about twigs) there are only two branches from each point so the arrangement is called a **binary tree**.

Software which allows children to create and use binary decision trees, and to print the equivalent biological key, is well known to primary school teachers. A simple version called ANIMAL was part of the set of programs which accompanied the original DTI machines provided for primary schools. More flexible decision tree programs can be used to classify and then to identify far more than animals – in fact anything from nursery rhymes to food, from clothes to clocks. Children find this software especially useful for 'sorting' things which they have collected or observed: birds, common pond animals, minibeasts, leaves, things from the seashore, and so on.

Apart from creating sorting trees for their own collections, children can also be provided with collections of objects and asked to create a set of questions which will allow them to discriminate between one object and another by observing their physical characteristics. For example, what questions would enable you to identify an object from a set containing a pencil lead, a rubber, a bobbin, a jam jar, a paper clip, a piece of card, a pebble and a paper towel?

One group of four girls used the computer to create a decision tree for a selected sample of cheeses. The labelled products were in front of them, and as they tasted these they pulled faces and made comments.

Amy: I think we should start with the Parmesan first. It's very dry and hard.

Kate: It tastes salty! This one's different too. It's bright orange.

Susan: Hey, look at this! it's all crumbly.

Amy: My mum always buys Cheddar. She says it's good for grating and it melts on toast.

Denise: Ugh! I wouldn't buy those.

Amy: What's up with you.

Denise: Ugh! That mouldy one. I'll have to go and get a drink.

Kate: I told you they'd be strong. I like them.

Denise: They're mouldy.

Susan: No, they're not. It's good for you. Look, this one has got green in it, and this one has got red veins. They can't be mouldy.

Kate: Well, what shall we start with? What about Brie and Cheddar? [*She types them in.*]

Amy: What shall we say?

Denise: Is it soft and creamy?

Susan: Has it got a downy skin?

Amy: Is it firm and yellow?

Susan: That's daft. They're both yellow. They're just different yellows.

Denise: No, this one's creamy. Creamy is about how it feels as well as how it looks. Let's put 'Is it soft and creamy?'

Susan: OK. Now it's my turn. Let's do this one with holes in.

Decision tree programs can be used in a surprising number of ways. If a suitable tree of questions is already available then children can use the tree for identifying things. At the other extreme, they can build their own trees starting from scratch. In between these two possibilities lies a third. If, say, a field trip involving pond-dipping is planned, then a 'starter' tree of the most common pond animals can be created in advance, using information from books or from photographs. The binary tree can be designed so that its main branches represent the major groups: nymphs, larvae, snails, worms, and so on. The preliminary research involved in creating this starter tree helps to focus the children's observations when they are collecting their pond animals. New finds can be added as and when they are discovered, so the tree can continue to develop over a period of time.

Scientists argue constantly amongst themselves about the best ways of classifying things. In their use of a decision tree program children need to concentrate on close observation of detail, on making comparisons, and on phrasing questions which will distinguish clearly between one thing and another. The structure of their tree – which depends on their criteria for classifying – will not be unique. By exploring and comparing different classifications of the same set of things children start to develop an understanding of why things are classified the way that they are.

Another way in which the computer can enhance scientific investigation is making use of it to control models which have been built, perhaps a house of the future or a machine which will wash, rinse and spin dolls' clothes. The computer can be instructed to alter the environment in some way – adjusting the temperature, switching on a fan, operating a buzzer, driving a motor – so that children can observe for themselves the kinds of changes which happen as a result.

The computer can also be used to monitor a scientific experiment in which something needs to be counted, timed or measured. Older primary children find this especially helpful when their experiment or investigation is a lengthy one. One group of upper juniors who wanted to compare the daytime and night time activity of their classroom hamster set up the computer to count the number of times the hamster left its sleeping box at night. Another group, working with their teacher Ivor Broad at Coryton Primary School in South Glamorgan, linked a temperature probe to their computer so that they could conduct some experiments which recorded temperatures at regular intervals over a period of several hours. Their investigation was part of a whole school project on the theme of 'hot and cold'.

Before they used the computer the children at Coryton had tried lots of different ways of measuring temperatures using various kinds of thermometers, and had researched different methods of trying to keep things hot or cold. The temperature probe was attached to the computer, and a piece of software was used to display the measurements being taken at regular time intervals.

The children's first experiment involved two cans of water, one very hot and the other very cold. By adding cold water to the hot or vice versa, and by making the time intervals of the readings very short, the children were able to see immediate and spectacular changes in the graphical display on the screen.

The children then set up an investigation with a thermos flask which contained very hot water (Figure 6.14) and set the program to take readings at 10-minute intervals over a period of 3 hours (Figure 6.15).

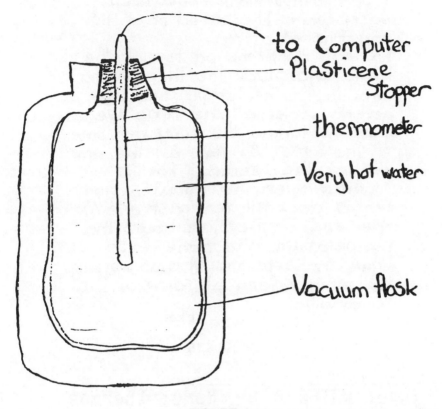

to Computer
Plasticene
Stopper
thermometer
Very hot water
Vacuum flask

FIGURE 6.14

The results of this experiment were printed so that everyone could see the details represented both in graphical form and in tabulated form (Figure 6.16).

There were several questions for the children to consider – how much the temperature of the water had dropped, whether it had dropped at an even rate during the 3-hour period, and so on. The results stimulated them to pose further questions. What would happen if they only filled the thermos flask half full? Would similar results be obtained with a different thermos flask? Would the same temperature drop be observed if they started with warm water, rather than very hot water? Is a thermos flask as good at keeping things cold as it is at keeping things warm? The children were surprised and very interested to see the results when they packed their thermos flask with ice instead of hot water (Figures 6.17, 6.18).

Our thermos flask Experiment

We did this Experiment to find out
if a thermos flask could keep
water warm. It Started of at 94°
and finished at 76°.
We put Plasticene on top of the
flask and Stuck the thermometer
through it. The temperature was
getting cooler all the time. We
were watching the computer Some
of the time but not all the time
We Set the readings for 20
readings every 10 minutes from
ten O'clock till ten past one. At
the end of the three hours the
temperature had gone down.
While the experiment was working
we were looking at some of the
readings.

                              Marc

FIGURE 6.15

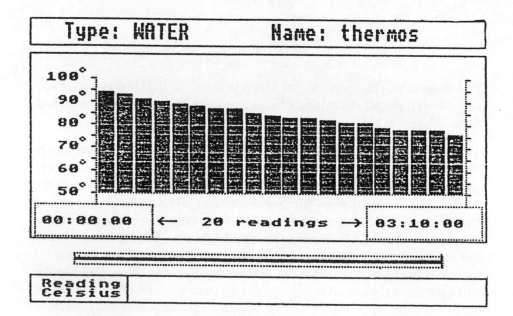

FIGURE 6.16

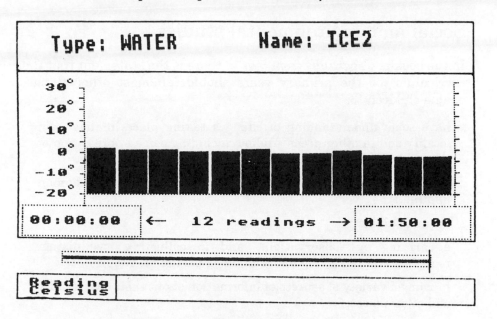

FIGURE 6.17

I have just discovered that a
thermos flask is better at keeping
ice cold. I found out that the
ice stayed cold for nearly three
hours.
Stuart Smith brought in some ice.
It was in pieces shaped like
cubes. We weighed it in a
plastic carton and it weighed 300
grams. I thought that it would
have melted after three hours but
I was wrong. The ice was still
there and it weighed 280 grams.
The pieces were still shaped like
cubes.

Gillian

FIGURE 6.18

Social and environmental studies

In the booklet *Geography from 5 to 16* there is the statement that the curriculum for the primary years should, amongst other things, enable children to:

> have some understanding of changes taking place in their own locality and in other areas studied, including some appreciation of the ways in which human decisions influence those changes;

> gain some appreciation of the importance of location in human affairs ... ;

> acquire skills in:

> a. carrying out observations, and in collecting, organising, recording and retrieving information as part of an enquiry;

> b. using a variety of sources of information about their own locality and other places;

> c. communicating their findings and ideas, with varying degrees of precision in writing, pictures, models, diagrams and maps.

Geography, like history, is often planned as part of a broader programme of topics and activities within a primary school social or environmental studies curriculum. For example, the study of a coastal resort might focus on the present character of the place, the ways in which the holiday trade takes advantage of the site and the surrounding area, and how the weather conditions influence the influx of visitors. The study might also be examined from a historical perspective, to see what changes have taken place over the previous century and the possible reasons for them: the type of work done, the clothes worn, the layout of streets and the architectural features of buildings.

The use of a computer simulation is one way to help children gain some understanding of the way that human decisions can influence change and development. Ideas of 'best location' are well suited to this approach since it is easy for a computer to calculate the outcomes of the decisions which are made. As part of a broader study of the environment, the children might use such a program to locate a medieval castle in an appropriate position, or to determine the best site for a fire station. What routes to the castle will be possible? Where will drinking water come from? How will protection from invaders be afforded? Should the fire station be positioned near the homes of fire officers, or near the fire hazards? Will all sections of the community be fairly served by it? Will the building of the fire station be acceptable to conservationists?

Those simulations which feature animals and their lives can help children to develop an appreciation of the environment from a different perspective from their own. A program in which, for example, children make decisions from the point of view of an urban fox requires them to decide on a strategy for exploring possibly hostile surroundings and on ways of using available resources to ensure survival. In the process of finding food, water and shelter a map of a city suburb is uncovered, complete with all its hazards: people, dogs, cats, roads and railways, and even snares.

When such a program is used sensitively as part of a project it can provide children with an insight into a way of life very different from their own. Sarah, aged 10, imagined herself as a fox searching for food. She wrote:

Last night I was hungry. The moon came up so I waited in the shadows of the trees at the end of the garden. I could hear cars in the distance. When it seemed quiet I ran silently through the garden towards the dustbin. One quick tug and the lid came off. It clattered on the ground making a loud tinny sound. Suddenly a curtain was thrown back and a pool of yellow light spilled on to the grass. A window opened. "What's that?" said a voice above my head. "It's just a cat," said another. "Shut the window. It's cold." The window closed and it was all dark again. When it was quiet I searched in the dustbin for food. Sweet papers, coke cans, bottles. Egg shells, newspapers smelling of fish and chips, empty cereal packets. The human beings had not been hungry, but there was nothing for me.

In history, as in geography, there have been some radical changes in teaching approaches over the last ten years. Nowadays there is much more emphasis on encouraging children to pose and test hypotheses about the past, to develop empathy with the people who lived long ago, and to use and understand the nature of the firsthand evidence that provides information about these people and their lives.

Data is therefore important in the teaching of history: real data, found in census records, in parish registers, in newspaper reports, in school log books, in street and trade directories, and so on.

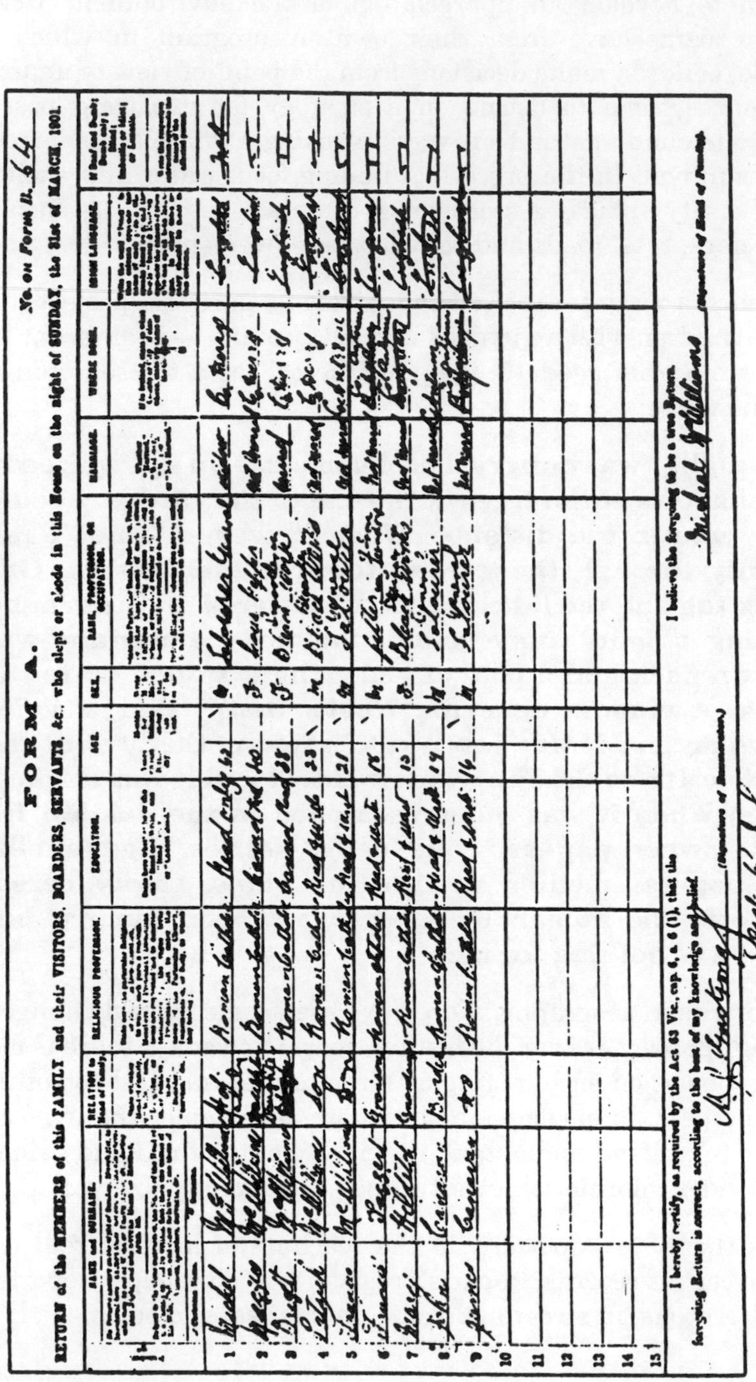

CENSUS OF IRELAND, 1901.

(Two Examples of the mode of filling up this Table are given on the other side.)

FORM A.

No. on Form B. 64

RETURN of the MEMBERS of this FAMILY and their VISITORS, BOARDERS, SERVANTS, &c., who slept or abode in this House on the night of SUNDAY, the 31st of MARCH, 1901.

NAME and SURNAME	RELATION to Head of Family	RELIGIOUS PROFESSION	EDUCATION	AGE	SEX	RANK, PROFESSION, OR OCCUPATION	MARRIAGE	WHERE BORN	IRISH LANGUAGE	If Deaf and Dumb; Dumb only; Blind; Imbecile or Idiot; or Lunatic

I hereby certify, as required by the Act 63 Vic., cap. 6, s. 6 (1), that the foregoing Return is correct, according to the best of my knowledge and belief.

(Signature of Enumerator)

I believe the foregoing to be a true Return.

(Signature of Head of Family)

FIGURE 6.19

Rather than reading in a twentieth-century book about the nature of employment of children in the mid-nineteenth century, today's children can start with their own hypothesis: 'Is it possible that children aged 10 were chimney sweeps in the 1860s in England?' They can then go to the census records, search the data and find the facts. Indeed, 8- or 9-year-old boys were often no longer living with their families, but were already apprenticed to a sweep-maker. What must life have been like when such conditions were regarded as normal? What empathy can the 10-year-olds today develop for the 10-year-olds living a century ago?

Joe Johnson, working with the children at Stadhampton Primary School in Oxfordshire, embarked on a study of the village as it was 100 years ago. He obtained the 1881 census records for the village from the Public Records Office in London. Thirty-four photocopies of the records for 373 people cost £34, but he was convinced that it was money well spent.

```
FORENAME      SURNAME      AGE  OCCUP
-------------------------------------------------
CHARLES W     CARTER       11   FARM BOY AG LAB
JAMES         GREGORY      12   HELPER IN GARDEN
ALFRED        SPENCER      12   FARM BOY
THOMAS        PAGE         12   FARM BOY AG LAB
ARTHUR        SPENCER      13   FARM LABOURER
EDWARD        ALLEN        13   FARM BOY
SUSAN         GREGORY      13   TEACHER
FREDERICK     CHALKLEY     13   GARDENER
ELIZABETH     SCALES       13   NURSEMAID
JOHN          DRAPER       14   FARM BOY
ALFRED        DAVIS        14   FARM BOY AG LAB
ANNIE M       KING         14   TEACHER AT SCHOOL
ALFRED        HORNETT      14   BOY CARTER
WILLIAM       GREGORY      15   FARM BOY AG LAB
JOHN          FLETCHER     15   FARM BOY
CHARLOTTE     EPHGRAVE     15   DOM SERV
MARY A        TINGAY       15   BARMAID
ALFRED        BENNETT      15   FARM LABOURER
ARTHUR        BROWNSELL    15   FARM LABOURER
ELIZABETH     COLLINS      15   GEN SERV
JOHN          PEARMAN      16   FARM LABOURER
FANNY         MAYNARD      16   PUPIL TEACHER
JOSEPH        WALLER       16   FARM BOY
ARTHUR        BURGESS      16   STABLE BOY
MARIA         TAYLOR       16   DOM SERV
FREDERICK     PHIPP        16   FARM LABOURER
SOLOMON J     SHADBOLT     16   FARM BOY
ELIZABETH     BRUNTON      16   DOM SERV
WILLIAM       CHALKLEY     16   LABOURER IN SAWMILL
BENJAMIN      HORNETT      16   CARPENTER
```

FIGURE 6.20

The children were first taken to the churchyard to look for names of any people who were buried in the graveyard and who had been alive in 1881. They found twenty-one gravestones, and from these they recorded the details of first name, surname, sex, year of birth, year of death, and age at death (Figure 6.20).

Back in school they started to look for matching details on the photocopies of the census sheets. It was a laborious job. They found that not all the information on the census return was relevant to their enquiry and, in addition, the copperplate handwriting was very difficult for them to read. Joe discussed with the children the information that would be useful to them, and they designed a record sheet made up with relevant headings listed in the right order. He then enlisted the help of some parents who spent some considerable time deciphering the census returns and transferring the relevant information to the new record sheets.

This was the children's first experience of using a computer database to store information, and Joe decided on this occasion not to involve the children in entering the data from the census returns. The sheer quantity of information was simply too great. Over a weekend he entered all the information himself. The children did, however, make a small data file of all the information taken from the twenty-one gravestones. That enabled them to print it out very easily so each child could have a copy. They then took turns in small groups to questions the census data file to see if any records contained the same details.

Their first surprise was to find that there were only four gravestones for people who had actually been resident in the village in 1881. Where had the other seventeen people come from? Where did all the other people included in the census go? Did they move away from the village, or were they buried without stones? The children never discovered any satisfactory answers to these particular questions, but later other questions emerged. Which houses did the four people live in? How big were their families? What jobs did they do? The school's ancilliary helper went with a small group of children who were interested and took rubbings of some of the gravestones. One of the people commemorated on these headstones turned out to have a descendant who was still alive and living locally. Jack Dandridge, aged 86 and the oldest man in the village, was the great nephew of Philip Dandridge, buried in the churchyard and named in the 1881 census.

Another rubbing made by the children was of Thomas Woods's gravestone. They decided that it would be interesting to find out how many other people with the surname Woods there were on the census file. There were twenty-one, and they found Thomas amongst them and put a ring around his name.

The children already knew a family called Woods. Every fortnight a senior citizens' club met in the hall during school hours. Vic and May Woods, who were regulars at the club, were an old couple living in the village. Vic was in his early eighties and May was in her late seventies. The children asked Vic if his family had lived in the village for a long time. He said they had, so they asked him if he knew any of the people listed in their computer printout of all the Woodses in the 1881 census. Thomas Woods was his father! Mary Woods was his great aunt! Suddenly there was a direct connection with 100 years ago. History came alive for these children – it was not just something that you read about in a book. Vic's father had been 4 years old in 1881; Vic himself was born in 1901. He identified uncles, aunts and grandparents, and talked about them, where they lived, and what they did.

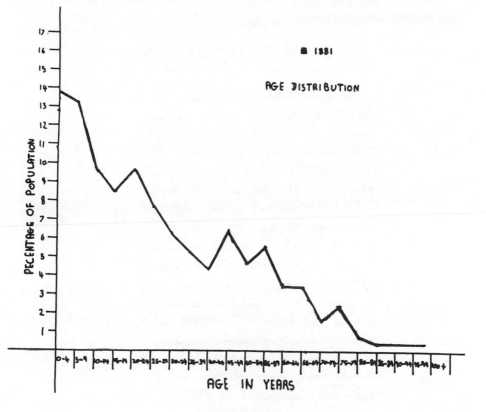

FIGURE 6.21

All sorts of other questions and possible answers were thrown up. The age spread of the village population in 1881 was a strange one. There were so many children and so few old people. Mary Holdway, aged 15, was listed as a school teacher, and Anne Marks, a widow aged 54, as a coal merchant. The parish registers showed that a number of children, including three children aged 5, 8 and 9, from the same family, had all died within three months of each other in 1874.

The children displayed their work and the results of their investigations in the library. At one end were the rubbings of the four gravestones, accompanied by tables printed from the computer showing all the members of each family. At the other end of the library they displayed their bar charts, histograms, pie charts and frequency tables (Figure 6.21). These were accompanied by descriptions written by the children explaining the significance of the printouts (Figure 6.22), by photographs and sketches of the cottages in which the people had lived, and with a display of 100 year old objects loaned by the children's families.

It is hard to see how work of such quality could have been produced without the aid of a computer.

AGE DISTRIBUTION

The age distribution in 1881 was a lot different from what it is today. The biggest age group in 1881 was the 0 to 4 year olds, their percentage was 13·80%. But as the children grew older the number declined because children died from what were incurable dieseases such as T.B and small pox. This rapid decline continued until they were about 22. At this point it was 6% of the population, less than half the original number. Then the decline would become less rapid but it is noticeable that less than 10% of the population were over 60 years old. This shows that in 1881 you were more likely to die between the ages of 0 to 24 than to die of old age. In the 18 hundreds people did not live to a very old age. The oldest age lived to in 1881 was 96.

FIGURE 6.22 .

Creative arts

Music making in the primary school can be experienced effectively without recourse to any kind of formal musical notation. Young children enjoy playing by ear, inventing melodies for singing or dancing, and improvising from real or 'scribble' music. They are able to record and play back their compositions using an audio tape recorder without the need to use 'dots' to write a score. A tape recorder with, say, four tracks will also enable some simple editing to take place. A tune can be recorded, then some chords fitted round it, with different things being tried out on different tracks.

However, the editing facilities on the tape recorder are limited. What happens when you just want to change one chord, or would like to retain the musical language but vary the sound? It is now clear that computer technology can be a great aid to the musician who is composing and recording work, whether she or he is a complete beginner or an experienced professional.

One example of the way in which a computer can assist young children who are composing their own music is a program which allows them to create and to store short musical phrases, and to arrange and re-arrange the phrases until the melody is satisfying to the ear. The phrases can be used repeatedly, and arranged in any order or any combination. At any point, a single phrase can be deleted or inserted, or replaced by another. Each phrase is represented and selected by a pictorial symbol – again, the children can create their own symbols to represent the sounds of their musical phrases.

One program offers eight different ready-made sets of phrases, spanning two octaves in range, with a selection of simple and compound time signatures. Each set has a different musical style: jazz, Indian, Chinese, and so on. But it is when children start to draw on their own culture and feelings about music to invent phrases and picture symbols for themselves that the program reveals its true strength. The resulting sound effects or musical composition can be saved on a disc either for further editing or for replay in a class performance or a school assembly.

A program like this encourages children to listen carefully and to make decisions about what to alter or what to retain based upon what they hear.

In exploring their ideas for individual phrases they can consider questions like:

- Would this phrase make a good ending?
- Would it make a good beginning?
- Is it a slow phrase or a fast one?
- Would it repeat well?
- How many times could it be repeated before something different is needed?

In considering two or three phrases linked together they can ask:

- Do these phrases go well together?
- What would they sound like if we changed the order?
- Can we find three phrases to make a complete tune?
- Can we sing the sequence of notes or clap the rhythm as the tune is played?
- Does the accompaniment improve or detract from the tune?
- How do these phrases make you feel? What do they make you think about?

When they are ready to create longer sequences of phrases it is possible to ask:

- How can we compose a piece that starts off slowly and finishes quickly?
- How can we compose a piece that sounds sad, happy, angry, peaceful … ?
- Could we compose a tune to go with this story, poem, picture, dance … ?
- Could we write some words to sing or to say in accompaniment to the music?
- Would it improve the tune to accompany it with other instruments?

The best music software allows children to create, edit, manipulate and mix sounds, and either to hear each note or phrase as it is added, or to listen to the entire composition. The sounds or 'electric instruments' which are created can have widely contrasting effects which can be recorded and used as they are, accompanied by voices, or combined with other acoustic instruments in the classroom in performing activities.

Modern multimedia computers have high quality sound production, capable of effectively emulating a variety of different musical instruments. However, to make the most of the computer as an aid to music making a synthesiser and speakers need to be attached to the system so that having created a tune children can hear it performed to a high instrumental standard. The synthesiser also allows sounds to be manipulated – played in different tonal qualities and textures. As with other forms of control technology, an interface box (called a MIDI box) is needed so that the keyboard and the computer can be linked together. MIDI stands for **Musical Instrument Digital Interface**, and any kind of keyboard which is to be linked to the computer needs to have a pair of sockets labelled MIDI in and MIDI out. It is common nowadays for synthesisers and keyboards to be built with MIDI capabilities.

Music making with the aid of a computer is a complement to, not a replacement for, other kinds of music making. Children who are making music need to have access to a full range of equipment which includes all the major ways of making sounds: things to hit, bang together, blow, pluck, scrape, rattle or shake, with a range of different tones and textures. To this great variety of instruments can now be added the electronic keyboard or the synthesiser. As more primary schools acquire a keyboard – preferably one with full-sized keys – more will be able to heed the advice offered by HMI in *Music from 5 to 16* (page 7).

> Those concerned with children's music education should encourage sensitivity towards and discrimination about sound in general and every opportunity should be taken to stimulate and sustain children's fascination with sounds of every kind ... The increasing availability in schools of computers and other electronic devices can arouse interest in the potential of synthesised sound.

Just as software can aid the composition and refinement of a piece of music, so software can allow children to create, adapt and modify a variety of designs, pictures and patterns: 'Computers are now used for drafting ... and in future computers are increasingly likely to be useful modelling aids' (*Craft, design and technology from 5 to 16*, page 15).

Painting with a computer was not really a viable proposition until the development of the mouse. A keyboard is not a very suitable tool for producing pictures or designs but software is available for older machines which uses the arrow keys for pattern making.

First there are simple design programs with which even the youngest children can create and manipulate regular shapes to produce computerised fuzzy-felt pictures (Figure 6.23).

Next, there are the programs which allow children to build up pictures or patterns by colouring **pixels** – small squares on a grid (Figures 6.24 and 6.25).

FIGURE 6.23

Although children can experiment with pixel designs by working directly at the computer they can be helped to think about their pictures or patterns if they first make freehand sketches and then transfer them to squared paper.

The same principle of colouring small squares can be used to design a unit tile, which can then be repeated in different orientations to cover the screen. The sizes, shapes, colours and symmetries of the patterns which are created in this way can all be controlled and investigated. Ideas for wallpaper or wrapping paper, patchwork, weaving, fabric printing, knitting and free embroidery can all be explored by the use of a program like this, as well as mathematical ideas of reflection, rotation, enlargement and tessellation. (Figures 6.26 and 6.27)

FIGURE 6.24

FIGURE 6.25

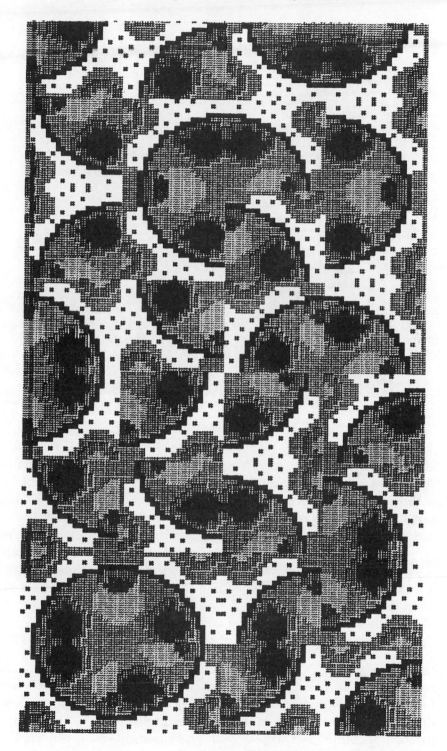

FIGURE 6.26

FIGURE 6.27

But modern computers with large memories can do so much more. The mouse is used in place of a brush or pencil to paint or draw freely as the cursor on the screen traces the path of the mouse on the table top. Fine control of the mouse for delicate painting is a skill that must be learned just like use of a brush or crayon, so children's paintings still look like children's paintings even when they are done at the machine. However, the software can provide tools which give more control over certain elements of the picture than children have when using traditional media. For example, any closed shape can be filled with smooth or graduated colour or a range of patterns and airbrush effects can be achieved at the click of a button (Figure 6.28).

For design work, regular shapes such as circles, rectangles, ovals and polygons can be drawn with precision and moved, resized, filled or distorted in a wide variety of ways. These objects can be precisely aligned on the screen and made to overlap in any order. They can be grouped together and copied and pasted, rotated or reflected to produce repeating patterns (Figure 6.29).

Kate Govier age 9 years

FIGURE 6.28

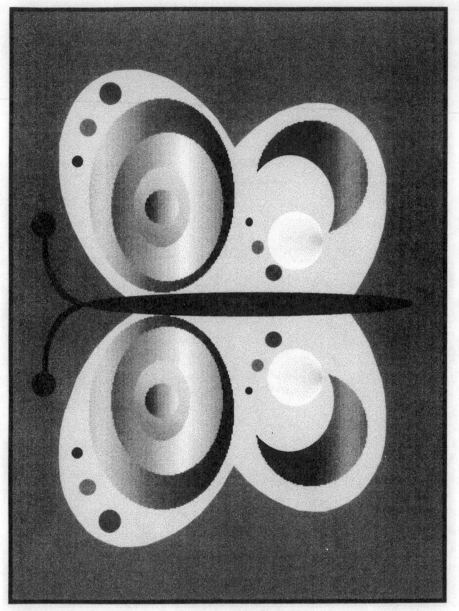

FIGURE 6.29

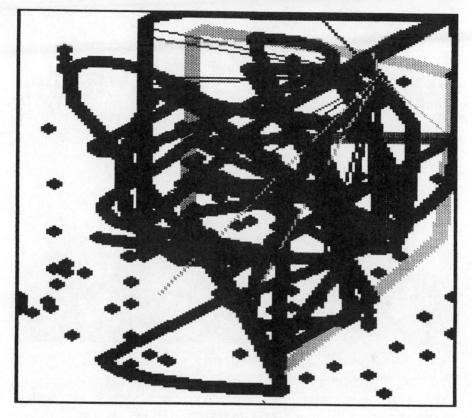

FIGURE 6.30

Clip art, ready made pictures available on disc or CD-ROM, can be pasted into children's work and modified in most of the ways described above. With additional equipment such as digital cameras or scanners photographs taken by the children themselves or pictures from any other source can be imported into the painting program and manipulated to achieve many different effects.

Once created, pictures can be saved to disc for later modification, printed out in black and white or colour, incorporated into multimedia presentations (see Chapter 7) or perhaps sequenced to make an on-screen slide show. Specialised programs are available for making banners, posters or greetings cards (Figure 6.31).

Painting programs can be used by anyone from the age of 3 onwards. The very youngest children will produce scribble designs and can explore this new medium in much the same way as they explore finger painting and painting with a large brush.

As the children gain better control of the mouse their designs grow in sophistication, and pictures and patterns of increasing quality can be produced (Figure 6.32).

FIGURE 6.31

Other kinds of software link together various aspects of art, design, music and story making. These programs can be used to introduce young children to film and video making, and software of this type is often capable of extending and enhancing children's topic work (see Chapter 7).

One example is a program in which children work in groups designing and creating a figure, a background scene, and a musical accompaniment. The figure is then animated against the background, in synchronisation with the music. Another example is some software which allows children to make a 'cartoon' film on video tape. Pictures are created on the computer, and an appropriate sequence for them is chosen. Once the duration for the display of each scene has been specified, the picture sequence can be transferred to video tape and a sound track added in the usual way.

One group of children who decided to make a spooky film using the cartoon program made the following comments about it afterwards.

> **Our cartoon was all about a witch. It was a really really creepy cartoon. It wasn't too scary for big children like us but for babies it would be.**

FIGURE 6.32

I liked watching it to see if the voices came out sounding eerie and if you didn't like the voices I liked going back and changing it all again. We changed ours 7 times I think and we had to go back after play as well!!!

It was kind of funny when Nathan said the skeleton was body popping. The pictures were dark and that with bats and things and stars and moons. It was the middle of the night and spooks and ghouls came out. I wasn't frightened though because I've seen the midnight horror movie. Even that doesn't frighten me much.

When we wrote the story I didn't think we were going to do something that exciting. We even had to change out of our PE kit! When the door creaked open and the voice said 'Open the door and come in' I wouldn't go in. Maybe if I had a gun I would.

The pictures were really weird and made the shivers go down my spine. The ghost popped up and it made me jump like when I went to an orchestra and the men banged the cymbals together and I didn't expect it.

When we watched the cartoon in class everybody was laughing and that made me feel shy but I felt like you do when you go on stage and come off when they are clapping. It makes you feel proud and clever.

Further reading

MUSE Report No 5. 1984. *Microcomputers in primary schools*. Heinemann Computers in Education. ISSN 0263–4783.

Ball, D. 1987. *Microcomputers in maths teaching*. Hutchinson. ISBN 0 09 160801 5.

Chandler, D. (ed.) 1983. *Exploring English with microcomputers*. MEP Reader 1. Council for Educational Technology. ISBN 0 86184 102 6.

Kemeny, H. (ed.) 1990. *Talking IT Through*. NCET. ISBN 1 85379 100 8.

Stewart, J. (ed.) 1985. *Exploring primary science and technology with microcomputers*. MEP Reader 5. Council for Educational Technology. ISBN 0 86184 136 0

7 Cross-curricular topics

Many different terms are used in primary schools for work which combines elements of learning from a variety of subjects. Topic work in one school is called project work in another; some schools refer to thematic work, others to integrated studies. The terms may be different but what they involve is common to them all – amalgamation of subject matter right across the curriculum. The topics may be historical, geographical, religious or a mixture of these; they may have a strong technological bias as in the study of transport or bridges; they may be concerned with sociological matters such as dress or custom. They are all very likely to involve the children in making visits and carrying out research using reference materials of all kinds: books, newspapers, pictures, charts and films.

Well-planned topic work gives abundant opportunities for extending, practising and applying the skills of speaking, listening, reading, writing, dealing with numbers, measuring, designing and making, drawing, painting, producing maps, diagrams and graphs, and using the methods of science. It also provides the need and the motivation for using the school library, learning how to find the books required and the appropriate sections in them; learning to change reading style from quick scanning to close study; learning to look beneath the surface of a message, to detect bias or over-generalisation; learning to compare one account with another. It requires children to deal with information as life often presents it, rather than neatly packaged as it often is in textbooks.

Integration of subject matter in a well-planned project is not easy to achieve. The Thomas Report, *Improving Primary Schools*, published by the Inner London Education Authority in 1985, describes situations where

> ... topics are often undertaken in isolation from each other and any cumulative effect is hard to discern. Children's work is corrected when it is to be displayed but is not often regarded as a prime indicator as to what should be taught next in language, mathematics, science, art or craft; nor is the work designed in part

to develop powers in these. The grouping of children, when it is employed, is often on an ad hoc basis simply on the compatibility of members rather than to provide circumstances through which to help children understand the advantages and difficulties of combining their efforts.

Today in England and Wales the National Curriculum demands a more rigorous approach and with careful planning it is possible to choose connected themes for the children to study from term to term and from year to year. The fact that many possible topics are suitable does not make them all equally suitable. In making a choice, the most effective teachers bear in mind what has been done previously. For example, one school based the children's project work on the environment and developed a sequence of themes:

- ourselves;
- our homes and families;
- our street, town or village;
- our borough or county;
- places far away.

Another school asked each class teacher to develop termly projects by choosing particular examples from each of three broad themes:

- people, their customs, beliefs and work;
- the characteristics and care of animals and plants;
- materials, their properties, and what can be made from them.

What is more difficult is to ensure that within each theme the developmental needs of the children are met in terms of the skills and understanding which the project demands. In any project that is planned for a whole class consideration needs to be given to children who have reached different stages of intellectual development. The more able need to be provided with sufficiently demanding levels of work just as children who find learning difficult should be helped to make a worthwhile contribution.

A good way to start is to encourage the children themselves to think of questions that interest them. Within the theme of food, for example, the following questions might arise.

- What are the favourite foods of children in the class? Are they similar to the favourite foods of adults?
- What fruits and vegetables can be seen in local shops? Where do these fruits come from? How are they grown? How far are they brought?

- What does a runner bean look like while it grows? Does it always look the same? Does it grow the same amount each day? Do all runner beans grow at the same rate?
- How many different ways of stacking and packing foods are there?
- How do shopkeepers know when to order more things?
- Which packet cereal sold locally represents the best value for money?
- Are local people satisfied with local shopping arrangements?
- What did the high street look like 100 years ago?
- How many different types of food were eaten yesterday? How many meals were eaten?
- How often do people feel hungry? Are some people in the world more hungry than others? Why?
- Which foods are good for you? How do you know?

The questions indicate three possible parts to the project: growing food, buying and selling food, and eating food. The first part might involve visits to an allotment or farm, and watching a film about how corn is grown and turned into flour; the second part might include a visit to a food processing factory or to local shops, and seeing a film strip of street life in the 1870s; the third part might involve a visit to the kitchen, dining room and gardens of an historic house, and looking at Unicef photographs of the basic foods in people's diets or Oxfam posters on the causes of hunger.

Finding answers to the questions will require some practical work:

growing food identifying foods and spices by taste or smell, drawing and measuring the growth of plants from seeds, designing and building a model mill or food transporter;

buying and selling food setting up and keeping accounts for a school tuck shop, comparing local prices for everyday foods, sketching, mapping and modelling the local shopping area, researching old maps and street directories, interviewing local residents;

eating food experimenting with different ways of keeping food, planning and cooking a meal for a family, collecting and comparing information on labels of food packets and tins, considering food advertisements.

Not all these activities are appropriate for all children. Different children are at different stages of development in their understanding, skills and knowledge. Each activity and its possible outcomes needs to be considered in advance, and the relevant skills and concepts within it identified. It is then possible to select activities within the topic, and match them to the developmental needs of particular children.

Topic work involves social skills as well as intellectual skills. It offers opportunities for children to work either in small groups or in larger teams; it requires children to listen and to take into account the contribution of others. It can also provide opportunities for children to be grouped in considered ways: to mix children from varied ethnic groups so that they grow accustomed to working together; to give support to a child whose command of English requires that his or her peers use simple and clear language; to mix girls and boys for what have traditionally been regarded as girls' tasks or boys' tasks.

The computer has an important role in topic work in two kinds of ways. On the one hand it is possible for a piece of software to provide the focus or starting point for a particular project, with other activities linked to it and developing from it. An adventure game in which the players act as castaways trying to survive on a desert island might well provide the initial stimulus for the project on food.

On the other hand a project based on any theme will involve information-handling skills of all kinds, from finding and communicating information to organising it in order to test hypotheses. The programs which are free of content, and into which children can place their own information and ideas, can assist the children in their research and in the presentation of their findings. In the food project a decision tree program might be used as an aid to the identification of fruits or spices; a database might help to handle data collected from cereal packets, or to analyse opinion polls of local residents; a spreadsheet might assist older children in keeping accounts for the tuck shop; a word processor could be used to record interviews with local shopkeepers, to express attitudes about foods, to report the outcomes of investigations, or to write an imaginative description of the inside of a café. It would also be possible to set up and reveal a piece of text or poem about food using a 'developing tray' type of program. For example, a passage for younger children might be taken from *The very hungry caterpillar* by Eric Carle, while older children might prefer the description of Mr Willy Wonka and his sweets in Roald Dahl's *Charlie and the chocolate factory*.

From program to project

Programs which create an environment based on fantasy are known as adventure games; those which create an environment based on fact are known as simulations. Both are types of modelling program which allow pupils to explore a model of a real or imaginary situation. In each kind of program children need to make decisions and use logical thinking to discover connections in the world in which they find themselves.

At Guthrie Infants' School at Calne some 6 year olds became involved with an adventure game in which a four-storey house must be explored in order to help a frog find its way back to the garden. Through a process of discovering the implications of certain actions, and finding an appropriate sequence of visits to the rooms in the house, the problem can be solved.

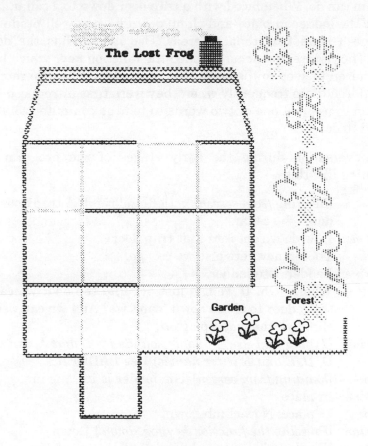

FIGURE 7.1

For their work with the program the children were grouped in mixed sex groups of twos or threes. The groups contained children of similar general ability, but the most important consideration in forming the groups was that each group contained one relatively good reader. During the course of a week each group had a session lasting about half an hour at the keyboard. In that time each child had a turn at operating the keyboard, reading aloud from the screen and recording any important information. In some of the groups the children read aloud together to help each other. All the children were included in the discussion and in deciding upon the next move. The computer was in the classroom the whole time and each group's turn was part of its activities for the day.

At the very beginning of the game the children were confused about the words that they should type. Some help was needed to encourage precision, since there is a limit to the deciphering that a computer program can do! When faced with a trap door down to a cellar, typing in 'Put the ladder in place and climb down it' may well produce the message 'I cannot do that' whereas 'Use ladder' has the desired effect. The children's teacher labelled the function keys which helped the children to keep to the permitted vocabulary. She also reminded the children quite frequently when they were first introduced to the program to use just one or two words to tell the computer what they wanted to do.

The conversation during the early stages of the program went something like this:

Martin: [*Reading from screen*] '... left and right. A trap door leads down the cellar.'
Catherine: How do we get into that trap door?
Martin: There's nowhere else we can go.
Catherine: Ladder. Use ladder.
Martin: Where? Oh! If we can just get into the door we can use the ladder to climb down, can't we? And we can use it to climb all the way up again.
Catherine: [*Typing and using phonic sounds for L and A, but giving D, D, E and R letter names*] Use LADDER.
Martin: [*Reading from screen*] The ladder is in ... is in ...
Catherine: In place.
Martin: In place. Now climb down.
Catherine: [*Pressing the function key for 'down'*] Down.
Martin: [*Reading from screen*] 'You climb down safely.'
Both: [*Sighing with relief and reading together from the screen*] 'You are in the cellar. It is very dark. You can see a key.'

Martin:	Hey! Key!! We can use the key to open the locked door.
Catherine:	Yeah, but we have to ...
Martin:	Take key!
Catherine:	But first we have to use the torch to see where we are going.
Martin:	Yeah. So use torch. Take key. Up. Then we can try and use the key to open the door.
Martin:	[Typing and using letter names] Use T O R S ... no C, C H.
Both:	[*Reading from screen*] 'You can see the ladder now.'
Martin:	Let's go up, then.
Catherine:	No!
Martin:	Oh! Take the key.
Catherine:	[*Remembering that they are already carrying the maximum number of objects*] No. Drop something.
Martin:	Take.
Catherine:	Drop.
Martin:	All right then. We'll drop something.

During the six weeks which they worked with the program Catherine, aged $6\frac{1}{2}$, made a plan of the house, which she had visualised and pieced together bit by bit (Figure 7.2). Martin, aged 6, developed a strategy for collecting, using and dropping objects in sensible places, since the program limits the number which can be carried at any one time to five. Together the children made plans for creating their own adventure game, including a detailed map and a tabulated list of objects which could be found, and where they should be used.

It was perfectly possible for the whole class to use the program during a six-week period. Each group had regular turns at the keyboard, and while they were doing so other groups were making models of the house, writing stories about how the frog came to be lost, making flowers for the garden, and finding out about breeds of large dog.

Some of the other activities in which these children became involved were:

- keeping diaries recording their search for the lost frog;
- talking about who the house could have belonged to, why the frog had got lost, and whether it would be right to give a mouse to a cat;
- painting some pictures of the garden and the rooms in the house;
- using Logo to draw a plan of the house and garden;

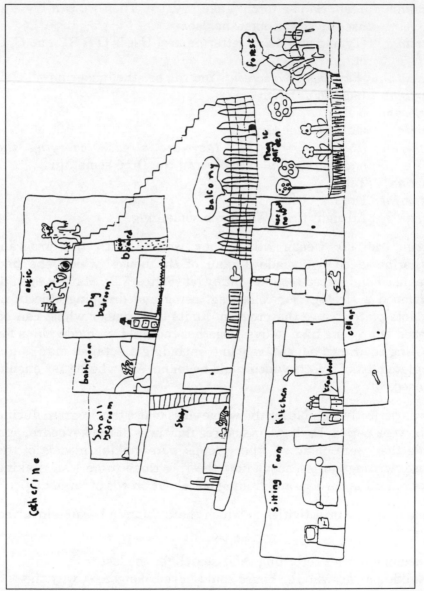

FIGURE 7.2

- planting seeds to make a garden, and measuring their growth;
- discovering different nursery rhymes which mention garden plants;
- watching frogspawn grow into tadpoles;
- linking some frog crouching and jumping movements together into a dance;
- hearing Alf Proysen's short story about Mrs Pepperpot in the Magic Wood;
- writing and illustrating their own adventure stories like those written by Hannah (Figure 7.3) and Matthew (Figure 7.4).

```
Hannah

in the magic garden I bit a

magic apple and I could fly

and my mummy was looking for

me and I could see all around

the world and the people were

tiny and when I was flying it

felt like a bird
```

FIGURE 7.3

At the junior school, the 10 year old children used the same program, but the activities which were stimulated by the use of the program were very different. One group found out as much as they could about frogs and toads, and developed a database in order to keep a record of their research. They made up quizzes for their friends who then used the database to help them to find the answers to the questions (Figure 7.5).

Matthew

when I was in the magic garden

I bit an apple and I turned

tiny I saw a grasshopper   I

gat on the grasshopper the

grasshopper took me to a

castle in the castle there was

a man he said go home there is

many dangers

FIGURE 7.4

FROG	Size	Colour	Skin	Warts
TREE FROG	4 cm	GREEN	SMOOTH	NONE
MARSH FROG	15 cm	GREEN	ROUGH	BIG
EDIBLE FROG	10 cm	BLACK	GRITTY	TINY
SPANISH FROG	6 cm	YELLOW	SMOOTH	TINY
ITALIAN AGILE	6 cm	GREY	SMOOTH	SMALL
COMMON FROG	9 cm	VARIED	GRANULAR	FLAT
GREEK FROG	7 cm	BROWN	SMOOTH	FINE
NATTERJACK	8 cm	GREEN	ROUGH	ENORMOUS
SPADEFOOT	8 cm	BROWN	SMOOTH	SMALL
MIDWIFE	4 cm	GREY	ROUGH	ON EYELIDS
PARSLEY FROG	4 cm	BROWN	SMOOTH	TINY
PAINTED FROG	7 cm	YELLOW	SMOOTH	TINY
YELLOW BELLIED	5 cm	GREEN	SMOOTH	ON BACK
FIRE BELLIED	5 cm	GREY	ROUGH	ON BACK

FROG	Home	Found	Croak
TREE FROG	EUROPE	TREES	LOUD
MARSH FROG	EUROPE	LAKES	IN RAIN
EDIBLE FROG	EUROPE	RIVERS	DAY, NIGHT
SPANISH FROG	SPAIN	WOODS	VERY WEAK
ITALIAN AGILE	SWITZERLAND	WOODS	UNDERWATER
COMMON FROG	EUROPE	FIELDS	LIKE TRAIN
GREEK FROG	S.EUROPE	MOUNTAINS	WEAK
NATTERJACK	EUROPE	SAND DUNE	LOUDEST
SPADEFOOT	EUROPE,ASIA	SAND DUNE	SCREECH
MIDWIFE	SPAIN	SAND DUNE	LIKE BELLS
PARSLEY FROG	FRANCE	PONDS	NIGHT
PAINTED FROG	MED.ISLANDS	PONDS	WEAK
YELLOW BELLIED	EUROPE	PONDS	IN RAIN
FIRE BELLIED	EUROPE	LAKES	BLOW TUBE

FIGURE 7.5

Another group, intrigued by the plan of the house, went out to look at buildings and made some pen and ink observational drawings of these (Figure 7.6). They noted the number of storeys, looked at brick patterns and roof designs, and the different ways in which roofs are covered. Back in the classroom they used Logo to reproduce some of the brick and tiling patterns for themselves. They also tried out insulation tests, trying to find out what kept a house warm.

The children of Bryn Deri Primary School in Cardiff used the option which accompanies the same program to create their own adventure game for the computer. One group created a setting in the Houses of Parliament; another group chose a Cornish tin mine (Figure 7.7).

More research, planning and model making followed. The children particularly enjoyed inventing and describing the hazard which the players of the game would meet, and which they would need to find ways of overcoming. Lisa wrote her description for the hazard in the tin mine using a word processor.

SPRIGGAN

There was a strange noise behind me. It sounded like something or somebody was walking near to me. I turned round slowly. My whole body was trembling with fear, my stomach was churning over. I had a feeling that something was hovering over me.

A sinister shape loomed in front of me. It had a transparent outline and shimmering body. Its skin was pale and its veins protruded. Its hands were frail and bony, its clothes were stained with blood and torn from jagged shafts. It had a tired, worn face much like that of an old miner.

He glided towards me, slowly, slowly. His feet didn't touch the ground. I tried to dodge him but there was no escape. Its teeth were damaged, chipped and covered with yellow. It opened its mouth and bellowed loudly, filing the mine with screeching noises. I covered my ears frantically with my shaking hands. My heart was beating fast, perspiration was trickling down my forehead. I tried to scream but no sound could I utter.

I felt that I was choking. I pulled at the collar of my shirt. Without realising, I pulled my cross and chain from around my neck. The object stopped coming towards me. It seemed to start shaking on the spot where it stood, but

although I could see that it was shrinking I could not run.
My feet felt like very heavy weights, as though they were
stuck.

I watched, amazed, as the object finally disappeared. All
that was left was a pile of fine silver coloured sand.

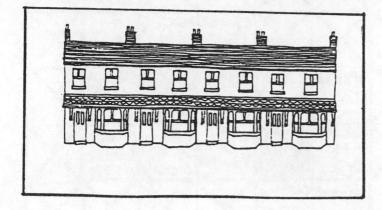

FIGURE 7.6

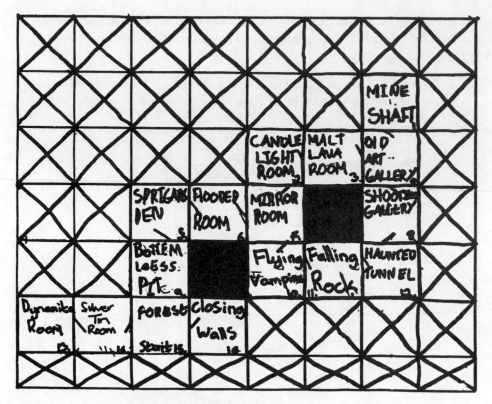

FIGURE 7.7

From project to program

The computer can of course be used to support a wide variety of cross-curricular topics. The themes of projects vary considerably from school to school, but one that is common to many is that of Christmas. It is a time of year when stories of the nativity are told and illustrated; when plays and carol concerts are performed for parents; when classrooms are decorated, presents made, and parties held. Christmas in a primary school is a joyous occasion; it is also a time of considerable hard work for the staff who need to ensure that throughout the festivities the children maintain their progression of learning.

The staff at St Mary's School in the northern part of Hampshire decided that they would be able to integrate the use of the computer with their preparations for Christmas. The school at that time had sufficient computers for each pair of classes to share a system between them. All the staff made suggestions about the ways in

which the computer could support the children's work so everyone
was involved in the planning.

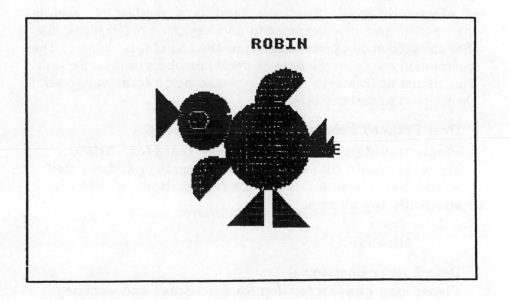

FIGURE 7.8

All the infant classes had been looking out for birds which visited their bird table throughout the winter months. The younger children decided to make designs for their Christmas cards using a picture-building program. First of all they used sets of flat shapes to make bird-shaped patterns. Next, they each sketched plans on paper showing how they intended to use the shapes in the computer program to make their pictures. Last, working in pairs, and with two designs to work from, the children took turns to create bird pictures. Once the designs were composed on the screen they could be adjusted to produce more pleasing effects: the colours were changed, the triangular beak rotated, the shape of the feet altered, the body made a little smaller, until the children were satisfied with the result (Figure 7.8).

After some very cold mornings, the top infants used the word processor to write poems on the theme of winter. The whole class together discussed the ways that things looked different when it was snowy or frosty. They thought about the things that caught their attention that normally they did not notice: footprints of birds, the edges of leaves, individual blades of grass. Over a period of a fortnight they worked in ones or twos on their poems, printing out each draft and taking it away to work on ready for the next session (Figure 7.9).

The school was also taking part of a local project evaluating the use of **electronic mail**. Electronic mail is a method of sending information from one computer to another using a telephone line. (See the section on Communication at the end of this chapter.) The information can be in the form of words, numbers or even pictures. The infants at St Mary's decided it would be an ideal way to send their letters to Father Christmas.

Dear Father Christmas

Please would you have a spare Tiny Tears for Christmas. My mum would like some diamond earings and my dad would like a watch. My mum's friend, Betty would like two fluffy toy kittens.

   Love from
      Michelle

Dear Father Christmas,

Please may I have a toy dog for Christmas and a scene of the stable of Bethlehem with Mary, Joseph, Baby Jesus in the manger, and the kings and shepherds.

   Love from
      Polly

It is a frosty morning.
The trees are nearly bare.
Winters coming.
The leaves have a tingling line of
white round them.

Alison (aged 6)

It is winter time.
The snow is falling.
The grass looks like sticks of glass
The road is covered with a white
sheet for cars to draw on.

Spencer (aged 7)

Snow flutters quietly
Covering the ground like white
    butterflies.
We walk through the cold
    crunchiness
Leaving our footmarks
By the small spiky footmarks of
    the birds.

Keith and Peter (aged 7)

The playground is white.
Snowballs are going everywhere.
There are cars stuck in the snow.
People are pushing them.
I'm glad that I'm in the warm.

Jamie (aged 8)

FIGURE 7.9

Dear Father Christmas,

Please can I have a Wrinkles dog, some sweets, an alarm clock, and a Wuzzle. I would also like a Mother Pound Puppy, and a Mouse-trap Game. Is it too much to ask for but I have been quite good.

  Lots of love and thank you from
     Emma

Dear Father Christmas,

My mum would appreciate a brass kettle and a stand for the kettle. We have a toy train for my mum's friend's baby. My cousin wants some records. I don't know what my nanny wants for Christmas but she is a nice person.

  Love from
     Daniel

Dear Father Christmas,

Please may I have a motorbike suit and please Father Christmas please give a present to my Dad. He would like an electric drill.

  Love from
     Patrick

All the children in the school had been listening once again to the familiar nativity story. Earlier in the term the lower juniors had been looking at the terse styles of newspaper headlines and front page stories, and had noticed how nearly all of these stories were made to appear more authentic by the inclusion of quotations from the people connected with the event. They were asked to think how local people in Galilee would have received the news if newspapers had existed at the time of Christ's birth. Armed with reporters' notebooks they made sketches and wrote front page stories for 'The Shepherd's Star' (Figure 7.10) and 'The Outlook' (Figure 7.11).

The same classes were also keen to use the computer to help them to design their Christmas decorations and wrapping paper. Their first task was to look at different star shapes and to think about the ways that they could be drawn. Some stars could be traced with a single line; some were formed by taking a shape like a triangle and rotating it about its centre. Some stars had all the connecting lines drawn in; others simply traced round the perimeter edge. Small groups of children set to work to produce star shapes using Logo (Figure 7.12). They were soon asking for calculators to help them to work out the angles. By Christmas they had collected several different designs and their work continued well into the Spring term. 'I never realised how complicated stars could be,' said one 9-year-old.

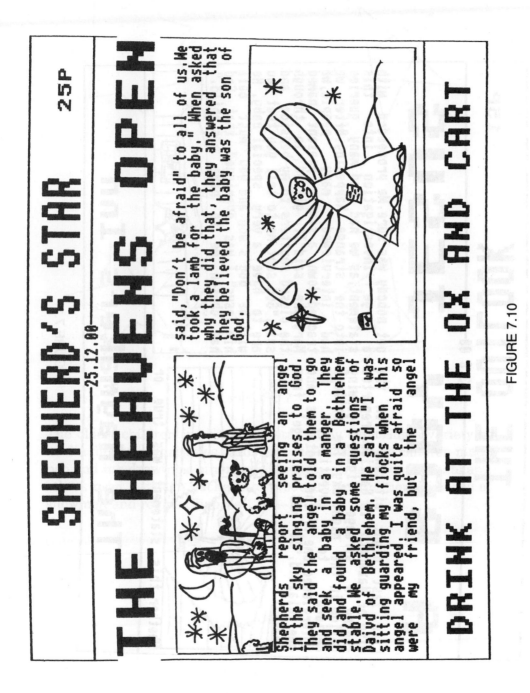

SHEPHERD'S STAR

25P

25.12.00

THE HEAVENS OPEN

Shepherds report seeing an angel in the sky singing praises to God. They said the angel told them to go and seek a baby in a manger. They did, and found a baby in a Bethlehem stable. We asked some questions of Daivd of Bethlehem. He said "I was sitting guarding my flocks when this angel appeared. I was quite afraid so were my friend, but the angel said, "Don't be afraid" to all of us. We took a lamb for the baby." When asked why they did that, they answered that they believed the baby was the son of God.

DRINK AT THE OX AND CART

FIGURE 7.10

FIGURE 7.13

FIGURE 7.14

FIGURE 7.15

FIGURE 7.16

After Christmas, the children used the word processor to record their reflections upon the occasion. Samantha, aged 11, revealed that she had a very generous grandmother (Figure 7.17).

My Gran

When my Gran came we had a party. All my relations came and Gran told them all that she was very well thankyou. They all had lots to drink and so did Gran. One man is always over the limit but he has never been stopped for drinking and driving. Gran doesn't drive. People didn't have cars when she was young. In the morning we wanted to open our Christmas presents but we had to wait for Gran. She came down very late. Then I saw my present and it said Happy Christmas and lots of love from Gran. I unwrapped it and I saw a keyboard! I wondered how she had known to get me a keyboard. She can't really be as old fashioned as she makes out.

FIGURE 7.17

Multimedia productions

When a computer is used for word processing or desktop publishing it is a production tool only, since the final product will be printed copy which may be read away from the machine. Multimedia authoring packages are programs that can be used to create sophisticated on-screen productions enabling children to explore new ways of communicating ideas. Being content free, this software can be used in any area of the curriculum and offers an exciting new dimension to the presentation of topic or project work.

Typically a multimedia production consists of a number of 'pages' which may be linked together in various ways. Each page can contain text, pictures, sounds, photographs, animations or video clips in any combination, all of which may be created from scratch or imported from other packages such as CD-ROM enclycopaedias or clip art collections.

The various elements of the production are linked together through the use of 'buttons' or 'hot spots' which may be created anywhere on the screen. Clicking on these with the mouse will cause something to happen. For example, a linear story might simply have buttons labelled 'turn over' and 'go to first page' but there might also be buttons which trigger animations or cause the text to be read out loud.

Children will have seen ready made multimedia materials, such as talking books or collections of information and most find the prospect of creating their own very exciting. However, even with the friendliest of packages, this is quite a demanding task, requiring careful planning and an appropriate allocation of time. A multimedia presentation cannot just be dashed off in an afternoon but it can be the result of collaboration between many children, with each pair producing their own page which is then linked in to the overall production.

One class of twenty four 10 and 11 year old children produced a multimedia *Guide to Islam*. This was an informative and comprehensive report which both presented the results of their research and could be used by others as an introduction to the Islamic faith. The production included a lot of information and much careful thought was put into its presentation. Children's drawings and original photographs were used and the text was kept brief with a spoken glossary for unfamiliar words accessed by clicking on the word itself. The materials included audio reports of personal experience and concluded with an interactive quiz. This was also well planned with repeated wrong answers taking the user back to the relevant pages of information and with correct answers winning elements of a mosque which was fully built when the quiz had been successfully completed.

Communication

Topic work can be given an extra dimension by the use of the computer for communication and although such use is not yet widespread a number of imaginative experiments in the use of communication systems in primary education have already begun. For example a number of UK primary schools are using electronic mail to communicate with children in schools in other English-speaking countries: Tasmania, mainland Australia, Canada and the United States.

To do this, a special piece of equipment called a **modem** is needed. This is a small black box which links the computer to a British Telecom telephone socket (Figure 7.18). As well as the modem, it is necessary to subscribe to an electronic mail service. The service's main computer sets aside a mailbox, rather like a pigeon hole, for each of its subscribers. When you use the special piece of software to connect up to their big computer, you can put a message in anyone's mailbox by typing a message straight from the keyboard, or by sending one which you have previously prepared with a word processor and have saved on a disc. You can also look at the messages in your own mailbox, but since electronic mail uses a system of personal passwords, you cannot look in a mailbox belonging to anyone else.

While the school computer is connected to the main computer, you pay the same rate as you would for a local telephone call. In spite of the expense of the necessary telephone link for very short periods, the immediacy of a letter from Alaska which tells you that most Eskimos live in homes built from wood or galvanised iron, and not in igloos, is worth more than one thousand out-of-date reference books telling you something different! Children around the world are now exchanging information about school life and home life, about weather patterns, local industry, transport systems, architecture and fashion, and items of local news.

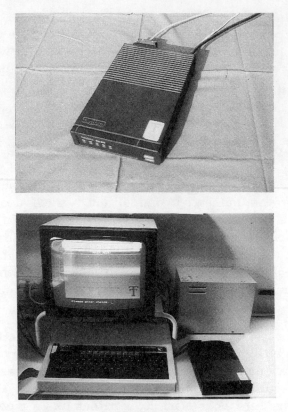

FIGURE 7.18

One primary school in Birmingham has set up a link with another primary school situated outside Sydney in Australia. In November, the English children wrote their first letters to their new friends.

Our school is situated in Birmingham's inner ring. We have lots of children whose parents have come from India and Pakistan and we enjoy celebrating the festivals of these countries as well as the traditional British festivals. During the first week in November we celebrated Divali, the Hindu and Sikh festival of lights. We hope that you will enjoy hearing about it.

Elizabeth Parry

The girls who danced were wearing special clothes. They were wearing saris and shalwar kameez. Wahida and her sister Nahida wear shalwar kameez every day. In the afternoon we made Divali candles and the wax ran all down them.

Sima Joshi

Mrs Parry told us a Divali story about Rama and Sita. She had some children to help her. There was a monkey king in it and a demon. Afterwards we sang two songs. We liked everything, especially the smell at the end when she lit the incense.

Nicola

Divali means festival of light. In Divali you need Rangoli patterns and mango leaves and fruit and flowers. If you leave those things outside then Lakshmi will leave you a present. This morning four girls in our class dressed up in saris and shalwar kameezes to show us a special Divali dance. Some girls and boys lit candles and the rest of them sang a song.

Diana

Today was Divali and it is the Hindu children's festival. We had a very nice assembly. Peena told me that Lakshmi gives us presents and we give her fruits. While we were singing some of the children lit candles. Mrs Henderson picked the best children who were singing. She picked me.

Wahida

After they had blown out the candles it started to stink.

Asia

The children in Birmingham were delighted when they got replies describing the Australian school, also with two hundred children, including several from Italian and Greek families. Later, they received letters describing an Australian Christmas which would be very different from their own.

Hello everyone. The summer is getting pretty hot now and there are lots of flies. The sprinklers are going on the grass the whole time. The plants in my back yard are beautiful right now. My poinsettia is ten feet tall and a red and blue parrot sits in it every day. From the school we can see the Pacific Ocean and there are yachts in the distance. We are all looking forward to the Christmas break. It's just too hot to work! Best wishes for Christmas from us all.

Chris Hagerty

This will just be a small goodbye letter before we break up. We break up on Thursday the 18th for 8 weeks of Christmas holidays. I hope we go to my Uncles farm. Both of my Uncles live on farms so I will go to one of my Uncles for 1 month and the other one for another month.

Kylie

I shall be inviting Brett and Nick down to the shack for Christmas this year and we will all go scuba diving around our rocks.

Tom

I expect it will be very hot at Christmas. Last year it was 30. We will probably go to the ocean beach and have a picnic. My mum will cook a turkey on the day before Christmas and it will be cold when we eat it. We will also have salad and lots of fruit and mangoes and pineapple and kiwi fruit and some nice nuts called macadamia nuts.

Maria

You are lucky because you will have snow at Christmas and you can go ice skating. I have never seen any snow but I think it would be soft and cold. Sometimes we go to the mountains at Christmas because it is not so hot in the mountains but it is a bit boring because there are only gum trees there and you have to be careful that you don't start a fire.

Harry

Another primary school has been using a communication system in a different way. Some fourth-year juniors at Gabalfa Primary School in Cardiff have been comparing their observations of the weather with pictures which they obtained on their computer from Meteosat, a weather satellite launched by the European Space Agency in 1981. From their pictures they were able, for example, to deduce the speed at which clouds moved, and to make comparisons with the wind speed on the ground. Their work emphasised to the children how important it was to make careful observations and to make accurate notes. They also appreciated how difficult it was to interpret the data in order to predict what the weather would be like in a few hours' time (Figures 7.19–22).

What have the children gained?

It is not easy to say whether cross-curricular topic work stemming from or supported by the computer is better than work which takes place without it. Some excellent work took place before primary schools had computers, so what difference has the computer made?

It is likely that children who are using the computer will work on their own in a small group while the teacher attends to another group working elsewhere in the classroom. The computer acts as a focus for the discussion and decision making which inevitably take place, in a way that would otherwise be difficult to provide. The interchange of ideas, and the collective efforts of the group, play an important part in their work. Convincing a friend that your ideas are sound ones means that your intentions must be communicated clearly and must be backed up by a reasoned justification for them.

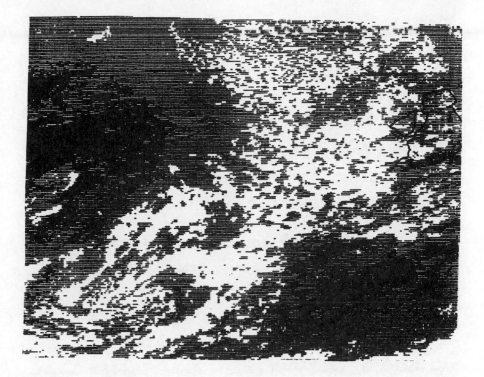

CO2   11:05   7/10/87
12:50   Grey clouds and quite windy.

FIGURE 7.19

Knowing that they are contributing to a long-term project, and so have time to develop their ideas, the children often become so involved with their work at the computer that they want to continue with it at lunch-time or after school. A sense of enthusiasm and commitment to one aspect of work in school frequently has beneficial effects on other aspects of the same group's work, as well as on the work of the whole class.

Apart from these social and personal gains, it is possible that the computer has been used within the project for the purposes of writing, drawing, calculating, organising, and so on. The computer then takes its place alongside other approaches: using pencil and paper, working with a set of paints, taking photographs, setting up a card index system .... It is through comparing one method with another in this way that children come to appreciate the versatility of the computer, and begin to understand why it will be important in their lives.

Meteosat is a satellite which can tell you what the weather is going to be all over the world. It was launched in June 1981. Meteosat can provide 24 hours of pictures each day.

You need special equipment as well as a computer in order to receive the signals from Meteosat.

The signals make a picture on the monitor and then you can interpret the pictures. For example you can try to see clouds and then say what you think the weather is going to be like.

Suzanne Chittenden

After learning the basic things about Meteosat we took more notice about what the weather was like. We would spend a day on Meteosat to record the interesting signals. About every hour we would take notes of what the weather was like so when we printed the pictures we knew what type of clouds to look for. We usually saved CO2 and CO3 because that showed Britain.

Jenny Street
Sarah Bird

FIGURE 7.20

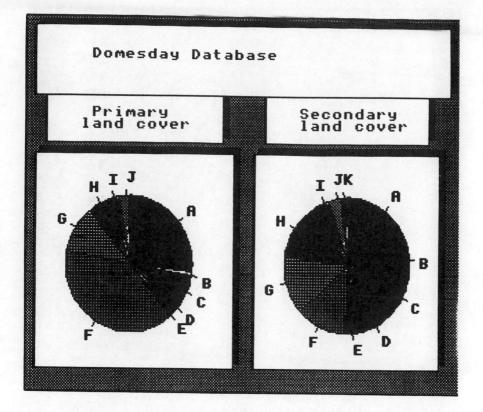

	Category	Primary land cover	Secondary land cover
A	Residential	26%	18%
B	Public use	1%	8%
C	Industrial	6%	11%
D	Urban recreational	2%	7%
E	Derelict land	2%	4%
F	Crops	36%	12%
G	Grassland	11%	14%
H	Woodland	4%	13%
I	Uncultivated	3%	4%
J	Extractive industries	2%	2%
K	Water	0%	1%

FIGURE 7.21

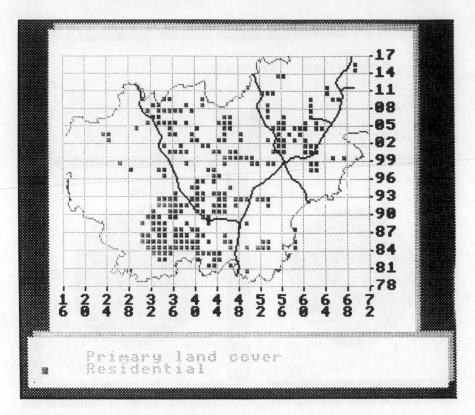

FIGURE 7.22

Further reading

Blyth, A. 1976. *Place, time and society 8–13: Curriculum planning in history, geography and social science.* Collins

Gunning, S., Gunning, D. and Wilson, J. 1981. *Topic teaching in the primary school.* Croom Helm

8 Planning and organisation

If computers are to be used as a resource to enhance and extend children's learning then they should be permanently available in all classrooms, and all teachers should be involved in using them. Although there are primary schools which have at least one computer system in permanent use in each class there are also schools in which computer use is patchy and dependent on the enthusiasms of individual members of staff.

If smooth transition from one situation to the other is to be achieved then each school needs to formulate a planned policy for the development of computer use. The policy will need to consider curricular aims and the provision of software, the acquisition, use and maintenance of hardware, and the in-service education required for the staff.

In creating a policy it is important to make sure that it is a realistic one – one that teachers can manage. There must be realistic targets, with a realistic time scale. It is often best to concentrate on achieving small but regular steps forward, rather than trying too much and failing. It is also important that the policy is a coherent one, so that children do not repeat things, and so progression and development are ensured.

One way of expressing a set of **aims** for the use of computers in primary schools would be to enable all children:

- to enjoy their work with a computer and to feel positive and confident about it;
- to appreciate what a computer can do and why it will be important in their lives;
- to develop the necessary technical skills so that they can operate hardware and software for themselves;
- to develop the social skills and personal qualities necessary for both independent and cooperative use of the machine;
- to extend their skills in:
    communication,
    handling information,

> monitoring,
> controlling and modelling,
> problem solving,
> creative and imaginative work;
* to develop their strategies for using the computer to support enquiry, investigation and experiment.

The staff at Liden Junior School in Swindon developed their policy to introduce computer work into the eight classes in their school in a five-year plan. They decided that their aims for their own professional development were very similar to their aims for the children, and that the best way to help all the children to feel positive and confident about using computers was for all the staff to feel the same way. They elicited the support of parents, and gave some priority to computer use on their occasional day closures for in-service work.

Year 1

One computer in the school, to be kept in the staff-room for the first half term. Staff to be encouraged to take it home over weekends and holidays. All teachers and all children to use the computer in the classroom for short periods.

Year 2

An additional computer to be bought. Each class to use a computer for a continuous period of two or three weeks each term.

Years 3–4

Two more computers to be acquired. Classes to be paired to share a computer between them. Each teacher to choose one major piece of software for use over half a term; three different packages to be used in a year. Meetings to develop coherent plans for use of adventure games, word processing, Logo and database work throughout the school in the following year.

Year 5

Two more computers to be bought. One each for the Year 5 and 6 classes. Year 3 and 4 classes to continue to share. Whole staff to review maths and language guidelines for the school to take information technology into account.

The pre-requisites for the success of a policy of this kind are based on an understanding that:

* clear curricular aims need to be specified;
* there must be sufficient hardware for everyone to use;

- the school must have sufficient good software for teachers to make a choice;
- teachers need time and support when they are planning the use of software with their classes;
- teachers need to know what is being done both in their own school and in others;
- teachers need to use a selection of software, both on their own and with children in the classroom, before they become involved in a complete curriculum review.

Management of the equipment in the school

It is important to establish procedures in the school for organising and maintaining the computer hardware. Equipment which is incomplete, kept in a disorganised manner or poorly maintained is an obstacle to even the most confident and determined of teachers. The checklist which follows may provide some pointers.

- An aim should be to provide each class with one or two up-to-date computer systems, depending on the size of the class and the space in the room. Apart from planning the capital expenditure over a period of time, some thought needs to be given in advance to the furniture that will be required, and the positioning of power points.
- Financial allowance needs to be made both for repairs and for the purchase of further equipment. Computers, like other electronic devices, will very occasionally develop faults and will need to be repaired. New models, costing less and with better facilities, are constantly being developed. However, software which runs on one machine will not necessarily run on another and more programs may need to be purchased as well. Nevertheless, when choosing a new computer it is best to get the most up-to-date model in line with the recommendations of the local education authority.
- Aim to purchase complete computer systems with a disc drive, colour monitor and a printer. If the local authority does not already insure the equipment then it is worth the school doing so. The policy should provide cover against fire, theft or accidental damage; the best policies will provide similar cover for teachers who are using a school's computer at home.
- Label clearly all the equipment and cables which belong to each computer system. Colour code all the plugs and sockets. This makes assembly much easier and helps to prevent damage.

- Ideally, equipment needs to stay in place in a classroom and to be covered at night to prevent dust settling on it. If equipment needs to be moved to a storage area each night for security reasons then make sure that it is easy to collect, assemble and return, and that everyone knows what the procedure is.

- A large trolley can be helpful for transporting the equipment if there are no steps to negotiate. However, most trolleys are not adjustable, and once inside the classroom it is usually better if the keyboard is placed on a table that is the same height as the children's normal worktops.

- In high security risk areas it is often better to purchase a small safe for each computer, rather than having to carry things up and down flights of stairs twice a day. One school positioned a safe in the corner of each classroom, with its back to the window and adjacent to a power point. A hole was bored in the wall of the safe so that an extension cable could be passed through it. The monitor, which was kept on the upper shelf of the safe, was never moved. Each morning the safe door was opened at right angles and a table was placed to stand against the upper shelf and the inside of the open door. The rest of the equipment was lifted from the lower shelf on to the table. The door had information for the children pasted on its inside and it helped to form a partially screened computer corner in the classroom.

Selecting software

The most successful curricular policies are those which set out to enhance and extend children's educational experience by integrating computer work into areas of the curriculum in which the school is already successful. The use of the computer is not then seen as a new skill, unrelated to other things which are happening in the school.

With this aim in mind, the most important criterion for choosing software is to look for ways in which teachers and children can exploit it, not the ways in which the software exploits the technical features of the machine. Very often reviews of software commend the speed at which a program works, the way it incorporates graphics and colour, and the use of sound. Indeed, such features can be very appealing. But teachers do not need software which shows how clever the machine is; they are interested in software which extends the possibilities for learning and teaching. Some of the very best educational software works slowly and quietly, has no pictures, and uses a minimum number of colours.

At one time primary schools suffered because there was a shortage of good software to choose from. Nowadays there are different problems. One that exists in some schools is that so much software has been acquired that it is impossible either to decide which of it is worthwhile, or to organise it and use it in a way that ensures progression and development for the children. Another problem of a different kind is that although good software exists for all the makes of computer which are commonly found in primary schools, not all schools know about this software or have copies of it.

One solution to both these problems is to set out a framework on the lines of Figure 8.1. The columns in the diagram represent the major applications of computers in primary schools. The numbers on the left indicate the levels at which particular pieces of software might be useful.

The levels might correspond to those of the National Curriculum. Level 2 indicates the attainment of an average 7-year-old; level 4 the attainment of an average 11-year-old. Level 5 materials would thus offer extension work for more able pupils at the upper end of the school.

LEVEL	Programming Control	Data Handling Measurement	Text Handling DTP	Graphics Music	Adventures Simulations	CD-ROM Multimedia
1						
2						
3						
4						
5						

FIGURE 8.1

The next step is to enter on the framework the relevant software which the school already possesses. Any blanks on the framework will indicate what might need to be acquired at some stage in the future, and where some guidance might be needed about what to buy.

For example, the column which is headed 'Programming/Control' would have Logo in it, and a set of procedures for control technology. It might also contain software in which children can 'program' a sequence of actions: for example, lifting an elephant onto a lorry (Figure 8.2), moving through a maze, or guiding a barge through a set of lock gates.

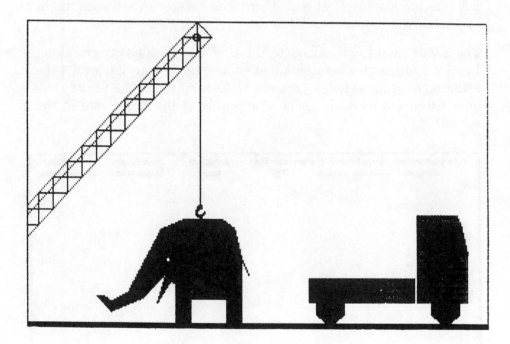

FIGURE 8.2

In the column headed 'Data Handling/Measurement', it would be possible to put databases – both those of an introductory nature and those which are more sophisticated, such as graph-drawing packages, decision tree programs and spreadsheets. Here also would go materials for monitoring and measuring temperature, light, sound and other aspects of the environment. In the column headed 'Text Handling/DTP' would go word processors and dictionaries, desk top publishing packages, developing tray or code-cracking programs, programs which animate text as it is typed, or which generate

LEVEL	Programming Control	Data Handling Measurement	Text Handling DTP	Graphics Music	Adventures Simulations	CD-ROM Multimedia
1	PIP JUMBO EARLY LOGO	MY FACTS ALL ABOUT ME MY WORLD BARSET	PODD MOVINGIN WRITER	KIDPIX PICTURE BUILDER	TREASURE HUNT MAGIC ADVENTURE ALBERT'S HOUSE	MY AMAZING BOOK OF OPPOSITES MY FIRST AMAZING DICTIONARY
2	PIP JUMBO EARLY LOGO LOGO	OUR FACTS SORTING GAME BODYMAPPER	WRITER STORY INFANT TRAY EASY WORKS	KIDPIX PICTURE BUILDER COMPOSE	LOST FROG GRANNY'S GARDEN BUSY TOWN	TORTOISE AND THE HARE JUST GRANDMA AND ME
3	LOGO CONTROL LOGO FACTORY	OURFACTS NOTICEBOARD DATASHOW BRANCH INFORMATION WORKSHOP	CLARIS WORKS TRAY FRONTPAGE NEWSBULLETIN BANNER	CLARIS WORKS MUSICBOX DRAW	DRAGON WORLD MALLORY DRAGON DROOM	CREEPY CRAWLIES GENESIS HYPERSTUDIO
4	LOGO CONTROL LOGO FROGS BOAT REVERSE	BRANCH CLARIS WORKS SENSOR PIGEONHOLE	ION CAMERA CLIP ART	MUSICAL INSTRUMENTS	MARTELLO FLOWERS OF CRYSTAL L MYST	ANGLO SAXONS GENESIS HYPERSTUDIO
5	→	→	PAGE MAKER	→	→	ENCARTA ILLUMINATUS NATIONAL GALLERY

FIGURE 8.3

arrangements of words or phrases. In the column headed 'Graphics/Music' would go picture-building and pattern-making programs, programs in which pages of graphics can be designed, cartoon-making and music-making packages, and the software which allows free drawing. The column headed 'Adventures/Simulations' speaks for itself and the column headed 'CD-ROM/Multimedia' would cover all available CD-ROM titles and multimedia authoring programs. One school completed the plan as in figure 8.3 although there is plenty of alternative equivalent material which the staff could have considered.

The programs which are included on the framework diagram – both those already in the school and those which it is proposed to buy in the future – should form a large core of the school's software library. To the core, each teacher might like to add half a dozen or so smaller programs – puzzles, games of strategy, perhaps a useful practice program – which they would find useful on particular occasions with certain children.

If a software library is planned in this way, it will not become too large and will be one that can readily be managed. It will not need to be implemented all at once – it will be possible to think about the strengths and interests of the teachers in the school and to develop complementary strands of the framework. A school where language work is well established might choose text management and adventure games; a school which makes a feature of its environmental studies might go for data handling and simulations; a school where teachers are confident about mathematics might choose Logo. Once the computer has become firmly established as a support for one area of experience throughout the school it can readily be extended to other areas at a later date.

The management of the school's software

Like all communal resources in the school, the software and its documentation need to be properly organised. This is a much simpler affair when all the school's computers have inbuilt hard discs or are networked. Then the appropriate software can be installed in each classroom or on the relevant area of the network so that software management is reduced to storing and organising the documentation and backup discs.

However, most schools continue to have at least some computers which use floppy discs. They need systems for cataloguing, storing, collecting and returning software so that teachers can rely upon a particular program being available when they want to use it. The suggestions listed here may help to act as a reminder about what needs to be done.

- If it is permitted by the publisher, make back-up copies of program discs as soon as they arrive in the school; label the copies clearly using a felt pen. Make photocopies of any function key strips or information cards that could possibly get lost or damaged. Keep all the copies in a safe place away from the computer.
- Maintain a list of all the software in the school and issue the list to each member of staff. It is helpful to indicate in the list the type of each program and the age range for which it is suitable. Update the list when a new program arrives in the school. The easiest way to produce such a list is by using a database.
- Make sure that all staff and all teachers are aware of the need to handle floppy discs carefully, to keep them in their envelopes when not in use, and to avoid touching the exposed magnetic material. Smaller discs for newer machines have a firmer covering and are easier to handle but they too should not be left in the sun or on a radiator.
- Keep all the program discs and some blank formatted discs in a proper storage box with a lid so that they are stored in their envelopes in an upright position. Arrange the discs in a sensible way so that they can be located easily in the box, perhaps alphabetically or in sections. Some reminders about the 'do's and don'ts' of looking after discs could perhaps be listed on the lid of the box. Keep the protect labels on the discs unless it will be necessary to save files on the same disc.
- Have a storage folder or zip-up bag for each piece of software. Keep in it the software documentation, extra copies of function key strips, information sheets, and so on. Add to the folder any notes about how the program has been used, including articles cut out from magazines or journals. Encourage the staff to add their own notes to these as well.
- Keep the folders and the box of program discs in a central place so that they are easily accessible. Ask each teacher to sign out for the programs which they are using with the children.
- At the end of the school year create and circulate a list of the software which each class has used so that teachers will be aware of the children's previous computer experience. Staff will also be able to consult each other when they are preparing to use a particular program.

- Add references to particular pieces of software to the school's curriculum guidelines.

Management of equipment in the classroom

Although it is hard to avoid them altogether, technical issues should not dominate what happens in the classroom. If the problem is that the sun is shining on the monitor screen, then the best solution is to turn the computer off and to go outside and investigate the lengths of shadows! Good organisation and management of the equipment in the classroom is one of the ways of minimising technical problems and of fostering successful computer work. It also frees teachers from organisational queries so that more time can be spent discussing the children's work. One of the secrets of successful management lies in encouraging the children to become as autonomous as possible. They need to be encouraged to be responsible for both equipment and discs, just as they are responsible for the care of a classroom animal.

Some of the technical things which children should be able to do are:

- setting up a system ready for use;
- handling and inserting discs correctly;
- knowing where letters and numbers are on the keyboard, how to obtain upper and lower case letters, how to use special keys like the delete key or the escape key, and the role of function keys;
- understanding the general terms used in connection with computer use: for example, print-out, screen dump, bug, program, file ... ;
- operating for themselves software like a word processor, a database or Logo, so that they can load and save files, and use the printer, without calling for help.

The checklist which follows may provide some ideas for the management of equipment in the classroom.

- Place the computer inside the classroom rather than in a corridor or in a separate room so that computer activities can be integrated with other things that are going on. The children will then accept that the computer is a resource like any other. They will also become aware of each other's work at the computer; the attention of the class can be drawn to the computer work of a particular group just as it is to any other piece of work.
- Position the computer in a permanent place so that the room does not need to be reorganised whenever someone uses the

machine. Make sure that cables are connected firmly and that they are kept well out of the way. Face the monitor screen away from the window to avoid reflections. Make sure that there is sufficient space near the machine for notebooks, maps or plans, and anything else that the children will need.

- Make sure that the children are instructed in safety aspects, that they know how each piece of the equipment is turned on and off, and how to adjust the monitor for brightness.
- If the computer is to be left overnight in a position where chalk dust might settle then it is best to cover everything with a piece of sheeting.

Using software

Teachers need to become familiar with software which is to be used either by taking it home or by finding time to look at it in school. It is also helpful to know from other teachers how they have used it. There are often ideas for classroom use contained in the software documentation and it is well worth reading this before making a start.

In the earlier chapters of this book there are some checklists to help with the use of databases, word processors and programming. The more general points listed here may be helpful to teachers who are using a piece of software for the first time.

- Prepare any information or instruction cards which the children might need: for example, instructions about loading and saving files or about using the printer. Keep the cards close to the machine.
- Prepare any materials which the children will use: for example work folders, squared paper, coloured pens or pencils. Duplicate any record sheets which the children will need to maintain during their work with the program. Make sure that all the resources which the children may need are readily accessible. Encourage the children to get things for themselves and to put them away when they have finished with them.
- If the software is to be used as part of a broader project, then plan the project in full and decide how and when the software will play a part.
- Decide how the software will be introduced initially to the children and how they will continue to use it.

- Group the children for their computer work. Pairs, or threes, are suitable for most activities. Sometimes groups of similar ability are best, sometimes groups of mixed abilities and talents – like other classroom activities, it will depend on the nature of the task. It is important to ensure that boys do not dominate, so single-sex groups may be appropriate at times.

- Decide on some kind of timetable and give the children an indication of when it will be their turn to use the computer. It is sometimes useful to prepare a list showing the order of the groups. The children can then tick off or date the list when a turn is completed which helps to keep a check on their computer time over a period.

- Discuss with the children how individual tasks at the keyboard can be carried out (for example, typing, reading from the screen, maintaining a record) and how these tasks can be shared.

- Encourage the children themselves to be responsible for switching on hardware, loading software and getting started with the program.

- Remember to allow sufficient time at the keyboard for each group – time for them to think, discuss, plan, try out an idea and try again if the idea does not work. More than anything else, time is required for children to be thorough. The time is often a lot longer than the time which is generally allowed for more traditional, non-computer tasks. Even the youngest children may need as long as 30–40 minutes, with substantially longer periods for older or more experienced pupils.

- Try to spread expertise amongst the children. Strategies like 'If you need help don't ask me until you have asked at least two friends' help to foster independence in the children and provide some breathing space for the teacher.

- As in all problem-solving activities, it is important to build up the children's confidence in themselves. If they ask, 'Shall I try … ?', or 'Will this work?', then suggest, 'Try it and see what happens.'

- During their sessions at the keyboard try to find time to observe the children and to listen to them without intervening in any way. Children working with a computer often reveal either misunderstandings or abilities that their teachers had not anticipated.

- Allow time for discussion and reflection with the children at the end of a session. Sometimes it is helpful to arrange a whole class discussion so that children benefit from sharing their findings and combining as a class to try to solve a problem.

Planning for staff development

If computers are to be used in all primary classrooms by all primary teachers then it is essential that all the staff of the school have the opportunity to learn and to try things out and that they are assured of continued help and support.

In some schools, one teacher has taken responsibility for the use of the computer. The nominated teacher has attended in-service courses, organised arrangements for using the computer in classrooms, coordinated the selection and purchase of software, and generally guided the development of work with computers in the school. Although there are advantages to such a system, there can be disadvantages too. Often the teacher concerned has been one of the few male members of staff, reinforcing the image for other teachers and for the children of men as computer experts. Another disadvantage is that if the nominated teacher leaves the school, there may be no other member of staff with similar expertise to take over.

Other schools have tried to make sure that computer use is not the responsibility of just one person, but a collective responsibility. The staff as whole have set out to devise ways of supporting each other, of sharing ideas, successes and failures. All the staff are encouraged to attend courses on computer uses and to report back on good ideas and good practices learned.

Teachers who are developing new professional skills do so at several levels. A period is needed in which an awareness of the need to change and a sense of commitment develop; time is required for learning new skills, some of which will be of a technical nature; time is also needed for thinking about educational principles, for applying them in the classroom and for evaluating their effect. These levels are not sequential or hierarchical in any way: they overlap and interact with each other (Figure 8.4).

In some ways the level of awareness raising – a feeling of conviction about the need to change and the development of commitment to it – may be what is most important. The proverb 'Where there's a will there's a way' is a true one; once they are really convinced of a need primary teachers are always very willing to try out new ideas, and they are adept at overcoming practical problems which stand in the way. Evidence of a lack of conviction and the lack of confidence associated with it, was made plain in a study of computers in the primary curriculum carried out in 1987 by the University of

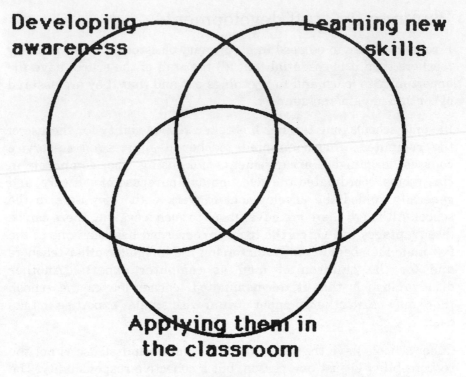

Developing awareness

Learning new skills

Applying them in the classroom

FIGURE 8.4

Sheffield. Primary schools offered all sorts of reasons why their computers were not being used.

> It hasn't been out over recent weeks because in the summer term we're tied up with all sorts of other things.

> It's the effort of getting organised. We have two buildings and there are lots of steps so we can't have a trolley.

> Our rooms have only one power source and unfortunately it's next to the blackboard. Unless we trail terrific long wires around it's the centre of attention near the front of the class.

> It's the chickens. The children are hatching chickens just now an we are using the only suitable electric socket for the incubator.

> Well, we used to use it when Mr Brown was here, but he left.

Awareness can be raised in different ways, some subtle and some less so. What is needed is some stimulus for discussion about needs, issues or problems. If one or two teachers in the school are enthusiastic they can pin up an occasional article on the staff notice board, raise computer use as a topic of conversation over coffee, relate humorous anecdotes, mount exciting and interesting displays of children's work in their own classrooms and more public places like corridors, and so on. It is also possible for the staff as a whole to use some time after school, basing their discussion on video films, or extracts from written material.

When very little is happening, and a stimulus is needed from outside the school, then progress may well be slower. The first aim might be to interest just one or two of the staff. A visit from an advisory teacher offering practical help with organisational problems can be a good start, especially if the visit is followed by a series of others in which the advisory teacher works with one or two class teachers in their own classrooms with their own children.

Once awareness has been raised, a period of confidence building is required. A teacher education programme might be developed in three stages in which new skills are learned and tried out in the classroom.

Stage 1: Becoming familiar with the equipment   All teachers need to learn how to connect up the equipment, how to insert a disc and view the disc directory, how to load a program, how to load and save a datafile, and how to use a printer. One of the easiest ways to learn how to do these things is by using a simple word processor. It is also helpful for every teacher to know how to format a blank disc, how to make a back-up copy of a whole disc, how to copy a single file from one disc to another, and how to remove an unwanted file from a disc. At this stage it is useful to learn how to do things in a small group, but it also helps to try things out alone, perhaps by taking a computer system home for a weekend. Knowing that a helpful colleague is close by, or at the end of a telephone, can be very reassuring.

Stage 2: First steps in the classroom   The next two stages are similar in pattern. Stage 2 involves finding out about and evaluating a small number of programs, then planning how to use one or more of them in the classroom. A word processor is again a sensible starting point, or a developing tray type of program. Infant teachers might like to think about a maze puzzle, or an easy-to-use picture making program. Junior teachers might prefer to try some decision tree software or a simple adventure game. Plans need to be made for the organisation of the classroom, and any support materials need to be prepared. Hearing about the experiences of other teachers, or making visits to their classrooms, is very helpful. The most important feature of this stage is that each teacher has support with any problems that occur once the children have begun to use the software, including an opportunity to reflect on what happened with others. This stage is one that therefore needs to take place over a period of time, so that ideas can be tried out in the classroom and afterwards discussed.

Stage 3: Developing new ways of working   The third stage is for considering one or more of the major software tools. First of all teachers need time for learning how to operate the software and for thinking about possible applications across the curriculum. The experiences of other teachers are again very helpful: in person, on video film, or in written case studies. Next the software needs to be tried out in the classroom, so that the attitudes and reactions of both children and teachers can be considered. At this stage, the teacher needs to become a researcher in his or her own classroom: making time and space for exploring new styles of learning and new styles of teaching. Again, the sharing of ideas with others is an important aspect so that big issues can be discussed: new skills, new concepts, the curriculum changes which are becoming necessary, and changing forms of assessment.

The timing of the in-service education requirements for the staff will depend very largely on the decisions that have been made about the use of the present computers and the purchase of future equipment. Not everyone necessarily needs the same level of support at the same time or in the same way. For example, a teacher of top infants may become interested in Logo, perhaps through attending a course at a teachers' centre. She may decide to start activities with the children in her class during the following term. After a while she may join a support group of other teachers, perhaps meeting at the teachers' centre, exchanging experiences, sharing problems and gaining ideas. At the same time she keeps her colleagues informed of what she is doing by chatting about it informally in the staffroom. Sometime later she might invite the teacher who will be responsible for the children during the following year to spend regular sessions with her watching the children at work. The second teacher might watch an appropriate video, do some reading, and take the computer home at weekends during the summer term to work on Logo by herself, knowing that if she encounters problems her colleague will help to sort them out on the Monday morning.

Where to go for help

Most local authorities offer an advisory service for schools. Many of them have a computer centre where courses are run and where software can be viewed. Advisory teachers based at the centres are often available to visit schools, either to work alongside teachers in classrooms or to help a school establish its priorities and policies for computer use. Local authorities often make arrangements for licensing or bulk purchase of good software so that schools can obtain copies at very low cost or even without charge; the centre staff should be able to provide information about any such schemes.

Both short and long in-service courses for teachers are run by local colleges, polytechnics and universities. The staff of these institutions are often prepared to visit a school to work with teachers in classrooms, or to help with in-service arrangements on a day closure.

From time to time there are schools' television broadcasts which are intended to be used as an in-service resource. Watch out for any that are about computers in primary schools.

There are also national associations which run annual conferences and publish very helpful quarterly magazines. They will also provide advice about insurance schemes for schools who are not covered by a local authority scheme. The association which is specifically for primary school teachers is MAPE (Micros and Primary Education). Application forms for membership can be obtained from the Computer Centre, Newman College, Bartley Green, Birmingham B32 3NT.

Further reading

Ellis, J. 1987. *Equal opportunities and computer education in the primary school*. Equal Opportunities Commission, Overseas House, Quay Street, Manchester M3 3HN. ISBN 0 905829 98 0.

Schenk, C. 1986. *Hands on: Hands off. A computer activity book for schools*. A&C Black. ISBN 0 7136 2707 7.

9 Children, parents and teachers

Children, like adults, have different approaches to the use of a computer. Some are prepared to be passive, to let others make comments or to take decisions; others will want to dominate, to do all the talking and to take all the decisions themselves. The personal skills which all children need to develop when they are working with computers apply to the whole curriculum, not just to work with the computer, but without them it is very difficult for any kind of learning to take place.

Positive attitudes It is vital that all children develop positive attitudes towards the computer and that girls as much as boys feel confident about using the machine.

Social skills Learning with a computer, like other kinds of learning, provides opportunities for children to gain from each other by working together collaboratively in a group. To do this productively they must be able to take part in collective decision making, to listen to other people, and to have respect for each person's contributions to the work of the group.

Good work habits For computer work to be successful children need to feel responsible for the equipment and software. They also need encouragement to be systematic when they work, to keep orderly notes and to present their work well.

The teacher's role

One of the best ways to help children to develop these personal skills when they are working with a computer is to encourage them to use the computer as a resource to solve problems and to answer questions. It is not an easy step for teachers to stand back from their traditional role of always being providers of what children do and learn. Yet if children are to become autonomous learners and good problem solvers they need to take increasing responsibility for the question to be answered or the problem to be investigated, as well as decisions about who they work with, how they work, and how they present their results.

For some teachers a 'standing back' role is easier to achieve by making use of the computer in the classroom than with the use of traditional resources. Good software makes it easier for teachers to observe children and to listen to their discussions since the focus for the children's learning is provided on the monitor screen and is managed by the computer program. The teacher can become an equal participant in the group, or a silent observer at the back.

Suggesting a role of standing back is not of course intended to imply that children are left to their own devices and are not provided with help if they become 'stuck'. Teachers need to play a positive part by helping children to refine the problems which they suggest, by asking questions at the appropriate moment, by challenging children to justify their arguments, and by encouraging them to reflect on what has been achieved.

In the initial stages of identifying the problem and clarifying its important aspects it is possible to ask children:

- What is the problem really asking you to do?
- What are you hoping to achieve?
- What information do you already know?
- Is there enough information? Could you get any more?
- Is there too much information? Which bit might be the most important?
- Could you write down the problem in a different way?
- Would it help to draw a diagram either to represent the problem or what you hope to achieve?

At the stage when children are attempting to attack the problem teachers can recommend that children draw on their previous experience, use intuition or even proceed by trial and error. Strategies which can be suggested if a group of children is short of ideas can include:

- What did you do last time?
- What about first trying a particular case?
- Have you broken the problem down into smaller parts?
- What about getting as far as this in the first place?
- Have you thought of changing any variables one at a time?
- Have you thought of working backwards?
- What about making a guess and seeing what happens?
- Have you made a list of the things that you have tried and that you know won't work?

Brainstorming may help at this stage, with ideas being noted on a large sheet of paper. Once the suggestions start to flow, it is important that no one in the group intervenes, or criticises any of the suggestions, however far-fetched they are. The ideas are kept until nothing new is being put forward. Their feasibility can then be discussed, and a short-list prepared for more detailed consideration. If children ask, 'Will this idea work?' then rather than say, 'Yes' or 'No' suggest that they 'Try it and see what happens.'

A tentative choice for a way of proceeding will be made by the children, tried, rejected or modified, and a route to the solution will gradually evolve. As it does so, children can again be helped by using prompts like:

- Have you used all the information?
- Are you taking this condition into account?
- Have you already done something which would help here?
- Have you considered changing the ... ?
- Would it help to put things in order?
- Would a graph help? Or a diagram?
- Do you notice any patterns?
- Are there any general trends?

If the children's plan is sound then it needs to be carried out carefully. Children need to be encouraged to check the steps they have taken and at this stage the teacher can ask:

- Is the result sensible?
- Have you solved each part of the problem?
- Will it always work?
- Have you satisfied all the initial conditions?
- Are there any other possible solutions?
- How can you be sure you've considered them all?

Finally, children can be urged to reflect on their experiences through questions like:

- Is the result what you expected?
- Which was your crucial step or discovery?
- Could the solution be shorter, more efficient, more reliable, more elegant ... ?
- Would the outcome be different if ... was altered?
- What other problems can you solve now?

Consider the strategies which were used by one infants' teacher when three children were about to make their second attempt at an adventure game in which they were searching a house for a frog. She skilfully focused their attention once again upon the problem, helping them to think about what was unsuccessful on the previous occasion, allowing time in the conversation for the children to think, and never herself telling the children what to do.

Teacher: Is there anything that you can remember from last time? Things you did?

Child: I can remember that we went into the kitchen, and we went into the office.

Teacher: Mmm. Was that what you called the study?

Child: Yeah. Into the study. And we went up the steps where there was a cat. We went down, but we got stopped by a dog.

Teacher: Why couldn't you get past the dog?

Child: Because we didn't have any of the things that he wanted that time because we'd already given him it ... or we'd dropped it.

Teacher: You dropped it? You dropped the thing that it needed?

Child: Mmm. I think we'll have to go back up for it. We'll have to use the ladder on the balcony.

Teacher: [*After a pause*] What do you two think?

Child: Maybe this time we could make sure we don't drop it.

Child: Or we could use the rope to go up again.

Teacher: [*After a pause*] Is there anything that you think that you might do this time that might help you?

Child: Um ... We could try and plot out the places we've been to.

Teacher: Yes?

Child: And ... and we could write down the places we can't go, like going down into the cellar.

Teacher: [*After another pause*] And how do you think you are going to get past that ... what was it that you say?

Child: A cat. It was a cat.

Child: Mmm. Not sure.

Teacher: What things did you try that the cat might like?

Child: We tried the ladder. We tried the honey. We tried the hammer. Tried the torch. Tried the bell. We tried everything.

Teacher: And didn't it like any of them? ... So that's really where we got stuck, wasn't it?

Child: Mmm. Maybe ... maybe there's something we haven't found yet?

Teacher: What sort of things do you think cats usually like?

Child: My cat likes milk and she likes Kit-e-Kat.

Child: Our next door cat likes to catch mice.

Child: I think that cats like fish.
Teacher: I wonder what this cat likes? Shall we start again now,
             and see what happens today?

Observing children

It is all too easy to assume that, by careful grouping of the children
and by allocating each group the same amount of computer time,
each child will participate and take equal responsibility. A child's
involvement when working with the computer will probably be
dependent on a number of different factors: the nature of the
software, the composition of the group, the child's gender, ability,
personality and confidence.

Time spent observing children working at a computer and listening
to their discussions is time which is well spent. Sometimes children
reveal misconceptions which the teacher had not appreciated;
sometimes they exhibit talents which indicate that their work away
from the computer is insufficiently challenging. One typical example
is that children working with Logo often use numbers in the
hundreds, comfortably adding or subtracting such numbers in their
heads, while the published mathematics scheme in use restricts
them to using pencil and paper to manipulate numbers up to 20.

The time spent observing is also an opportunity to concentrate on
reactions within the group. It is worthwhile looking out for some of
these circumstances.

- One child may dominate the group, perhaps by making decisions
  without consulting, by telling others what to do, by operating
  things before other children are ready, or by monopolising the
  keyboard or mouse. Such a child may need to be asked to play a
  supportive role rather than a leadership role, or to work with a
  partner who is similarly confident. It is also possible that the
  child needs to undertake a more challenging task than the one
  that has been provided.
- One child may be left out. The child may not understand what is
  going on, or may have lost interest, or may have opted out
  because of a disagreement with the others in the group.
  Sometimes the child may simply be ignored by the rest. If the
  behaviour of the group as a whole is unacceptable then it is
  important to intervene. If the task is too easy or too difficult for
  one child then that child needs to work with another group.

- There are also circumstances which fall between these two extremes in which particular children do not have an equal share in one way or another, sometimes willingly, sometimes unwillingly. There may be children who are not operating the keyboard for their fair share of time, some who choose to read the screen or maintain the record rather than type, or children who are quite happy to allow other children to tell them what to do. It may be necessary to emphasise to all the children in the group that they have a collective responsibility to take equal turns. Another strategy may be to move the willing followers to a group on their own.
- There may also be circumstances in which children behave in a way that is well meaning, but misguided. For example, a group of children may feel that is 'kind' to help a child in a wheelchair by doing all the typing for that child, or to help a child who is not quite fluent at reading English by reading from the screen on that child's behalf. Issues like these need to be discussed openly with the children so that they can appreciate what is appropriate help and what is not.

Gender issues

A report entitled *Computers in the Primary Curriculum* published by the Microelectronics Education Programme stated (paragraph 1.1.4): 'There are increasing signs that computers are being used more by boys and male teachers than by girls and female teachers. Primary schools may need to take positive steps to ensure that both sexes have equal opportunities'.

This statement is borne out by a number of indications. In January 1988, in figures supplied by the Department of Education and Science, 78.7% of the 171,397 full-time qualified primary school teachers in England and Wales were women. In the same month, in a small survey carried out in 314 schools in the London area, 243 said that a particular teacher took responsibility for work with computers (very often in conjunction with other responsibilities); 70.8% of these nominated teachers were men. It is hardly surprising that 'Shall I go and ask Mr So-and-so?' is a comment which is often heard from children when the machine is misbehaving.

Not long ago I watched a group of five primary children using a Robotix kit to construct a model which they were planning to control from the computer. The girls diligently assembled the framework whilst the boys busied themselves with the winding motors and subsequent computer control. This was not due to a lack of interest on the part of the girls. They were bustled out of the way and were too polite to bustle back. They wanted to be invited to use the equipment. Once they were allowed to the fore they were as excited and as adept as the boys (Figure 9.1).

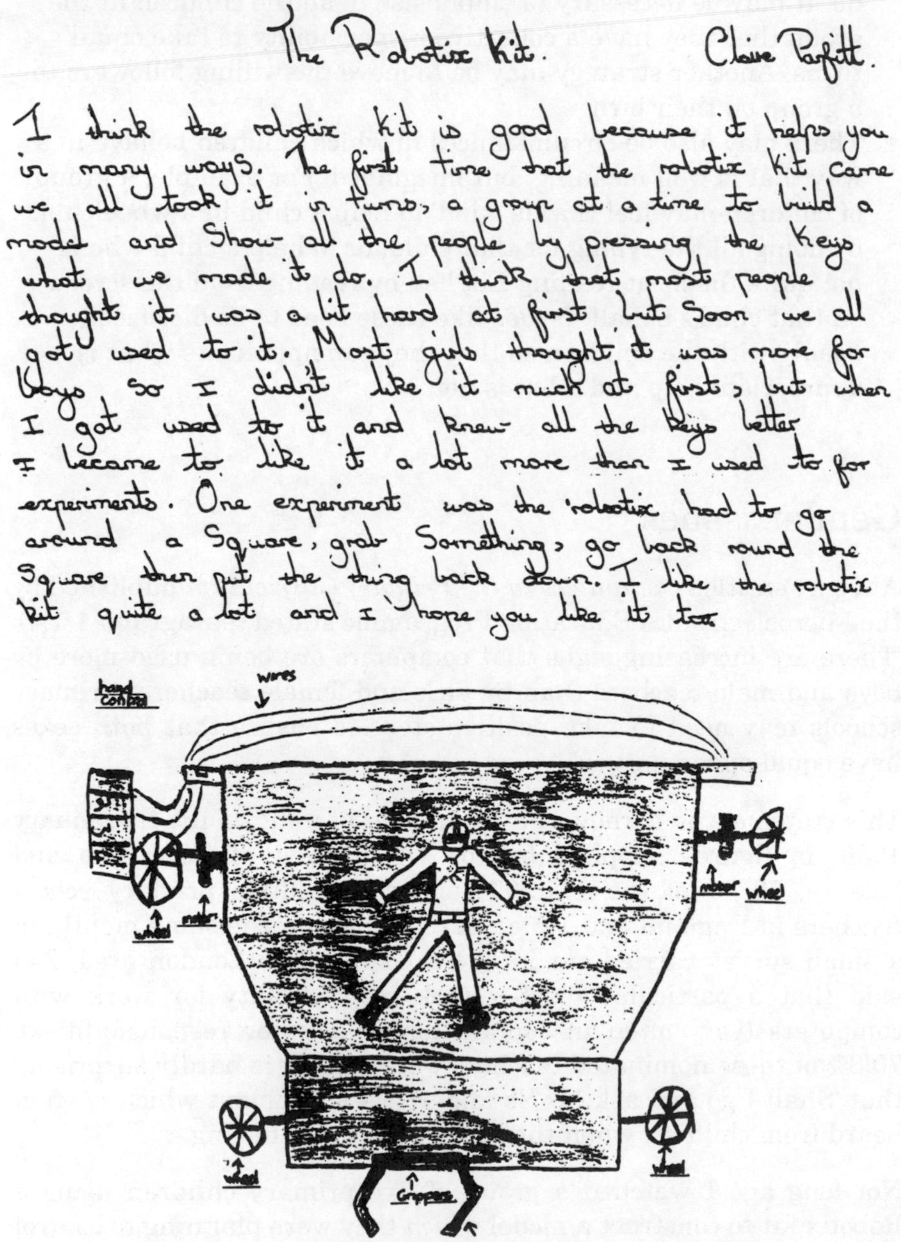

The Robotix Kit.   Claire Paffitt.

I think the robotix kit is good because it helps you in many ways. The first time that the robotix kit came we all took it in turns, a group at a time to build a model and show all the people by pressing the keys what we made it do. I think that most people thought it was a bit hard at first but soon we all got used to it. Most girls thought it was more for boys so I didn't like it much at first, but when I got used to it and knew all the keys better I became to like it a lot more than I used to for experiments. One experiment was the robotix had to go around a square, grab something, go back round the square then put the thing back down. I like the robotix kit quite a lot and I hope you like it too

FIGURE 9.1

Attitudes like those in Claire's class are not just evident with older juniors. A class discussion with some 5-year-olds in a small infants; school in Berkshire uncovered some interesting attitudes towards the roles of girls and boys with computers.

Teacher: Do you think that computers are more useful for girls or for boys?
Malcolm: Boys!
Teacher: Why do you think that is?
Malcolm: Because boys can do more complicated things than girls.
Teacher: Why can boys do more complicated things than girls?
Malcolm: They know better things.
Teacher: What makes you think that?
Malcolm: My Daddy told me.

This remark was at least countered by one of the girls in the group.

Teacher: What do you think, Ellen?
Ellen: Girls!
Teacher: Why do you think that is?
Ellen: Girls play nicer games than boys.
Teacher: Really?
Ellen: Yes. My Daddy told me.

The conversation continued.

Teacher: Martin, you have a computer at home, don't you? Who uses it?
Martin: Daddy.
Teacher: Does Mummy use it at all?
Martin: Sometimes.
Teacher: Does she? What does she use it for?
Martin: Not much. She really does the housework because Daddy's too lazy.

The credence one can place on statements made by children of this age is of course somewhat limited, as was demonstrated by Anneka, an extremely able child.

Anneka: Girls are better with computers because they've got longer hair, and they wear prettier dresses, and computers like girls better than boys.

The influences which lie at the root of these attitudes are many and varied, but the effect of pre-school and home experiences cannot be ignored. The choice of toys which children have access to at home is probably one of social tradition, and changing this is an inevitably slow process. Many parents and grandparents, educated a generation ago, have unthinkingly purchased a toy crane, a train set and a construction kit for their small son, and a doll's pram, a washing-up set and a nurse's uniform for their young daughter.

In a survey carried out in 1986 by Janine Blinko in the London Borough of Havering, 600 children aged between 6 and 12 years were asked to identify their favourite toys. The most popular choices and the numbers of children nominating them are shown in Table 9.1.

Table 9.1   Favourite toys listed by children aged 6-12 years

Girls		Boys	
Care bear	31	Computer	49
Doll	25	Transfomers	32
Teddy	16	Lego	23
Computer	13	Remote control car	21
Cindy	12	Model cars	14
Barbie	12	Atari	7

The Havering statistics were confirmed by some top infant children at Sir Thomas Abney Primary School in Hackney. In December 1987 they made a survey of the presents which children were hoping to receive for Christmas. Their graph, and some of the children's explanations for it, are shown in Figures 9.2 and 9.3.

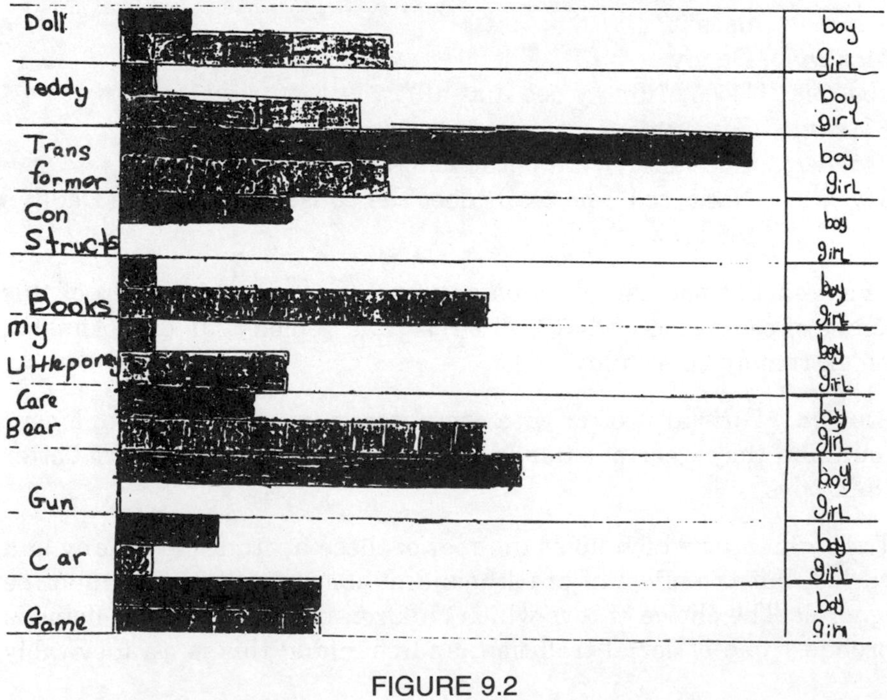

FIGURE 9.2

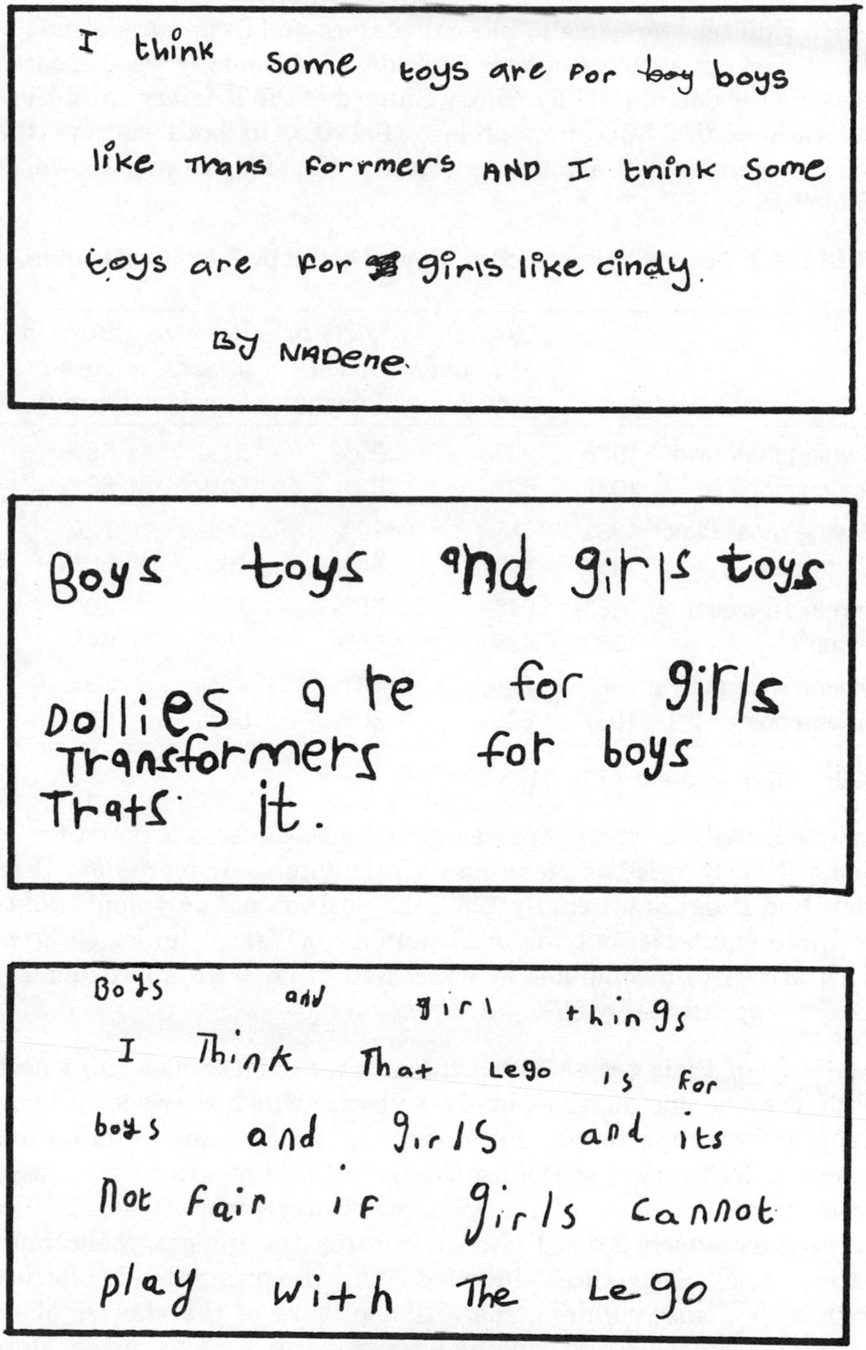

I think some toys are for ~~boy~~ boys like Trans forrmers AND I tnink some toys are for girls like cindy.

BY NADene.

Boys toys and girls toys

Dollies a re for girls
Transformers for boys
Trats it.

Boys and girl things
I Think That Lego is for boys and girls and its Not fair if girls cannot play with The Lego

FIGURE 9.3

The access which children have to technology at home will also influence the confidence with which they approach the equipment in school. In the early part of 1985, in order to ascertain the extent to which children were able to use calculators and computers at home, We carried out a survey of Year 5 children. The survey was repeated towards the end of 1987 by Hilary Shuard of the Primary Initiatives in Mathematics Education project (PrIME). In both surveys the schools were spread across the country. The figures are shown in Table 9.2.

TABLE 9.2 Access to new technology at home by 9 to 10-year-olds

		Girls in girls-only family	*Girls in mixed family*	*Boys in mixed family*	*Boys in boys-only family*
Owning their own	1985	28%	29%	54%	58%
calculator	1987	63%	50%	50%	58%
Having a calculator	1985	66%	72%	74%	72%
in the family	1987	79%	84%	79%	80%
Owning a digital	1985	51%	55%	79%	80%
watch	1987	43%	55%	68%	64%
Having a computer	1985	27%	36%	48%	59%
in the home	1987	50%	53%	56%	57%

1985: 2186 children; 1987: 1186 children

In 1985, twice as many boys as girls had access to a computer at home. Nearly twice as many had a calculator. Far more boys than girls had a digital watch. By 1987, the position not only appeared to be more equitable, but the total number of Year 5 junior children with access to a computer at home had risen from approximately 42% to approximately 55%.

Apart from their access to machines, children are also influenced both at home and at school by the software which they see and use. People feature strongly in adventure games and simulations intended for primary school use. Many of these programs are biased towards males: some of them do not feature women at all. The vocabulary which is used often reinforces the images: 'policeman' rather than 'police officer'. In one popular program intended for use with very young children, there is a picture of the shelves of an empty toy cupboard and children are invited to put toys inside. More than half of the 25 possible choices could be regarded as biased towards boys either by name or by association.

Boy biased toys   soldier, football, rocket, crane, car, He-man, plane, robot, boat, dinosaur, drum, Mr Man, jack in the box   (13)

Girl biased toys   doll, pony (My Little Pony)   (2)

Neutral toys   kite, castle, house, bricks, ball, duck, books, paints, crayons, teddy (10)

Software which is designed for the home market is much more likely to be orientated towards boys. Many programs focus on themes of space travel, war and violence, or sports like football or car racing which are generally regarded as the province of men. Nearly all of these programs involve competition in one form or another.

What then are the steps which could be taken by a primary teacher faced with such circumstances? Hazel Taylor, writing in *Girls into maths can go*, suggests that girls' attitudes towards mechanical or constructional toys or gadgets can be improved by setting activities with them into an imaginative context or into a story theme. The other suggestions which are listed below may provide some ideas for what could be done to increase the self-confidence of girls.

- Have a discussion about the issues with the children themselves, and raise them at a parents' evening.
- Make girls the 'monitors' who are responsible for getting out the computer each day and connecting it up.
- Supervise to make sure that girls and boys get equal amounts of computer time, and equal amounts of typing experience at the keyboard.
- Consider single-sex groupings for some activities. Give a group of girls the first turn at the computer and mix the order of single-sex groups.
- Make sure that girls have frequent opportunities to show their computer work to other children.
- Make sure that any software used in the classroom is of equal interest to both sexes, and wherever possible that it portrays girls and women in active, positive roles.
- Choose a girl to demonstrate the use of a new piece of software to other children in the class.
- If there is a technical difficulty with the computer, either refer it to the girls in the class to sort out or, if adult help is needed, send for a female staff member rather than a male.

In the ways in which the computer is used in the school as a whole, there are other questions to consider.

- Who is in charge of the computer? If the post is held by a male teacher, would it help to share the responsibility between a man and a woman?

- Which teachers use the computer? If there are disproportionately few women, could more be done to encourage them to participate?
- Which teachers attend courses? Are there any teachers who would like to do so but cannot because they are held at inconvenient times or inconvenient places? Could consideration be given to these teachers for daytime release? Or would it be possible to set up a course in the school itself, perhaps in partnership with a neighbouring school?
- Are all the staff aware that courses which are run for primary teachers usually concentrate on the applications of software rather than on the technical details of the hardware?
- Who runs any in-school workshops for the staff? Could women teachers lead more of them?

Involving parents

It is important that parents are involved in the development of computer use throughout the school. They need to know what is being offered to their children; if they understand what the school is trying to achieve then they will be more able to support and encourage their children at home. Parents may also have insights to offer about their children's experiences with new technology at home and about the ways that their children like to set about doing things. It is not just a question of teachers informing parents of what is happening in the school. A real dialogue is a two-way process, with parents making an active contribution to it.

It often comes as something of a surprise to parents who themselves work professionally with computers, particularly to those who work in the computer manufacturing industry, that primary children are not undertaking 'computer studies' but are learning to make use of the computer as a resource. Once they understand this, parents generally are very interested in the computer-related work which children do in school, and pleased to find that their children are gaining competence in using the machine in various ways.

Sometimes there will be sensitive issues which may need to be raised with parents. For example, there may be a mis-match between what you are trying to do in school about gender issues and what is happening at home. It is possible to say to parents: 'We know that as girls get older they tend to shy away from using computers, from taking examinations which involve computers, or from opting for computing as a career. We are trying to make sure that in our primary school the girls have the maximum opportunity to become confident and competent at using new technology. Is there any way that you would be willing to adapt what you are doing at home in order to help what we are trying to do in school?'

Most schools already have arrangements for informal discussions with parents, for consulting parent governors and the parents' association, for open days and parents' evenings. Many schools nowadays have schemes to strengthen home-school links: inviting parents into school to work with children, or sending home books or games.

Parents who are helping children with computer work, either at home or at school, may need to be given some guidance about when to intervene and when to stand back. For example, it is important that children should do the typing and that they should be allowed to try out something even when the parent knows that it will lead nowhere. It is when children become frustrated because all thought seems to have deserted them that the odd idea contributed by the parent becomes helpful.

Parents can also help to make sure that the group working with the computer operates fairly. They can curb over-enthusiastic users and make sure that each child gets a fair share of typing at the keyboard. They can ensure that a collective decision is reached before proceeding, and can help to gauge when it is a good time to stop.

Some other strategies for extending parental involvement in the children's work with computers are listed below.

- Workshops for parents in small groups can be very helpful especially when there is an opportunity for discussion afterwards. Software which children use as the basis for a project generally provokes a good discussion; so does Logo.
- Arrangements where parents can observe children at work can be made. If possible, when a child's parents arrive, they and their child should have some time together at the computer, as well as an opportunity to look at the child's computer-related topic work. For parents who are unable to visit the school during the school day some slides or video film of the children at work can be shown, or some of the children can be asked to come back after school to work with their parents.
- Displays of children's computer-related work in the school entrance hall can help to inform parents and to stimulate their interest.

- A magazine which is produced by using a word processor and/or a desktop publishing package could be produced to describe for parents the work which children do with computers in school.
- Parents who can make a special contribution can be invited to work with groups of children in the classroom. For example, parents of children who speak English as a second language might be asked to work on an adventure game with a group of children who are talking in their community language.
- Children might borrow things to take home to share with their parents – perhaps calculator games, technical Lego or Robotix kits, or even software if the child has a computer at home and it is the same model as the one in school.
- Parents can be offered advice about software which could be purchased for use at home: for example, games of strategy like 3D noughts and crosses, or adventure games like The Hobbit. Logo is available for many of the computers commonly found at home, and so are word processing packages.
- Parents might be encouraged to talk with the children about their work with computers, or to accompany groups who are going on a visit to see computers in use at work.
- 'A technology trail' round the locality could be devised and sent home with the suggestion that parents walk round it with their children.

It is especially important to make sure that parents who may themselves feel tentative about the technology are made to feel welcome and at ease.

- If workshops are run for parents, try to make sure that mothers, in particular, are able to come by providing creche facilities, or play equipment for younger brothers or sisters.
- If the school has a parents' room in which parents can meet, talk, drink coffee, and so on, a computer could be placed in it for one afternoon a week, and two or three children could demonstrate some of the things that they have been doing.

Further reading

Burton, L. (ed.) 1986. *Girls into maths can go*. Holt, Rinehart and Winston. ISBN 0 03 910687 X.

Hammond, R. 1984. *Computers and your child*. Century. ISBN 0 7126 0460 X.

Cunliffe, J. 1984. *Play Logo: an introduction to computing for parents and children*. Deutsch. ISBN 0 233 97718 X.

10 Evaluation and assessment

Information technology has now established itself both in society and in education. Before the DTI hardware scheme in the early eighties few people would have imagined that computers would become commonplace in primary schools. When the equipment first arrived in classrooms teachers were excited, but they were also uncertain about the prospective role of the new technology. The last fifteen years or so have been a period for trial and for experimentation, for sharing good ideas and for rejecting those which seem less profitable. The computer is becoming established as a resource for learning across the primary school curriculum and, through this approach, is providing children with a broad appreciation of its versatility.

Both old ideas and new ones need to be evaluated by those who are trying them out. Self-appraisal involves asking questions about what is being done and why it is being done, deciding whether it is being done well, or whether the school should be doing something different. Some evaluation is taking place all the time as teachers look critically at their own work, but there is also a need for the staff as a whole to take stock of what has been achieved, so that plans for the future can be reviewed and crystallised.

This chapter suggests questions which the staff of a primary school could consider. The questions are not intended to be used as a blueprint, or to be followed in their entirety. The level of resourcing and of in-service provision, and the consequent level of achievement, will in any case vary considerably from one area to another. An individual school could base a discussion upon one or two of the listed questions, and could talk through some of the issues raised in the discussion with a member of the LEA advisory service. Groups of teachers from different schools might consider the broad headings at an in-service course, and evolve their own sets of questions to suit their local circumstances.

A. The curricular policy and classroom practice

The school's aims and its curricular policy are the foundation stones on which developments can be built. Each school needs to consider the value of its policy as well as its effectiveness.

Policy

- Are the school's aims for the use of information technology clear to everyone: staff, governors, parents, children?
- How do the children in the school learn about the computer itself and the significance that it is likely to have in their lives?
- Can teachers in the school describe occasions when the computer has been used in a way which gives children opportunities to:
    - exchange ideas through discussion;
    - suggest and then test hypotheses;
    - organise and analyse information;
    - experiment with and express creative ideas;
    - pose and find solutions to their own problems;
    - develop methods for themselves;
    - sort out their own mistakes?
- Do any teachers consider that they have used the computer to:
    - help them cope with the varied demands of the classroom;
    - help them to develop new teaching styles;
    - focus on how children learn rather on what they learn;
    - give better insight into children's thinking?
- Has there been any debate about the possible advantage of concentrating computer use throughout the school on one or more of the major applications: adventure games and simulations, word processing and text management, information handling, programming in Logo, control technology, graphics or music?
- To what extent has it been possible to review the school's curriculum guidelines for, say, language, mathematics and science in order to take information technology into account?

Continuity

- How do teachers know which software the children have used previously:
    - in another class;
    - at home;
    - in a previous school or playgroup?

- How do teachers in the school prevent unnecessary repetition of work with computers? What ways are there of ensuring that the children's experiences are progressively more challenging?
- Are staff aware of the ways in which other primary schools in the area are making use of their computers?
- What has been done to ensure that the children's future secondary school teachers are familiar with their computer experiences at the primary school level?

Classroom organisation

- When the use of a computer has been allocated to a particular class or group of children, what are the advantages or disadvantages of
  > positioning the computer in the classroom or work area;
  > using a corridor or a special computer room?

- How frequently, and for what purposes, should:
  > a teacher use a computer to work with a group of children;
  > a small group of children work at the keyboard, with the occasional but not constant presence of their teacher;
  > a child work individually with the computer?

- For each class, what proportion of time with the computer is spent by children on
  > basic skill practice;
  > extending skills of listening, talking, reading or writing;
  > solving problems;
  > organising, interpreting or presenting information;
  > creative or imaginative work?

- What organisational strategies do teachers use so that children can have time away from the computer to
  > plan and to follow up their computer work;
  > exchange ideas and explain their work to others?

Hills glitter on a winter's day,
Icy frosty icicles sparkle,
Silver snow-drifts dazzle,
Icicles twinkle,
Fields shine in the sunlight,
Houses shimmer like diamonds.

FIGURE 10.1

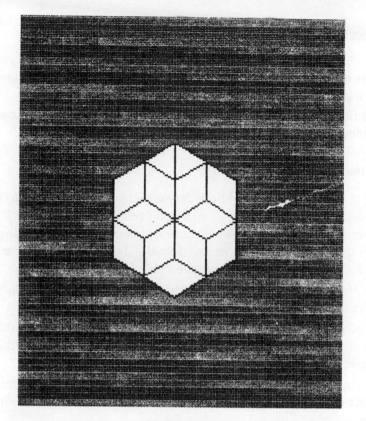

FIGURE 10.2

B. People

Curriculum innovation of any kind needs to take into account the needs, skills and sensitivities of all the people concerned. In the case of computers, the pressure on schools to adopt them can sometimes make the adults feel insecure, whereas children seem to be able to use the new technology with great ease.

Children

- How are children encouraged to feel that they have a part to play in the care of the hardware and the software?

- Is it necessary for the staff to take any special steps to encourage particular groups of children: for example,
    children for whom English is a second language;
    children who do not have a computer at home;
    girls?

- What do teachers do if they discover children who know more about computers than they do?
- Should there be occasions when the children in the class can use their own initiative in deciding to use the computer, without asking permission or being directed to it by the teacher?
- Should there be occasions when the children themselves decide which piece of software it would be appropriate to use?

Parents and the community

- What opportunities are there for parents and governors to gain an active understanding of what the school is trying to do? Are there workshops for parents and/or governors? Are they invited into the school to watch or participate? Is there any information in the school brochure about the role of the computer?
- Are there other ways in which the involvement of parents and others in the community could be extended?
- What advice does the school offer to parents who are thinking about buying a computer for their child, or who want to know which programs to use at home?
- How many girls and boys have access to a computer at home? What do they use it for? Are there implications for what should happen in school?

Staff development

- Are all the staff encouraged to take the computer home for preparation?
- What strategies have been used to share expertise amongst the staff in the school? Has it been possible to:
     double up classes so that one teacher can help another;
     have workshops after school;
     discuss successes or failures in the classroom;
     compare the work done by two age groups who have used
        the same piece of software;
     use some video film as a basis for discussion?
- When teachers attend courses, what arrangements are made for them to share their knowledge and skills with colleagues?
- What arrangements are made to support:
     probationary teachers;
     student teachers;
     teachers who are new to the school;

teachers who are using a new piece of software for the first
time in the classroom;

any staff members who feel they lack the skills needed for
computer use?

- Which teachers should take priority:
    for attending out-of-school courses or conferences;
    for visiting other schools to see what they are doing?

- What are the duties of the teacher/s who take overall
responsibility for the management of the computer? Are all staff
aware of these duties? Are the duties reviewed from time to
time?
- What steps are being taken to ensure that:
    the female staff are as involved as the male staff;
    the older staff are as involved as the younger ones?

Support services

Local authorities vary in the support which they are able to offer
their primary schools. What is important is that all primary teachers
are aware of the facilities which exist, and make maximum use of
them.

- Could the school make more use of the facilities and support
provided by in the locality? For example, by
    a computer centre or a teachers' centre;
    a software viewing or lending library;
    colleges or universities?
- Could more use be made of the help which has been or could be
offered by any advisory teachers?
- What procedure is there to draw the staff's attention to suitable
courses?
- How is any information sent to the school by the LEA or
publishers made known to each member of staff?
- Could the school make more use of the journal, software and
local events provided by MAPE? The address is provided on page
227.

C. Resource management

The way that resources are managed in a school is one of the key factors in determining the success of any curricular innovation. Resource management will need to take into account the hardware and software, the use of time, and financial planning.

Hardware

- How many computer systems does the school need?
- Is the present hardware well organised and well maintained? Are the staff generally satisfied with the arrangements?
- Is there a need to review the school's present policy:
      for the use of existing equipment;
      for the purchase of new equipment?
- Are there any ways in which changing the location of any of the existing computer systems would ensure that it is used more effectively?

Software

- Is there an efficient system for storing the software and its documentation? Is the system working effectively? How satisfied are the staff with the arrangements?
- Do staff have an easy means of knowing what software is available in the school?
- Which programs should form the core of the school's software library?
- What is the system for reviewing the software library? Has any inappropriate software been discarded?
- Does the school need to purchase more software? Why?
- When a new piece of software arrives in school what arrangements are made for each member of staff to appraise it and become familiar with it?
- Do the school's curricular guidelines for core subjects refer to appropriate pieces of software? If not, how could appropriate references be incorporated?

Time

- Would there be any advantages in using the computing resources with just one group of children for a substantial period of time?

- Are there other ways in which a re-allocation of computer time would ensure that it is used more effectively?

Financial considerations

Financial support for schools wishing to buy computing equipment varies considerably from one local authority to another. As well as any support provided by the LEA, parents' associations are often willing to raise funds for computers. Sometimes there are local trusts or businesses which will help. Occasionally there are special projects, initiated either by the LEA or by others, which can provide funds.

- Do financial plans cover:
        insurance and security arrangements;
        maintenance;
        future purchases and/or replacements;
        installation, including storage, furniture and wiring?

- Does the school have other important needs which should take priority over expenditure on additional computing equipment and software?

D. Questions for individual members of staff

The staff as a whole will be involved in the discussion of the questions listed above. Indeed, the discussion of some of the questions may involve others from outside the school: governors, parents, the local authority advisory service. But each individual member of the staff will also need to appraise his or her own role.

Questions for those in posts of responsibility

The headteacher, the deputy headteacher and any curriculum coordinator for information technology will of course play a major part in the consideration of the general set of questions. As they consider their own particular roles, it might be helpful to ask more specific questions:

- Are the staff likely to feel that I am interested in and concerned about the development of computer use in the school, and that it is high on my list of priorities?
- In the last month, how often did I set out to observe computers being used? Did I spend time talking to the teachers and/or children about my observations? Did I make it clear to them when I was pleased with what I saw?

- To what extent did the ways in which I observed the computer being used match the school's general aims for learning?
- What are the most/least exciting uses of computers I have seen so far? How do these uses compare with what I hear from colleagues in other schools?

	6 months	1 year	2 years
Hardware			
Software			
INSET			
Curriculum			
?			

FIGURE 10.3

- How often did I myself teach the children by making use of the computer?
- What time did I give to discussing computing policy individually or in groups with:
    members of staff;
    parents or governors;
    colleagues in other schools?

- What should our priorities for action be in the next six months/one year/two years? To what extent is my view of the necessary priorities shared by others? (Figure 10.3)
- What constraints are there which could stand in the way of developments? Are there ways of overcoming these constraints in any way?
- Who can or should initiate any necessary action?
- Do we need any outside support and advice? If so, what?

Questions for individual class teachers

As well as making a contribution to the overall evaluation by the whole staff, each individual class teacher will need to appraise his or her own role.

- When the computer is available for my class to use, do I:
  > plan and prepare adequately;
  > spend enough time observing children who are using the computer;
  > remember not to intervene when children are trying to solve a problem for themselves;
  > allow time for children to mull things over;
  > spend sufficient time listening to and talking with the children about their work with the computer?

- Could I improve the integration of the use of the computer with other classroom activities?
- Am I sure that the programs which my class have been using are flexible enough to match the needs of each individual child?
- Have I checked that each child gets an equal amount of time with the computer, and that particular children do not dominate within a group?
- How should I assess and keep a record of the children's progress with their computer work?
- Which piece of software should I next learn to use so that I can introduce it to my class? What plans do I need to make to achieve this?

E. Assessing outcomes

The outcomes of the school's planning and provision for work with computers determine what the children gain from it. Assessing a child or group of children through observation and questioning takes time, and is not easy. It involves considering the children's attitudes, observing them in the way that they set about their work, listening to what they say, and looking at what they produce.

There is a need to sit back and watch how children approach their work, whether they enjoy it, whether they persevere with it, whether it challenges them, what they do when they get stuck, how they organise themselves, and so on. There is a need for questioning which asks children to justify what they have done, to explain their methods, and to attempt to give reasons for their results. As well as observing them at work there is a need to have open discussions with the children about how they see their own progress.

Assessing children's attitudes

* Do all the children enjoy their work with the computer? How does their enjoyment of computer work compare with their enjoyment of other aspects of classroom work?
* Are all the children equally confident about their computer work? Do the girls think that they are as good as the boys?

Watching children as they set about their work

* Are all the children able to operate both hardware and software without help?
* Are the children well organised? Are they working systematically, and keeping any necessary notes in an appropriate way?
* Are all the children prepared to persist with a piece of computer work, over several sessions if necessary? How does their persistence with computer work compare with their persistence with other work?
* How do children react when what they are doing with the computer does not turn out as they had anticipated? Do they make a careful check of measurements they have taken, the sequence of the commands which they have used, or the way that they have entered data? Do they try to analyse the reasons for an unexpected result?
* Is each child learning to listen, to have respect for the contributions of others, to cooperate or to take responsibility within a group?

Listening to children working at a computer

- Do the children merely repeat the information which they see on the screen, or do they help each other to interpret, make sense of and absorb what they see?

- When they talk to each other, are they able to describe or explain a situation, to give information or instructions, or justify a decision, in a clear manner?

- Are they using logical connectives to reason with each other: if, then, otherwise, because, and, either, or ... ?

- Are they considering in advance the possible outcomes of their decisions, and predicting the results which they expect to obtain, or are they trying things out without forethought?

- Does their conversation reveal that they are looking for relationships: for example, do they use phrases like 'that's the same as ...', 'that's less than before', 'it should go in front of ...', 'they seem to be going up together ...'?

- Are they using unexpected mathematical skills or ideas: for example, large numbers, negative numbers, mental arithmetic ...? If so, what are the implications for their mathematical work away from the computer?

- When questioned, can they explain and justify their strategies? Can they describe and give possible reasons for their results?

Looking at recorded work

- To what extend does the children's recorded work (handwritten notes, print-outs) reflect the quality and totality of what was said and done at the keyboard? If not, does this matter?

- How does the recorded work compare with the children's non-computer recorded work?

- If the recorded work is sketchy, what would be gained by encouraging the children to extend it into a more complete description of their methods, strategies and conclusions?

- How do the children feel about their recorded work? Would they like to take it home to show parents, have it displayed for others to see, placed in a folder to add to later on ... ?

Conclusion

The questions about evaluation and assessment which have been raised in this chapter show that both the problems and the possibilities which have stemmed from the introduction of information technology into schools are much the same as those which present themselves when other aspects of the primary school curriculum are considered. Nevertheless, the questions should help to clarify objectives and priorities for the use of information technology, to identify strengths or weaknesses in the school's current work, and to highlight the actions which need to be taken for the future.

11 Into the future

A school curriculum has many functions. Most new ideas in education emerge in the first place to fulfil the present functions of the curriculum; often, as those ideas are explored and developed, new functions for the curriculum start to evolve. It takes time to acquire confidence with new equipment and familiarity with the operation of new software. It takes longer to learn how to exploit to the full the links between the software and those elements of learning that arise in most aspects of the curriculum: communication, information handling, problem solving, creative and imaginative thinking. Only then is it possible to consider how the balance and emphasis within the curriculum might need to change, or how new styles of teaching might give rise to new expectations for learning.

Crystal ball gazing is never easy. It is difficult, if not impossible, to predict what further developments in information technology will be made in the next few years. A period of 25 years can cover enormous changes. In 1935, television was known only to a few, and was certainly never envisaged as a common household item. Only a small number of homes had telephones. In 1960, a computer needed a large room to itself, and neither pocket calculators nor digital watches were known to anyone – the microchip did not exist – but television and telephones had become a reality in a majority of homes. By 1985, everyone who wanted one could afford a cheap calculator or digital watch, and nearly half of all children aged 10 owned their own. A microcomputer had found its way into every school, and into an estimated five million homes.

In the next 25 years we will probably see the appearance of all kinds of inventions of which we have no knowledge at present. Nevertheless, there are some broad trends in the development of information technology which indicate the general ways which things are likely to go.

Isaac Asimov, in his story 'Earth is room enough' published in 1967, imagined the schoolroom of the year 2155.

Margie always hated school, but now she hated it more than ever. The mechanical teacher had been giving her test after test in Geography and she had been doing worse and worse until her mother had shaken her head sorrowfully and sent for the County Inspector.

He was a round little man with a red face and a whole box of tools and wires. He smiled at her and gave her an apple, then took the teacher apart. Margie had hoped he wouldn't know how to put it together again, but he knew all right and after an hour or so, there it was again, large and black and ugly with a big screen on which all the lessons were shown and the questions were asked ...

Margie went into the schoolroom. It was right next to her bedroom, and the mechanical teacher was on and waiting for her. It was always on at the same time every day except Saturday and Sunday, because her mother said that little girls learned better if they learned at regular hours.

The screen was lit up, and it said: 'Today's arithmetic lesson is on the addition of proper fractions. Please insert yesterday's homework in the proper slot.'

Margie did so with a sigh. She was thinking about the old schools they had when her grandfather's grandfather was a little boy. All the kids from the whole neighbourhood came, laughing and shouting in the school-yard, sitting together in the schoolroom, going home together at the end of the day ...

And the teachers were people.

The mechanical teacher was flashing on the screen: 'When we add the fractions $1/2$ and $1/4$ ...'

Margie was thinking about how the kids must have loved it in the old days. She was thinking about the fun they had.

Since the publication of the first edition of this book there have been two major developments in the educational use of computers, both reflecting aspects of Asimov's vision while seeming to point in completely opposite directions. These are Integrated Learning Systems and the Internet.

Integrated Learning Systems

Integrated Learning Systems (ILS) appear to be very close to Asimov's mechanical teacher. They are carefully structured computer programs designed to teach basic mathematical and literacy skills through regular repeated practice. But an ILS is far more sophisticated than a teaching machine of the 1960's. It manages the delivery of curriculum material, presenting all learners with individual programmes of work tailored precisely to their specific needs. The system constantly assesses learner performance and provides continuous feedback and detailed records of progress for both children and teachers.

Because an ILS has clearly defined objectives it is relatively easy to evaluate its success. This is not true of much of the software discussed elsewhere in this book. Children using Logo for example, may become active independent learners, acquire mathematical understanding and develop general problem solving skills but none of these is easy to measure and researchers have found it very difficult to prove that Logo is a valuable educational activity. An ILS, on the other hand, aims to develop very specific skills broken down into small steps which are easily assessed. Evaluations of this kind of software both in the United States and in Britain show quite dramatic results, particularly in mathematics. Children using the system can make learning gains of around twenty months over a six month period of use and there is evidence that these gains persist over many years.

Integrated learning Systems do not fit comfortably into the philosophy which underpins most use of computers in primary schools in this country. They are used on a one-to-one basis rather than for collaborative groupwork, they put the computer in charge of the child rather than the other way round and they focus inwards on specific skills rather than leading outwards by offering diverse stimuli to imaginative or investigative activities. However, learning gains of this magnitude, found in a substantial body of research, cannot be lightly dismissed, particularly in a climate of incessant complaints that standards of performance in 'the basics' are falling. Such complaints are far from new, but today there are political imperatives which mean they are being taken more seriously.

For Integrated Learning Systems to become widely used in primary schools, political intervention would be needed because the systems are so expensive. To allow all pupils access for their daily 20 minutes work, requires a dedicated network of 8 computers which could cost around £40,000 to install and equip. Whether any government would be prepared to fund such systems on a large scale remains to be seen and without dedicated funding Integrated Learning Systems are unlikely to become widespread.

The Internet

The image of serried ranks of children sitting at individual terminals all locked into their own learning programmes is hardly an attractive one but the systems are only intended to be used for 20 minutes at a time leaving the rest of the school day much the same as it is now. Perhaps a greater threat to schools as we know them is the trend for linking cheap microcomputers with equally cheap communication devices allowing any pocket or classroom computer to connect to any other, or to a myriad of computerised databases around the world.

When the first edition of this book was published, in 1989, no-one had heard of the Internet. Now it is mentioned in almost every political speech, magazine and newspaper. If we are to believe the hype, the Internet will revolutionise education as it will revolutionise all other aspects of our lives. There can be no doubt that it potentially offers much that is attractive to schools: the opportunity to browse through an art collection or museum; access to every book that has ever been written in a form that may be searched, cut or edited; direct and immediate written communication with anyone in the world. But there are still very few primary school subscribers and ways of using all this educational potential are only just beginning to be explored.

The Internet is a worldwide computer network which links up thousands of smaller networks as well as millions of machines belonging to private individuals. Computers are linked through a telephone line which is connected to each one through a box called a modem (the most up-to-date machines may have the modem built-in). A variety of different 'service providers' supply the necessary software and give access to the Internet for an annual subscription fee. There are four main facilities likely to be of interest to primary education:

- Electronic Mail (Email) is a system whereby messages written at one computer can be sent to other computers around the world. This facility is already used imaginatively by some primary schools (See Chapter 7).
- Newsgroups are electronic discussion groups which work rather like email but post the messages on a 'notice board' where anyone can read them and add their own contributions. There are thousands of newsgroups on the Internet, often on esoteric subjects like motor-cycle maintenance or bee keeping, but primary teachers have yet to discover ways of using newsgroups effectively in the classroom.

- File Transfer Protocol (FTP) is a system whereby any document, file or computer program can be sent through the Internet from one computer to another. It is not yet widely used by schools but may herald a completely new future for computer use whereby all software is accessed in this way, making floppy discs, hard discs, and even CD-ROMs, redundant.
- The World Wide Web (WWW) is a vast collection of linked, multimedia, information pages which have been created in thousands of different places all over the world. These can be read using a piece of software called a browser which fetches and composes the pages on the screen . Experimental use of the WWW is underway in a number of primary schools with some even involved in compiling their own Web pages.

Other schools are involved in a project with Reuters news agency whereby a set of articles covering each day's news, are sent to the school computer overnight. In one school pupils are using this as just one among many sources of daily news. Each week between 4 and 6 mixed Year 5 and Year 6 pupils work as news hounds selecting and researching news items from a variety of sources including the computer program, local and national newspapers and tv and radio broadcasts. The following week the same group work on a separate computer to compile their selected items into a mini newspaper, suitable for an infant or lower junior audience. Each newspaper includes at least one article at each of four levels, school based, local, national and international. During the same week a second group starts the process, so that all pupils have the opportunity to produce a newspaper over the course of a term.

The extent to which the Internet will be used in schools of the future will depend upon the resolution of some of the current difficulties. The first of these is that ordinary telephone lines are not adequate to allow multimedia materials such as video to be transmitted at an acceptable speed for on-line use. This is one of the reasons that the Reuters articles are sent overnight and then accessed from the hard disc rather than over the telephone line. High speed transmission requires cable links to all schools forming 'broadband' networks with vastly increased speeds of data transfer.

A further problem for schools is the cost of using on-line services, not so much the subscription fees, which are fixed and can be incorporated in the budget, but the telephone charges which are an unknown quantity which could become very considerable.

As with ILS, the political will to solve these problems is a necessary prerequisite to further development.

Speech recognition and synthesis

Most primary teachers will have seen computerised toys like Texas Instruments' Speak and Spell which are pre-programmed to 'speak' a limited number of stored words. A more versatile system will attempt to 'say' anything that is typed, although the speech may sound like a rusty Dalek! Systems like these incorporate an electronic model of the vocal tract plus a code resembling English (perhaps 64 phonemes made up from 25 different consonant sounds, 36 basic vowel sounds, two pauses and a stop). Each phoneme is recited according to the code. For example, if you type HIS LAUGH WAS ROUGH the computer will have a reasonable go at it, but if you type HIS LARF WOZ RUFF it will get a lot closer.

A computer which 'speaks' has many uses, particularly for young children who are learning to read and write, or for people who are partially sighted. But getting a micro to 'listen' is potentially even more useful, and not just for the disabled. It is much quicker to talk than to type, and there are many circumstances when typing is impracticable – for example, when hands are dirty or when they are being used for something else. A 'listening' device is also much smaller than a keyboard, an important factor in determining the size of portable computers.

In voice recognition systems, coded sound patterns are stored and then compared with the user's speech. The closest match is assumed to be the intended word. The variations in the ways that people speak mean that each user must teach the machine the words that it must recognise, usually by repeating them several times. Obviously, a system like this must have a very large memory if it is to be effective at recognising more than a few words. It must also work exceedingly fast if it is not to leave unnatural pauses between words while it matches the patterns.

As a consequence of this, speech recognition systems are expensive pieces of software which require expensive hardware to run on. But a machine which produces a printed version of a story as it is being told is already a reality. Most modern multimedia computers already in schools are capable of running speech recognition software and the development of portable machines, at an affordable price, which can transform dictated speech into printed text is surely imminent. The impact of such systems on primary education could be enormous and the implications are only just beginning to be considered.

Conclusion

Computers have come into schools very quickly in the last few years. The information technology industry continues to develop at a fast rate and it is often difficult for teachers to keep up with it. Even throughout the writing of this book we have had the constant sense of being overtaken by events. To offer any glimpse of the future is to offer a hostage to fortune.

Most of the aids to education that have been developed in the post-war years, from the overhead projector to the language laboratory, were intended purely for educational use. Like the use of the initial teaching alphabet (ITA) or the teaching of French in primary schools, they were subject to educational fashion. But the microelectronic age has developed first and foremost outside schools; there is no evidence that it is a passing fancy.

New equipment and new software continue to be stimulated by industrial and commercial users, not primarily by the needs of teachers and children in schools. Often what is developed for the home, office or factory spills over into schools and, given time, alternative and imaginative uses for it are found. In the process, teachers and children develop new skills and new ideas. In this way whole areas of the curriculum will come to be re-evaluated and perhaps even replaced. We will not only change how we teach, but what we teach.

The microelectronic revolution has arrived in schools. Information technology and educational computing will continue to influence the ways in which learning and teaching take place. But whatever piece of new hardware or new software becomes available, its use as a versatile tool for learning rather than as an educational toy will continue to depend on the skill and imagination of the teacher.

Appendix

The National Curriculum

This book has been written without reference to the National Curriculum, but both the National Curriculum and the book have been informed by reference to good classroom practice in the use of information technology to support teaching and learning. It is thus not surprising that every aspect of the use of computers required by the National Curriculum is covered somewhere in the pages of this book.

Information technology (IT) has a rather special place in the National Curriculum because it is both a subject in its own right and a tool for use in all other areas. Although IT is not a 'core' subject, it is, in many respects, rather like mathematics or English – a core element which is fundamental to successful work in many parts of the curriculum.

IT in other subjects

The Common Requirements of the Programmes of Study for all National Curriculum subjects (except PE) contain the following statement:

Pupils should be given opportunities, where appropriate, to develop and apply their information technology (IT) capability in their study of ...... (name of subject).

Chapters 6 and 7 of *Children Using Computers* describe some of the ways in which IT may be used in English, mathematics, science, design and technology, history, geography, art and music.

In some subjects the National Curriculum demands more specific use of IT than that covered by the statement in the Common

Requirements. The following table summarises the recommendations and prescriptions for IT use in English, maths, science and geography, indicating which chapters of this book offer coverage of each area. Although there is no specific reference to IT in mathematics AT1 (Using and Applying Mathematics), many of the approaches to problem solving covered in Chapter 3 involve using and applying mathematics.

Subject	Reference	Quote	See Chapter
English	Writing KS2 (2b)	Pupils should be given opportunities to plan, draft and improve their work on paper and on screen	2
Maths	Shape Space and Measures KS1 (1b)	use IT devices, eg programmable toys, turtle graphics packages	4
	(3b)	understand angle as a measure of turn and recognise quarter-turns and half-turns, eg giving instructions for rotating a programmable toy	4
	Shape Space and Measures KS2 (1c)	use computers to create and transform shapes	4
	Handling Data KS2 (1c)	use computers as a source of interesting data, and as a tool for representing data	2
Science	Opportunities KS2 (1d)	use IT to collect, store, retrieve and present scientific information	6
Geography	Geographical Skills KS2 (3f)	use IT to gain access to additional information sources and to assist in handling classifying and presenting evidence, eg recording fieldwork evidence on spreadsheets, using newspapers on CD-ROM, using word-processing and mapping packages	2 & 6

The Information Technology National Curriculum

In addition to requiring children to learn about the uses of IT in school, home and the wider world, the subject 'Information Technology' in the National Curriculum has two strands. The first, Communicating and Handling Information, is extensively covered in Chapter 2 of this book. The second strand, Controlling and Modelling (and at Key stage 2, Monitoring), is covered in chapters 3, 4, 5, 6 and 7 as the following table shows.

Subject	Reference	Quote	See Chapter
Information Technology	1	**Pupils should be given opportunities to:**	all
Key Stage 1	1a	use a variety of IT equipment including microcomputers and various keyboards, to carry out a variety of functions in a range of contexts;	
	1b	explore the use of computer systems and control technology in everyday life; Pupils should be taught to:	
	2 **Communicating and Handling Information**		
	2a	generate and communicate their ideas in different forms, using text, tables, pictures and sound;	2
	2b	enter and store information;	2
	2c	retrieve, process and display information that has been stored.	2
	3 **Controlling and Modelling**		
	3a	recognise that control is integral to many everyday devices;	5
	3b	give direct signals or commands that produce a variety of outcomes, and describe the effects of their actions;	4 & 5
	3c	use IT based models or simulations to explore aspects of real and imaginary situations.	7

Subject	Reference	Quote	See Chapter
Information Technology	1	**Pupils should be given opportunities to:**	
Key Stage 2	1a	use IT to explore and solve problems in the context of work across a variety of subjects;	**all**
	1b	use IT to further their understanding of information that they have retrieved and processed;	**2**
	1c	discuss their experiences of using IT and assess its value in working practices;	
	1d	investigate parallels with the use of IT in the wider world, consider the effects of such uses, and compare them with other methods.	
		Pupils should be taught to:	
	2 **Communicating and Handling Information**		
	2a	use IT equipment and software to communicate ideas and information in a variety of forms, incorporating text, graphs, pictures and sound, as appropriate, showing sensitivity to the needs of their audience;	**2**
	2b	use IT equipment and software to; organise, reorganise and analyse ideas and information;	**2**
	2c	select suitable information and media, and classify and prepare information for processing with IT, checking for accuracy;	**2**
	2d	interpret, analyse and check the plausibility of information held on IT systems, and select the elements required for particular purposes, considering the consequences of any errors.	**2**

continued

Subject	Reference	Quote	See Chapter
3 Controlling and Modelling			
	3a	create, test, modify and store sequences of instructions to control events;	**4 & 5**
	3b	use IT equipment and software to monitor external events	**6**
	3c	explore the effect of changing variables in simulations and similar packages, to ask and answer questions of the 'What would happen if... ?' type;	**3, 4 & 7**
	3d	recognise patterns and relationships in the results obtained from IT-based models or simulations, predicting the outcomes of different decisions that could be made.	**3, 4 & 7**

References

Aspects of the Work of the Microelectronics Education Programme. 1987. Department of Education and Science.

Computers in the primary curriculum. Report of a conference held at Elcott Park. 1984. Microelectronics Education Programme.

Curriculum matters: an HMI series. HMSO for the Department of Education and Science.
The curriculum from 5 to 16. 1985.
Mathematics from 5 to 16. 1985.
Music from 5 to 16. 1985.
Geography from 5 to 16. 1986.
English from 5 to 16. 2nd Ed. 1986.
Craft, Design and Technology from 5 to 16. 1987.

Science 5–16: a statement of policy. 1985. HMSO for the Department of Education and Science and the Welsh Office.

Improving Primary Schools. Report of the Committee on Primary Education (the Thomas Committee). 1985. Inner London Education Authority.

National Curriculum. Department of Education and Science.
Science Working Group: Interim report. 1987.
Mathematics Working Group: Interim report. 1987.
Mathematics for ages 5 to 16. 1988.
Science for ages 5 to 16. 1988.

Report of the consultative committee on the primary school (the Hadow Committee). 1931. Board of Education.

Technology survey. PrIME Newsletter No 5. Autumn 1987. School Curriculum Development Committee.

Blinko, J. 'Calculated play'. *Times Educational Supplement.* November 1985.

Ellam, J. and Wellington, J. *Computers in the Primary Curriculum.* 1987. University of Sheffield.

Noss, R. 'Doing maths while learning Logo'. *Mathematics Teaching* No 104 1985. Association of Teachers of Mathematics.

Index

adventure games
  exploring a tower 136
  finding a frog 181
  cross curricular links 10
  making your own 99, 188
aims 211
Algorithms 80–4
areas of experience 4
assessment
  general 254
  children's attitudes 254
  children's conversation 255
  children's recorded work 255
  children's ways of working 254
attitudes 228

BASIC 142–3
Big Trak 75
binary digits 116
binary tree 150–1
bits 116
bugs 101
buzzers 120

calculators 80–1
CD-ROM 10, 24, 25, 42–5,
  130–1, 173, 202, 218
CDT from 5 to 16 126, 165
Ceefax 24
census data 157–61
Christmas 190, 205
classroom organisation 211,
  220–1, 244–5
classroom resources 6
clip art 173

collaborative writing 48
communication systems 257
computer control 108–27
computer poems 134
concept keyboard 51
content-free software 13
continuity 245
control
  automatic 108
  manual 108
control technology
  general 108ff.
  aims 126
  equipment 118
  helping children 124
  lighthouse 113
  model making 116
  what children gain 126
conversation 128
creative arts 4, 163–76
creative skills 15
cross-curricular work
  general 177ff.
  Christmas 190, 205
  finding a frog 181
  food 179
  giants 5
  raising a Tudor warship 12
  selecting themes 178
  the sense of taste 32
  tuck shop survey 26–8
curriculum
  content 17, 263
  process 17

data collection
  collection sheet 32
  planning a survey 26–8, 32
  questionnaire design 27–8
  skills 72
databases
  general 30–42, 58–9
  decision trees 149–52
  entering data 33
  frogs and toads 187
  graphs and charts 36
  helping children 42
  Jellicles 64–5
  life in 1881 160
  types of database 30
  using census data 157–61
  in science 146–8
debugging 101
decision making 71
decision packages
  general 163
  painting programs 165–73
  snowmen and robins 198
  tiling programs 141, 165–6
decision trees 149–52
design and painting
  packages 165–73
desk top publishing 13, 54
Divali 204
drill and practice 8, 127
DTI hardware scheme 1

electronic mail 192, 260
electronic notice boards 260
Email 260
English from 5 to 16 47, 128
environmental studies 155
equipment *see* hardware
evaluation 243–56
  general 243
  of children's
    involvement 247–8
  of classroom practice 253
  of continuity 244–5

of parents' involvement 248
  of policy 244
  of teachers' needs 248–9
fact finding 25–8
feedback 108
File Transfer Protocol 261
film making 174
finance 250
firsthand enquiry 145–6
Fischertechnik 111, 119
floor turtle 84–95
flowcharts 82
future trends 257 ff.

gender issues 233
geography
  siting a windmill 67
  study of coastal resort 156
  life of an urban fox 157
Geography from 5 to 16 155
good work habits 228
graphs and charts
  block graphs 36–7
  flowcharts 82
  histograms 36
  pictograms 36
  pie charts 36
  scattergrams 37
  structure diagrams 82–3
  tables 37
  Venn diagrams 37

hands on, hands off 7
hardware
  DTI scheme 1
  evaluating needs 250
  management 220
  mouse 163
  modem 204
history
  examples of projects 41
  life in 1881 159
  raising a Tudor warship 12
  study of coastal resort 156

teaching methods   17
using census data   157–61
home computers   2, 238

icons
information   17–29
children's definitions   18
collection   28
facts   17
nature of   18
processing   23
sources   20
different types   21
ways of sending   22
information handling
skills   15, 25–7
what children gain   58
information processing   23–5
interface box   113, 120
Integrated Learning Systems
(ILS)   8, 258–9
Internet   25, 260–2
electronic notice boards   260
Email   260
File Transfer Protocol   261
World Wide Web   261

language development
general   128–34
animated text   130
area of experience   4
arranging words   132
bilingual learners   48, 128
developing text   131
drafting writing   46–8
reading strategies   131
story-writing skills   46
Lego technic   111, 119
light bulbs   120
Little Professor   8
Logo
general   84–106
adventure game   99
control technology commands
116, 121

drawing a circle   93
drawing stars   197
helping children   100
making a quiz   98
mathematical links   105
number work   95
PE activities   86
plan of the school   88
printing words   98–9
snowman   88–9
sprites   95
turtle graphics   84
what children gain   104–6

mathematics
general   134–45
adventure game   136
area of experience   4
BASIC   143
graphs and charts   36
national curriculum   265
numerical skills   15
picture building   140
spreadsheet   144–5
strategic games   9, 62
tiling patterns   140–1
Mathematics for ages 5 to 16
145
Mathematics from 5 to 16   68,
134, 142
Meteosat   208
MIDI interface   165
model making   116
modem   203
moral education   4
motors   119
multimedia   13, 173, 202–3,
218
music   12, 163–5
Music from 5 to 16   165
music keyboards   164–5

national curriculum   264–8
levels of attainment   215
newspaper pages   54, 195

observing children   232–3
organisation   211, 245
overlays   51

painting programs   165–73
parents   240, 248
picture building   165
pixel   165–6
planning   211
policy   244
practice, value of   7
pressure pads   120
problem solving   60–73
   its value   7
   definition   60
   evaluating solutions   71
   helping children   70, 226
   links with programming   106
   problem posing   6–7
   skills   15, 70
   software   61
   what children gain   70
programming   74–107
   BASIC   142–3
   definition   75
   Logo   84–106
   links with problem
      solving   106
   robots   78–9, 109
project work *see* cross-curricular
   work
purpose of computer use   6

record in database   30
resource management   250–1
resources *see* hardware *and*
   software
Robotix
   buggy   114
   challenges   113
   use by girls and boys   235
   parts in a kit   111, 119
robots   78–9, 109

role of
   class teachers   228, 253
   headteachers   251–2

science
   general   145–55
   area of experience   4
   computer control   55
   examples of projects   41
   identifying cheeses   151
   identifying twigs   149
   investigating heat loss   154
   simulations   146
   bird table visits   146–9
Science 5–16   146
sensors   119
sequencing activities   75
simulations
   car racing   10
   in geography or history   157
   in science   146
   life of an urban fox   157
   raising a Tudor warship   12
   siting a windmill   67
skill development   14
skills   14–16
   algorithmic   80–4
   communication   15, 58
   creative   15
   decision making   71
   higher order   15
   information handling   25–8
   investigational   70
   numerical   15
   observation   15
   personal and social   16, 228
   practical   15
   problem solving   15, 70
   reasoning   70
   story writing   46
   study and research   15
small programs   9, 135

social studies
  general   156–62
  examples of projects   41
software
  content free   13
  gender bias   233–40
  management and
    organisation   218, 250
  planning framework   215
  problem solving   15, 70
  selecting   214
  small programs   8
  different types of
    software   8
  tips for first-time use   221
sources of help   226, 249
Speak and Spell   262
speech recognition   262
spelling   47
spelling checker   55
spreadsheets   144–5
sprites   95
staff development   222–6
  appraising needs   223, 248
  sources of help   226–7, 248–9
synthesisers
    music   164–5
    speech   262

talk   128
talking books   130–1
teacher's role   228
technology
  general   108, 145–55
  area of experience   5
  construction kits   111, 119
  control technology   108
  designing and making   110
  model making   111

The curriculum from 5 to 16
  4, 6, 110
time management   250
topic work *see* cross-curricular
  work
toys survey   236
turtle graphics   84 ff.
types of software   8

upper and lower case   51

variable   93
video making   174

weather forecasting   206
word processing   13, 16, 46–58,
  129, 201, 220
  snowflake story   13–14
  book review   49–51
  firework poem   48
  fonts   56
  Gran   201
  helping children   58
  developing reading skills   129
  developing writing skills   129
  designing newspaper
    pages   55, 195
  presentation of work   47, 51–2
  reluctant readers   130
  text development   131
  spelling checkers   55
World Wide Web   261